Gilbert Childs

Steiner Education
in theory and practice

Floris Books

First published in 1991 by Floris Books
Fifth impression 2005

British Library CIP Data available

ISBN 0-86315-131-0

Produced in Poland by Polskabook

Contents

11. The Dawning of the Intellect

12. After Puberty — the Upper School

13. The Curriculum

It is essential that we develop an art of education which will lead us out of the social chaos into which we have fallen. The only way out of this social chaos is to bring spirituality into the souls of men through education, so that out of the spirit itself men may find the way to progress and the further evolution of civilization.

Rudolf Steiner

1   Rudolf Steiner as Educationist

*What occupies people's minds today, in the widest circles, are
the social problems. However, they lack the intellectual strength
earnestly to study these problems, because in the present age the
intellectual power is as though paralysed. The belief prevails
that the social problems can be mastered by what is called
knowledge, but they can never be mastered if they are not
tackled from the viewpoint of spiritual science.*

Artist, scientist, philosopher

All too often Rudolf Steiner has been regarded as a mystic, but people
who so regard him merely betray their ignorance of his basic approach
to Spirit as well as Nature, which was that of the scientist. It is often the
case, too, that people have heard Steiner's name in connection with other
impulses stemming from his insights, such as the bio-dynamic system
of farming and gardening; the new art of eurythmy; ideas for a renewal
of art and architecture which manifested themselves so strikingly in the
first and second Goetheanum buildings; new conceptions of the art of
medicine; a new approach to theology and Christology which led to the
founding of the Christian Community; and so on. Such people often have
only vague ideas as to the very significant contributions Steiner made to
the whole realm of the social sciences, particularly education. Philosopher,
sociologist, educationist, artist, scientist — he was in very deed a man of
many parts. He averred that the impulse for his teachings sprang directly
from the spiritual worlds as needs of our time, and his ideas concerning
child education in particular are being taken up with increasing interest and
enthusiasm; moreover, they are being put into practice. Steiner claimed
that the system of education that he evolved was right for modern Man,
pointing out that previous ages of civilization had different educational
ideals and practices.[1]

The popular image of Steiner schools

Steiner, or Waldorf schools, particularly those in Britain, have been popularly categorized as "progressive" along with other schools which proceed, for one reason or another, along unorthodox lines, and even as "experimental." Progressive they certainly are, in the very best sense of that deplorably over-worked and much-abused term, but experimental they most certainly are not. More will be said in later chapters to vindicate this statement; for indeed the very opposite is true, as Steiner stressed time and time again that teachers should be capable of re-creating the Waldorf curriculum at any time within the spirit of the whole ideology that supports it. However, it must be said that the older-established Waldorf schools in the United Kingdom were founded on fee-paying lines, and as such became understandably confused in the public mind with other ordinary private or independent schools.

Furthermore, it must be admitted that Waldorf teachers and other British Steiner educationists have not been over-energetic in propounding their principles and practices over the decades. True, the basic educational lectures of Steiner have long been available in English translation, but these are difficult and obscure to the point of exasperation for the casual reader, and are all too often abandoned for this reason. The books by Steiner educationists that have appeared have been explanatory of practice rather than interpretive of principles, with parents and enquirers in mind rather than other educationists. Edmunds' book *Rudolf Steiner Education* is a valuable introduction to Waldorf education for the general reader, particularly in respect of its aims and methods. He speaks out of many years' experience both as class teacher and specialist teacher, as does his colleague, A.C. Harwood, whose little book *The Way of a Child*, which first appeared in 1940, has been reprinted many times. In this deservedly popular book, Harwood's love for children and his understanding of child nature are immediately apparent, and his much more substantial work *The Recovery of Man in Childhood* describes Waldorf methods in a style which is at once lively and authoritative. Moffat's little book *Forward toward What?* is convincingly written and very thought-provoking, containing wisdom distilled from more than twenty-five years' experience as a Waldorf teacher. The translation of Frans Carlgren's book under the title *Education towards Freedom* describes typical activities to be observed in all Steiner schools, and it has the advantage of being strikingly illustrated with examples of work contributed by pupils from many and diverse nations and cultures. All these books provide valuable indications for parents and others who wish to have further insight into Waldorf educational

2

practices without wishing to be burdened by the theoretical principles behind them.[2]

The recent sharp increase in new Waldorf schools in the United Kingdom is perhaps indicative of widespread public dissatisfaction and disillusionment with State education. Reports suggest that parents, casting round for alternatives to the State system, are impressed by the happy, relaxed atmosphere in Steiner schools they have visited, and the abundant evidence of close pupil/teacher relationships. That they like what they see is reflected in the energetic moves made by parents to help to provide for and support Waldorf schools, and available data suggest that the sharp upward trend in the numbers of Waldorf schools in Britain and throughout the world will continue.

The reluctance of Steiner teachers to "push" the children in their classes during the years between the ages of seven and fourteen, is fairly well known. The reasons for this lack of emphasis on purely intellectual achievements will be discussed in later chapters. However, it is at first sight very easy for a casual visitor to confuse the artistic activities which take up so much of classroom time, with "play-way" activities. Class teachers in Waldorf schools are acutely conscious of what they are trying to achieve with their class. They are in complete control at all times; for this is their primary responsibility - to be *conscious* of the reasons for dealing with their class as they do, and of the effects of their total behaviour on their pupils. A class of children is a social unit, a community in miniature, with its own peculiar characteristics, and therefore its own individual combination of qualities in terms of pupil/teacher interaction.

The essential unity of a class is considerably enhanced if its teacher remains with it for the whole of the eight-year lower school period: the sense of community is stronger, continuity is preserved, and personal relationships and loyalties developed and fostered. Children feel secure in an atmosphere of stability and trust, and it is such an atmosphere that Waldorf school class teachers set out to provide. The close personal bonds which gradually form between teacher and child reveal themselves to advantage whenever moral or disciplinary matters arise; the natural authority of the class teacher weighs much in such situations. The advantages of knowing the personal background and history of individual pupils, their temperamental traits, scholastic strengths and weaknesses and other characteristics which have been carefully observed over the years are obvious. Compared with the typical Waldorf school class teacher, the State primary and middle school teacher is clearly disadvantaged in these respects, and the same may be said of their pupils.

A threefold social order

Rudolf Steiner, throughout his lectures and writings on education, never tired of emphasizing that a proper pedagogy can grow only from a thorough knowledge of human nature, and particularly child nature. What he meant by human nature is far removed from the tenets of orthodox science, which regards the body as a mechanism, which doubts the existence of the soul, and which denies the spirit. Physiologists meticulously observe and record the workings of the body, denying the possibility that these workings are patient to a soul-spiritual agent. Psychologists assiduously experiment with the human being's mental and emotional phenomena as if they were solely attributes of the body. Theologians, whose proper concern is with the "spirit" of Man, invariably speak of it in psychological terms, thus confounding soul with spirit and degrading both to a common level, with the inevitable resulting loss of credibility. Unfortunately for them, theologians have no empirical grounds upon which to argue (as do the psychologists) which leaves their position extremely weak and vulnerable. Steiner contended that the apparent need to experiment with human beings clearly demonstrates that *real* knowledge of Man is absent, claiming that his system of spiritual science restores such knowledge. Educational aims and methods should be firmly and exclusively based on genuine knowledge of Man, and not arrived at by theorizing, devising taxonomies of aims and needs and similar intellectual exercises. In other words, proper knowledge of the needs of the child at any particular stage of development presupposes proper knowledge of how to meet them, and this is the seemingly immodest claim of Steiner pedagogy and didactics.

A good example of this, in that it can be expressed in sociological terms, concerns Steiner's ideas on the essential threefoldness of society. Put briefly from an historical point of view, western civilization has inherited its spiritual structure from the Greeks, and its State (legal) structure from the Romans; to these has been added a third structure — the economic, which is purely European in origin. These three elements, however, are chaotically mingled in modern social life, and it is necessary that order be brought in. Steiner's ideas concerning the Threefold Commonwealth regard the State as a trinity rather than as a unity: one autonomous sub-state should concern itself exclusively with the cultural life (spiritual structure); another should concern itself exclusively with Man's life of rights (legal structure), and a third with the production and management of goods and services (economic structure). These three areas of the social organism Steiner connected with the three great ideals of universal humanity: liberty, equality and fraternity. Liberty he connected

4

with cultural, intellectual and religious freedom; equality with the political sphere and legal rights, and fraternity with the ideal attitude which should prevail in all matters concerning the economic life. All this seems feasible and reasonable enough, but Steiner went further: he connected the three areas of social life and the three universally human ideals with the three main developmental stages of the growing human being — infancy, childhood and adolescence, and the educational principles which should prevail at each stage, namely, imitation, authority and independence. In his own words:

> Upon this threefold educational basis must be erected what
> is to flourish for mankind's future. If we do not know that
> the physical body must become an imitator in the right
> way we shall merely implant animal instincts in the body. If we
> are not aware that between the seventh and fourteenth year
> the etheric body passes through a special development that
> must be based on authority, there will develop in Man merely
> a universal, cultural drowsiness, and the force needed for the
> rights organism will not be present. If from the fifteenth year
> onward we do not infuse all education in a sensible way with
> the power of love that is bound to the astral body, men will
> never be able to develop their astral bodies into independent
> beings. These things intertwine. Therefore I must say: proper
> imitation develops freedom; authority develops the rights
> life; brotherliness, love develops the economic life. But turned
> about it is also true. When love is not developed in the right
> way, freedom is lacking; and when imitation is not developed
> in the right way, animal instincts grow rampant.[3]

The world-view of Waldorf teachers

Principals or head teachers of state and orthodox private schools often provide a strong unifying influence, which is generally thought to be beneficial. Steiner schools have none such, but they do have a powerful unifying principle in the ideology peculiar to them, based on anthroposophy (see Chapter 2). The world-view of Waldorf teachers is quite definitely orientated; their conception of life and the world is of primary importance, as discussed elsewhere.[4] What is also of great importance and significance is the fact that the Waldorf school movement is a worldwide one, just as the anthroposophical movement is, and this means that there is gradually coming into existence an international network of educational establishments working along closely similar pedagogical principles. In early 1991 the total number of Waldorf schools worldwide was well in excess of five hundred. The implementation of the Waldorf curriculum within the framework of the various national cultures presents no problem as long as the fundamental principles are maintained, and Steiner's insistence that the curriculum should be capable of being re-created at any moment is consistent with the realities of the situation. At international conferences, Steiner educationists and teachers speak the same pedagogical language, and such occasions afford the opportunity for them to exchange ideas on curriculum implementation. The social implications contained within Rudolf Steiner's educational philosophy are profound, as the brief quotation from one of his lectures made just now clearly indicates.

It has often been said that in the last analysis what a teacher teaches is himself or herself, and the need for the right kind of "life-philosophy in action" must have been in Steiner's mind when he spoke the words quoted at the opening of this chapter. Head and assistant teachers in orthodox schools, whatever their own personal ideas on education, find themselves at the mercy of policies which shift according to governmental decree, of the various findings of educational theorists and experimenters who bombard them with conflicting ideas, and of their own particular philosophy of life. The least that can be said about Waldorf schools is that the the distinctive ideology that underpins their pedagogical practices constitutes a powerful stabilizing factor; and the same may be said of the curriculum, which is essentially the same as it was seventy years ago. The framework is thus well established and strong, and there are few signs of ossification and traditionalism.

There has long been much talk among orthodox educationists about "educating for the future," "the social needs of tomorrow's citizens" and suchlike, as if we all knew perfectly well what the twenty-first century held in prospect for mankind and the world!

A C Harwood, a Steiner teacher for many years, contended that it is plainly impossible to educate for a new social order without some idea of what that social order should be, and that it is a pernicious form of education which puts in the forefront the ideal of moulding the next generation into some prescribed social form. The real object of education should be to leave the next generation in the best possible condition to create its own social forms.[5] According to Steiner, children are not ripe to exercise their own judgement until after puberty. If class teachers have done their job well, in that they have provided their pupils with concepts that are capable of further growth and development and not those which are fixed, rigid and closed, they have at the same time left their charges free to develop as they will, according to their own inherent characteristics and abilities. It mattered not at all, when the children were in their care, whether they were teaching future politicians or future shop assistants; whatever ideas class teachers transmitted should have been mobile and to a large extent unresolved or "open-ended," and not definitive and "once-for-all." To be labelled a "product" of this or that school should not be something adult people should be proud of; their early education should have left them free to "produce" themselves as individuals, able to exercise their birthright of as untrammelled a freedom as possible and to experience true autonomy.

2 Investigator Extraordinary

*My knowledge of the things of the spirit is a direct result of my
own perception, and I am fully conscious of this fact. In all
details and in the wider views I have always examined myself
strictly to see whether I have made every step, as my perception
advanced and developed, so that a completely conscious
mind accompanied these steps. Just as the mathematician
advances from thought to thought without the intervention of
autosuggestion or the unconscious, so must spiritual perception
advance from objective imagination to objective imagination
without anything living in the soul but clear, discerning
consciousness.*

Citizen of two worlds

Rudolf Steiner claimed that from an early age he was aware of a
supersensible world as well as the ordinary material world familiar to
us all. At around the age of seven he began to receive impressions
from a world other than the physical; manifestations of beings and
events in a world that was hidden from his family and people around
him revealed themselves. Even at that tender age the boy realized that
his unusual perceptions could not be understood by anyone else, and
therefore remained silent about them. This silence lasted for the best
part of thirty-four years. During these years he worked as a "spiritual
researcher" *(Geistesforscher)* with the aim of establishing a true "science
of the spirit" *(Geisteswissenschaft)*. His findings he incorporated into his
teachings for which he adopted the name "anthroposophy." Trained as a
scientist and possessing a profound respect for the principles of scientific
methodology, Steiner was meticulous in the application of such principles
to his spiritual investigations. This must be emphasized, as much of what
he had to say might well seem incomprehensible, even nonsensical, to one
unfamiliar with his "spiritual science" and its terminology. However, th'
powers of spiritual perception to which he laid claim Steiner declared tc
slumbering within every human being — they have only to be awoke
developed. His book *Knowledge of the Higher Worlds and its Att*
cribes in detail how this may be brought about. Never'
be equally stressed that no special spiritual powers ə

of anyone in order to understand the communications of the spiritual investigator; common sense and unprejudiced thinking together with a certain willingness to embrace new ideas and to tread new avenues of approach to familiar phenomena are all that is necessary.

Born on 27 February 1861 at Kraljevec, now in Croatia but then on the border between Austria and Hungary, Rudolf Steiner's early life was unremarkable enough. His father was employed by the South Austrian Railway as stationmaster at various small stations, and as such was poorly paid. Rudolf, as the eldest of three children, was obliged to help in household and garden, and he learned at an early age how to operate the station telegraph. Anything of a mechanical nature possessed a strong fascination for him; on the other hand, he was sensitive to the grandeur of the surrounding mountainous countryside which he loved so well, and he gladly immersed himself in the life of Nature with all her changing moods and seasons. Rudolf started school at Pottschach when his father was stationmaster there, but when he was eight years old the family moved to Neudörfl, just over the border into Hungary. School meant little to him, and by ordinary standards he was an indifferent pupil; he was a poor speaker and mastery of the written word was gained only by arduous effort, but by contrast reading came easily to him, as he was quick to grasp concepts and ideas. One day the assistant teacher happened to leave a geometry textbook in his room, and the young Rudolf plunged into it with enthusiasm and zeal. Little else than "the coincidence, the similarity, of triangles, squares, polygons" filled his mind for weeks on end.[1]

The finding of the geometry textbook was instrumental in influencing the whole course of Steiner's life. It was the first confirmation for him that, here in everyday life, could be found forms which were "perceived only within oneself, entirely without impression upon the external senses,"[2] and this discovery gave him the deepest satisfaction. Here at last, the young Rudolf perceived, was common ground between the material and the spiritual: the possibility of reconciling the two worlds he had been living in until now appeared more and more likely to him. Geometry seemed to him to be a knowledge which appears to be produced by Man but which, nevertheless, has a significance quite independent of him.[3] Thus was his experience of a spiritual world justified and confirmed, and it gave rise to profound relief and joy.

Of great significance to the young Steiner was the nearness of the church and churchyard. He became deeply attached to the church, its rites and liturgies, and he was often to be found in the company of the Neudörfl village priest, whom he greatly revered. Much of his attachment was due to observing the celebrant of the cult in mediating between the sensible and supersensible worlds.[4] Here was further confirmation that the two worlds co-existed; further confirmation, to Steiner, that the spiritual and material worlds were equally real. During this period the boy passed his life amid his home environment without really sharing in it, and he received no religious encouragement from his father, who was a freethinker.

Rudolf Steiner's father had intended that his son should become a railway civil engineer, so when the time came for his secondary education, young Rudolf was sent to the *Realschule* in Wiener-Neustadt in preference to the *Gymnasium*, though he himself was quite indifferent to the matter. Thus the foundations were laid for his further grounding in the natural sciences. At the age of fourteen he acquired a copy of Kant's *Critique of Pure Reason* and he plunged into it with boundless boyish interest and enthusiasm. He did not find it easy going, being obliged to read many a page more than twenty times in succession. But to Steiner's burning question: To what extent is it possible to prove that in real thinking spirit is the agent? he found no help whatever from Kant.

Precocious in the world of ideas, Steiner never attempted to hide the fact that he was slow in development as to the facts of the material world. Some idea of how difficult it was for him to grasp the substance of an ordinary elementary and secondary school education, and the ordinary problems of learning might be gained from the following:

> It was always difficult for me to fix in memory such external
> data, for instance, as must be assimilated in the field of
> science. I had to see a natural object again and again in order
> to know what it was called, in what scientific class of objects it
> was listed, and the like. I might even say that the sense-world
> was for me rather shadowy, or like a picture. It passed before
> my mind in pictures, whereas my bond of union with the
> spiritual bore always the genuine character of reality.[5]

Such, however, were his powers of application that in the summer of 1879 Rudolf Steiner matriculated with distinction, and in the following autumn took up the study of mathematics, natural history and chemistry at Vienna Technical College. He had decided to become a teacher in a *Realschule*, but even while still a student at Technical College he took up tutoring in his spare time to supplement his income. While still at the *Realschule* in Wiener-Neustadt he had taught himself the usual *Gymnasium* subjects as well as Latin and Greek, and he now found this accomplishment very welcome, as indeed he did later also.

During this time Steiner read every philosophical book he could lay hands on, and attended lectures on philosophy at the University in Vienna. He felt duty bound to seek for the truth through philosophy, and he had the urge to study mathematics and natural sciences, and to place their findings upon a solid foundation of philosophy.[6] It must not be forgotten that throughout he also beheld the spiritual world *as reality*, and the struggle to reconcile the two worlds continued ceaselessly. But he had begun to realize that the philosophy that he learned from others could not in its thinking be carried all the way to the perception of the spiritual world. At this point Steiner decided that he must formulate his own theory of knowledge.

Goethe's influence on Steiner

Significant for the further development of his ideas was his acquaintance with Karl Julius Schröer, who was Professor of German Language and Literature at the time. Schröer was a recognized authority on the literary works of Goethe, for whom he had an unbounded admiration, and his enthusiasm was infectious. Rudolf Steiner, however, was more attracted by the work of Goethe in the natural sciences, in particular his theory of colour. Once more, this time in the field of optics, did Steiner find further confirmation of the interplay between the spiritual and material worlds, which gave him still greater impetus to proceed with his work towards a theory of knowledge that would be comprehensible, and perhaps acceptable, to orthodox scientists. Further studies from a Goethean standpoint, carried on during his spare time, in botany and anatomy, gradually led Steiner to the conviction that contemporary natural scientific thinking, denying as it did the Spirit, could necessarily only understand what was dead in Nature, and never living processes. Consequently he applied himself with renewed zeal to a thorough study of Goethe's natural scientific writings in the hope of finding a bridge between the two worlds. Then in 1883, when Steiner was only twenty-two years old, he was invited by Professor Kürschner, upon Schröer's recommendation, to prepare an edition of Goethe's works in the *Deutsche Nationalliteratur*. This seemed to Steiner like a stroke of destiny, and he accepted the invitation gladly.

By now his college training had come to an end, and Rudolf Steiner's high reputation as a tutor brought a recommendation for a post with a family named Specht in which there were four boys. His main responsibility was for the education of the youngest, Otto, who was then ten years of age and, suffering from a hydrocephalic condition, was considered to be practically ineducable. Steiner welcomed the challenge; he was able to perceive the association between the soul-spiritual element and the

11

bodily element in his pupil, and it was then that he went through his "real course of study in physiology and psychology."[7] Within two years Steiner had successfully brought the boy to *Gymnasium* entrance standard; he continued with his normal education and eventually qualified as a medical doctor. This period in Steiner's life was also of great significance, as this pedagogical experience was of paramount importance in enabling him, in later years, to formulate a new art of education.

3   Origins and Development

*Of necessity our educational task will differ from the
educational tasks which mankind has set itself hitherto. Not that
we are so vain and proud as to imagine that we, of ourselves,
should initiate a new world-wide order in education, but
because from anthroposophical spiritual science we know that
the epochs of evolution as they succeed each other must always
set humanity fresh tasks.*

Material versus spiritual

Steiner was one of many thinkers who have pointed out the difference in
attitude between the medieval craftsman plying his trade and the twentieth
century worker tending his machine in the factory. The craftsman was
more integrated in society; his activities brought him into contact with
many people in their many roles; the rise of industrialism and the
harnessing of the factory worker to the capitalist system tended to sever
his links with society, leaving him isolated at his bench or machine. The
craftsman invariably saw his work through all processes from raw material
to finished product, and his job satisfaction was assured. Later, with the
Industrial Revolution, the division of labour and the fragmentation of
production by specialized processes gave rise to restricted horizons at
both personal and social levels.

The introduction of machinery during the early nineteenth century was
to bring about a world revolution which was at once not only industrial
but political, economic and socio-cultural as well. The structure of society
common to all European countries was dominated by the distinction
between townsman and peasant, with a handful of nobility as wealthy
landowners, and as such was relatively stable. This was to give way to a
social structure dominated by the distinction between the entrepreneurial
and industrial *nouveaux riches* as employers, and a new proletariat,
outrageously exploited and leading an existence of misery and squalor
in the newly-created urban slums, as employees. The urgent demands of
social justice led to the founding of the trades union movement which,

however, did little more than bring about some degree of amelioration in the worker's *economic* lot, and while in Britain the Chartists strove for their "rights" in order to satisfy their burning *political* needs, all over Europe there was revolution and strife in face of similar exploitation and repression. What sparse comfort there was in religion, as the main source of sustenance for Man's *spiritual* needs, eventually disappeared under the impact of Darwinism and the further extraordinarily rapid advances of scientific knowledge and the influence of scientific theory. Rudolf Steiner often pointed out that the rise of industrialism and technology, based as they are on firmly scientific modes of thinking and practice, were coincidental in this shift of popular conceptions of the universe from religious foundations to scientific foundations. In this the leading-classes, the employers, suffered far less than the following-classes, the employees; the middle and upper classes proved themselves to be more resilient than the working classes, and for sound reasons. The former managed to preserve their perspective mainly because they not only enjoyed more leisure time but possessed the financial means for cultural pursuits, whereas the latter possessed neither.

Steiner argued that, as all industrial-technological processes are based on scientific principles, the factory worker could not help but imbibe scientific lines of thinking, albeit unconsciously. Thus science became the new creed of the working classes; the old traditions were lost and forgotten, spiritual life a thing of the past. Nevertheless, the need remained, as well as the desire, for the proletarian to see his human worth against a background of spiritual values; hence there was a hankering after and a longing for them.[1] This striving after what Steiner called "human-consciousness" was thus left unsatisfied, to be replaced eventually by a "class consciousness" based on excessive concern with the economic realities of life. According to Steiner the worker believed — mistakenly — that a transformation of economic processes in his favour would automatically grant him his rights as an individual, wrongly divining that economic processes, operating according to the scientific laws of cause and effect, were deemed to be the only reality. Thus the spiritual life and the life of rights were seen in economic terms; they existed as mere chimera against the background of solid economic reality, dominated as it was by technology and capitalism. Steiner asserted that the life and processes of economics, devoid as they are of spirit and soul, cannot somehow miraculously engender their essential qualities. Rather must Man's *spiritual* yearnings and aspirations, dimly discernible though they may be, be heeded and attended; only thus may he find solutions to his manifold social problems.

Thus Steiner saw the ills of the body social as being due directly to the impotence of the spiritual life in modern society.[2] He saw the economic life of society as being granted importance and influence far exceeding its proper bounds and as usurping other equally important aspects. He stressed that, contrary to popular belief, the body social is not in essence unitary, but threefold. The healthy functioning of society, he declared, depended on the independent functioning of three spheres of activity: (i) the economic sphere which concerns solely the production, distribution and consumption of goods; (ii) the sphere of rights or political sphere which deals with purely human relations as between one person and another; and (iii) the spiritual sphere which comprises all those activities that spring from within Man as an individual human being. Each of these three spheres of activity should form a "state" which should be empowered to order its own affairs, negotiating with the other two "states" as sovereign bodies to produce the unity of the body social.[3] The guiding principles on which each of these three states should order its own affairs should be: fraternity in things economic, equality in things political, and liberty in things spiritual.[4] In order to appreciate Steiner's basic educational ideas it is necessary to understand the connections between his teachings about the threefoldness of the human organism and those of the threefoldness of the body social, and these will be discussed in due course.

The first Waldorf school

After the surrender of Germany to the Allies in the autumn of 1918, the country suffered from shortage of food, even famine, and demonstrations, strikes and riots were widespread. People were desperate in their search for a solution to urgent social, political and economic problems. In such a *milieu* Rudolf Steiner's ideas concerning a Threefold Social Order found no lack of supporters, and in May 1919 the "Union for the Threefold Social Order" was founded in Stuttgart. He and his collaborators were invited to speak to the workers in committee rooms, public houses and in the factories, and many prominent industrialists and businessmen invited Steiner to private consultations. Among these was Dr Emil Molt, managing director of the Waldorf-Astoria cigarette factory in Stuttgart, who decided that the time was ripe for a practical move. Molt was an industrialist with a keen appreciation of social problems, and was highly esteemed by his employees. He was convinced that catastrophes such as World War I were due to faulty and neglected education, and at a meeting with Rudolf Steiner and a few collaborators on 25 April 1919 concrete plans were laid for the founding of *Die Freie Waldorfschule*, The Free (or Independent) Waldorf School, in Stuttgart. His invitation to Steiner to organize and direct the school met with a ready response. Many years later Molt wrote:

> The original idea which led to the founding of the school was a social one, to provide for the children of workmen and employees the same teaching and education as that enjoyed by children of families with means. The insight was involved that the social chasm might begin to close if the problem of education were no longer dependent on money, and that our cultural, economic and political advancement would be possible only if all children, without distinction of the class to which their parents belonged, were permitted to share in the same educational system.[5]

Rudolf Steiner was convinced that much social unrest, and particularly the feelings of inferiority widespread among the working classes, was not due, as generally supposed, to frustration in political and economic matters, but to cultural deprivation. He deeply deplored the fact that millions of fourteen year old children in the industrialized countries of the West were wrested away from the real process of cultural development and thrust into commercial and industrial life of one form or another.[6] The only remedy for this, he asserted, was the participation in a free spiritual life, with full allowance to give each citizen the best chance of individual development. Furthermore, Steiner was equally convinced that the problem of education was primarily a problem of the training of teachers, and that a clear appreciation of the threefold structure of the human being and of the life-epochs marking his development through life would constitute a sound foundation for a pedagogy based upon the actual nature of the growing child and not on any abstract theories. He never tired of emphasizing that the purely *intellectual* approach to *any* social problem, including the problem of education, was unrealistic, going so far as to contend that Man's ordinary conceptual thinking is intrinsically anti-social.[7] Human beings are awake — fully awake — only in their thinking; in their life of feeling they are dreaming, and in their life of will they are asleep. Nonetheless, he declared, faculties and propensities from these deeper strata of the life of the soul must not be ignored if the life of society is to proceed harmoniously. Cultural impulses were in danger of being vitiated because of undue emphasis being placed on purely intellectual values, thus exacerbating the influence of cultural deprivation seen in Western industrial countries. Steiner believed

16

that the educational process in modern times needs to be a therapeutic process, and this he declared Waldorf pedagogy to be.

Work on the Waldorf School went swiftly ahead during the summer months of 1919, and in late August and early September Steiner held concentrated courses of lectures and seminars for the teachers-designate of the new school concerning the principles and practice of his educational ideas. Amid a festival atmosphere the first Waldorf school came into being on 7 September 1919. In his opening address Rudolf Steiner declared that if humanity is to live in a socially right way in the future, humanity must educate its children in a socially right way, and that a small contribution in this direction was now to be made by Die Freie Waldorfschule in Stuttgart.

Steiner spoke of the original Waldorf School as "a true child of care," and there is no doubt that it occupied a very special place in his affections, and in his life. As leader and director of the school his responsibilities were great; furthermore, he was at the same time heavily involved in the founding of an Independent College for Spiritual Science (*Freie Hochschule für Geisteswissenschaft*) at the Goetheanum in Dornach, a village on the outskirts of Basel in Switzerland. The first collegiate course was held there in the autumn of 1920, and during the years 1919 to 1924 he divided much of his time between Dornach and Stuttgart, when an illness which was to prove fatal in March 1925 put an end to his travels.

It was typical of Steiner that he concerned himself closely with the day-to-day problems of running the Stuttgart school, and none was too small that he would not give his attention to it if requested. He appointed the teachers, all of whom were anthroposophists but not all of whom were trained teachers, and he knew every child by name. He gave several supplementary lecture courses for the teachers as well as informal talks and advice. Quite often during the weekly teachers' meetings at which he happened to be present, a question or problem would draw an answer which would be expanded into a miniature lecture. The proceedings were taken down in shorthand, and the records of these conferences, known to all Waldorf teachers simply as the *Konferenzen*, are an invaluable fund of indications as to how Rudolf Steiner dealt with practical and theoretical problems as they arose, and they afford useful insights into his ways of thinking.

Expansion of Waldorf Schools

By the time of Steiner's death in 1925 another Waldorf school had been founded in Germany, at Hamburg, one at The Hague in Holland, and two in England: at Streatham, London, and at Kings Langley, Hertfordshire.

Gradually the Waldorf School Movement spread, and other schools opened; in 1928 the first American school was founded in New York City, and by the outbreak of World War II sixteen schools in all were operative, being distributed as follows:

Germany	3
United Kingdom	5
Norway	2
Holland	2
Switzerland	2
Italy	1
U.S.A.	1

Under the Hitler regime in Germany all independent schools were closed, including of course all Waldorf schools, and those in the occupied countries suffered the same fate. During the years of World War II the only Waldorf schools to remain open in Europe were those in Switzerland and the United Kingdom.

Within a year or so of the ending of the war in Europe, twenty-four schools in the then West Germany had been established or re-established, and the Waldorf School Teacher Training Seminary at Stuttgart had re-opened to receive record numbers of prospective teachers. Since then growth in the number of schools worldwide has accelerated, and by the end of 1990, the number of Waldorf Schools in 25 countries across the world had reached 521. During the few years towards the end of the 1980's the rate of expansion was more than one hundred new schools per year, and it seems set to increase even faster. Thus the international Steiner Schools movement can claim to represent the largest non-religious educational body in the world, and this serves to emphasize the truly universally human character of Waldorf philosophy, pedagogy and didactics. The seemingly inexorable manner of such rapid growth, particularly since the early 1970s, has given rise to some puzzlement among orthodox educationists, though not so much to Steiner educationists, for many and complex reasons.[8]

All Rudolf Steiner Schools pride themselves in being "free" (in the sense of being independent) and all establishments in Great Britain and the Commonwealth, as indeed in North America and English-speaking countries generally, are for the most part independent when it comes to finance. The independence they enjoy, and the autonomy it affords, is very highly valued; for strong feelings exist that the less interference by the State — or any other authority for that matter — the better, even if this means slow progress and financial hardship. All Waldorf Schools are non-profit-making concerns and charitable status often accompanies their highly-prized independence. They are all acutely aware of the desirability of arranging their financial structure so as to be in line with Rudolf Steiner's indications concerning social health, and which are to be found in his writings on the Threefold Commonwealth referred to elsewhere.

The superstructure of a typical Waldorf School consists of an Association, usually a non-profit-making company without shareholders limited by guarantee, a Council of Management, and a Finance Committee; and an important feature of these bodies is that parents and friends of the school actively participate in their deliberations. The infrastructure comprises a College of Teachers, which is responsible for the day-to-day running of the school, and a Teachers' Council, which meets in order to arrange detailed implementation of the decisions taken by the College of Teachers, which comprises invited individuals from the ranks of the Teachers' Council, both bodies being drawn exclusively from members of the teaching staff.

The nominal Head of the school is the Chairman of the College of Teachers, who may be elected either for a definite or an indefinite period. Senior members of staff corresponding to heads of departments in State schools are usually recognized as such by mutual consent rather than being officially appointed. Posts of responsibility do not carry extra remuneration, and there are no scale posts or grades; all teachers hold equal status. Thus the principle of "extended professionalism" is practised to a very great extent, as has always been done in Waldorf schools. The weekly meetings of the Teachers' Council, which corresponds to the general purposes of staff meetings in orthodox schools, invariably include a short study session of Rudolf Steiner's educational or related works.

Sports and games are not especially encouraged in Steiner schools for several reasons (see, for example, p. 107), including that of the competitive element involved, and there are no "houses" or other artificial means of segregating the children. The whole school meets, not every morning for assembly, but on festival days and other comparatively rare occasions, usually not more than three or four times a term. Before school starts, each class meets for a recital of the morning verse, and this, as are most class rituals, is powerfully consensual in character. Differentiating rituals and practices are avoided as much as possible; signs and tokens such as distinctive garments, cups, shields, prizes, stars, good and bad marks, house points and suchlike are entirely absent. There are no prefects in the usual sense; the students of Class 12 (equivalent to Upper Sixth Form) as a body are expected to assist in the supervision of the younger pupils on the playgrounds, and when festivals, plays or concerts are held.

Steiner considered that the greatest problem confronting education in the twentieth century and beyond was that of the training of teachers. To work through what he meant by this, and the implications contained therein would require a separate volume, but so much will be discussed *passim* as to give basic indications in this direction. Much has been made by his antagonists of Steiner's apparent lack of modesty in setting forth what might be taken to be a completely subjective view of the Universe and Man, and creating a whole system of pedagogy incorporating such views. He would of course claim that he was being entirely objective — more objective, indeed, than his critics — simply because he was aware of a supersensible world as well as a sensible, and therefore enjoyed a more comprehensive view of reality than they.

Certainly he required of Waldorf teachers that they embrace his world-view (*Weltanschauung*), and every teacher training programme in Steiner education includes, if appropriate, a course in basic spiritual-scientific tenets. Set books include not only the three fundamental courses given at the foundation of the first Waldorf School in Stuttgart in 1919, namely *Study of Man*, *Practical Course for Teachers* and *Discussions with Teachers*, but also such books essential to an understanding of anthroposophical principles such as *Theosophy*, *Goethe's Theory of Knowledge* and *Philosophy of Freedom*.

Part-time teacher training courses are offered by several of the twenty-five Steiner schools in the United Kingdom, the main fulltime centre being located at Emerson College in Forest Row in Sussex, which since its foundation by L. Francis Edmunds in 1962 has trained large numbers of prospective Waldorf teachers drawn from seventy different nationalities.

The College offers a Foundation Year for all courses, Education students, as prospective teachers, going on to a second year, from mid-September to June of the following year. The Education Course covers the following:

(1) A study of childhood as part of human development in body, soul and spirit.

(2) The Waldorf Curriculum in its creative-pedagogical approach to meet the needs of the developing child.

(3) The development of artistic and imaginative faculties in painting, drawing, modelling, speech and drama, music and eurythmy.

(4) The collegiate task beyond the classroom: school management and organization, relationship with parents, and the social needs in the wider school community.

Upon satisfactory completion of the year, students obtain a Course Completion Certificate, which is recognized as a valid qualification by Steiner Schools throughout the world. It need scarcely be mentioned that the part-time teacher training courses run by established Waldorf schools approximate to those run by Emerson College.

Of significant importance with regard to pupils and students in need of financial support for attendance at British schools and colleges based on the educational principles of Rudolf Steiner is the Godparents Association, a charitable organization founded in 1968 for this purpose. It consists of two separate funds, known as the Children's Fund and the Training Fund.

The purpose of the Children's Fund is to help finance children at Steiner or Waldorf schools in Great Britain. Individual applications to schools are not encouraged, the Association preferring to work in close co-operation with the Steiner Schools Fellowship which represents the schools. It goes without saying that donations, covenanted payments and legacies are welcomed, as indeed they are for the Training Fund.

The aim of the Training Fund is to help young people who are training in Great Britain, irrespective of nationality, to prepare themselves for practical work within the anthroposophical movement. Financial help is given in the form of interest-free loans to students doing training courses in a variety of fields, which include agriculture, the arts, education, eurythmy, and speech and drama. The money thus lent to students comes from the loan repayments of other students, and out of donations from other sources. Similar funds to the Godparents Training Fund exist in other countries, and representatives of some of these meet from time to time to consider common issues.

4   Premises and Terminology

*In education we must comprehend man as a whole; and man
in his totality is body, soul and spirit. We must be able to deal
with the spirit if we would educate.*

From philosopher to spiritual scientist

Rudolf Steiner was a philosopher of outstanding calibre, as his early
published works amply demonstrate. His first book, *A Theory of
Knowledge Implicit in Goethe's World Conception*, was published in
1886 when he was only twenty-five years of age, and he was granted his
Ph.D. from the University of Rostock in 1891 on a philosophical thesis,
later published, with additional material, as *Truth and Science*. His chief
philosophical work, *The Philosophy of Spiritual Activity*, followed in 1893,
and this work alone is sufficient to ensure a high reputation in this field.

Although he studied philosophy with a view to building a bridge
between the visible world of Nature and the invisible world of Spirit,
and wrote with this aim in mind, Steiner gradually came to realize that he
would have to employ different methods of approach and presentation
if he was to be understood by the general public and not be rejected
by them as he had been by contemporary thinkers. Consequently,
he adopted a non-philosophical approach, and rather than employing
complicated arguments involving problems of semantics he made skilful
use of analogy and paradigm, and rather than definitions he employed
characterizations and epithets. He was thoroughly grounded in the world
of the spirit, and was so consistent in his descriptions of that world, that
the difficulties he encountered in putting supersensible experiences into
ordinary language were gradually overcome. His ideas were seen to cohere
as well as inhere, and this assisted enormously in the development of his
arguments, most of which the majority of readers were obliged to take on
trust at first. However, confidence in his particular system of philosophy
having once been established, Steiner was able to develop it in his own
way, which was unique. He adopted some traditional terms current in
esoteric circles of former ages, and this proved to be unfortunate in some

instances, but he also invented his own technical terms, and these will be explained as and when appropriate.

It must be said that many of Rudolf Steiner's books, when opened by readers unfamiliar with the basic tenets and terminology of his spiritual science, may well be regarded, at worst as nonsense, at best incomprehensible. Those familiar with his published works know that Steiner often throws off apparently unfounded statements, fully expecting his readers to accept them; usually, however, seemingly aphoristic remarks may well be substantiated by reference to his other works. His written style was fundamentally different from his lecturing style; his books and articles are often models of careful, systematic presentation of ideas, whereas his lectures may appear, in print, to be loosely constructed and anything but systematic. In defence of this, it must be emphasized that Steiner never intended that his lectures be printed; quite often what he said and the way he said it was geared to the needs, wishes or demands of a particular audience at a particular time. His lectures to the workmen building the second Goetheanum were very dissimilar to those given to seasoned anthroposophists, for instance.

Bearing this in mind, it would not be proper for comment, critical or otherwise, to be levelled at any of Steiner's pronouncements without sincere attempts to accept, even tentatively, his premises and master his terminology. Willing suspension of disbelief is essential, for it takes considerable time and effort to become familiar with the teachings of anthroposophy (*anthropos-sophia* — wisdom of Man) the name Steiner adopted for them. He also used the term "spiritual science" (*Geisteswissenschaft*) interchangeably with that of anthroposophy, and in many ways this may be preferable, as it contains within itself reference to "science," and Steiner claimed to employ strictly scientific methods in his researches. It is invariably the case that the serious student soon sees ordered patterns emerge from the seeming chaos, and this is also true for the various "disciplines" of spiritual science which concern themselves with cosmology, pedagogy, medicine, agriculture, theology and Christology, the arts and sciences in general, or "pure" anthroposophy, namely, those aspects of spiritual science which cannot readily be applied to easily definable areas of human activity. Whole systems and sub-systems are seen mutually to support one other; they interpenetrate each other considerably, and inter-relationships can be readily detected.

Body, soul and spirit

For present purposes, however, we need be concerned only with Rudolf Steiner's ideas concerning the nature of the human being. First we shall consider those which postulate Man as consisting of body, soul, and spirit, and here it is best to quote Steiner at some length:

> Through his body he is related to the objects which present
> themselves to his senses from without. The materials from the
> outer world compose this body of his; and the forces of
> the outer world work also in it. And just as he observes
> the things of the outer world with his senses, so can he
> also observe his own bodily existence. But it is impossible to
> observe his soul existence in the same way. Everything in
> me which is bodily process can be perceived with my bodily
> senses. My likes and dislikes, my joy and pain, neither I
> nor anyone else can perceive with bodily senses. The region of
> the soul is one which is inaccessible to bodily perception.
> The bodily existence of a man is manifest to all eyes; the soul
> existence he carries within himself as his world. Through
> the spirit, however, the outer world is revealed to him in a
> higher way. The mysteries of the outer world, indeed, unveil
> themselves in his inner being; but he steps in spirit out
> of himself and lets the things speak for themselves, about that
> which has significance not for him, but for them. The human
> being looks up at the starry heavens, the delight his soul
> experiences belongs to him; the eternal laws of the stars which
> he comprehends in thought, in spirit, belong not to him but
> the stars themselves. Thus, the human being is citizen of three
> worlds. Through his *body* he belongs to the world which he
> also perceives through his body; through his *soul* he constructs
> for himself his own world; through his *spirit* a world reveals
> itself to him which is exalted above both the others.[1]

Such a description may seem at first sight excessively simplistic, but it is carefully worded, and amply repays careful thought and reflection. Steiner held that, just as Man's physical body consists of physical-material substances necessarily obtained from the earth, his "soul body" consists of "soul substance" and his "spiritual body" of "spiritual substance." He was careful to point out that the composition of Man's soul and spirit members out of soul and spirit "substance" is not merely analogous to the composition of his physical body from earthly mineral substance: just because soul and spirit cannot be detected by empirical means this does not signify that they do not exist. This is not the place to indulge in polemics; as remarked earlier in order to understand Steiner's ideas one must accept them, albeit tentatively, and be prepared to employ the maximum degree of empathy possible.

In ordinary parlance, distinctions between soul and spirit are not always made, and quite often the terms are used interchangeably. Within the ambit of Rudolf Steiner's spiritual science, the words are used in the manner of technical terms. Discussing the corporeal nature of the human being, he points out that our observation of the world around us by means of our senses reveals essential relationships with the mineral, plant, and animal worlds. Like the minerals, we build our body out of the substance of nature; like the plants, we grow and propagate our species; like the animals, we perceive the objects around us and build up our inner experiences on the basis of the impressions they make on us.[2] He is careful to point out, however, that Man constitutes a distinct kingdom of Nature, and is not, as scientific orthodoxy maintains, merely a higher member of the animal kingdom.

Steiner argues that even the simplest of sensations belongs to the realm of Man's soul, to his inner world as contrasted with the outer world, and that such sensations give rise to feelings of pleasure and displeasure. These, he declares, are the stirrings of our inner life, our soul life, and they incite reactions on the outer world through the medium of our deeds, our acts of will. The body becomes the foundation of the soul-being of Man in that he receives incitements from the outer world, but he creates in response to these incitements a world of his own.[3] However, unlike the animals, Man is not slave to such sensations and incitements, as certain aspects of his spiritual nature reach down, so to speak, into his soul-life and modify and regularize them. In other words, Man reveals his spiritual nature inasmuch as he is a *thinking* being: by thinking about his perceptions he acquires knowledge of his environment, and by reflecting about his actions he is empowered to introduce a reasonable coherence into his life.

The soul of Man, then, according to Steiner, is confronted by a twofold necessity: by dint of the fact that we possess a bodily nature we are governed by natural necessity, the laws of the change of matter; by dint of the fact that we possess a spiritual nature, we subject ourselves to the laws of thought. In a manner of speaking, therefore, just as the body is the basis of the soul life, so the soul life is the basis of the spiritual life. The very fact that a human being is able to reflect along these lines supports the view that Man is not a member of the animal kingdom. His highest feelings — altruism, for example — do not come of themselves, but are achieved by energetic and sustained thinking; no animal is capable of such conscious actions.

Having considered the being of Man from a threefold point of view, as comprising together body, soul and spirit, we may now look at Steiner's ideas concerning Man's constitution from another standpoint. Scattered throughout his educational writings and lectures are found references to a fourfold membership of the human being into physical body, etheric body, astral body, and ego.

The fourfold nature of Man

Through his physical body, Man maintains a connection with the inorganic mineral world. This is necessarily so, as the food he eats originates in the soil beneath his feet, but having first been conveniently transmuted by certain members of the plant world; in some cases, of course, certain members of the animal kingdom are by custom included in the food chain. The mineral world itself is lifeless: it cannot be maintained that mere chemical changes involve life-processes — they are essentially mechanical by nature. The physical body of Man, according to Steiner, is that which brings the substances of the mineral kingdom into mixture, combination, form and dissolution by the same laws that are at work in the mineral world itself. It need hardly be said that scientific materialism designates the physical body as being the one and only constituent of the human being, all associated phenomena of a psychic or spiritual nature being regarded as incidental.

Over and above the physical body, spiritual science recognizes a second essential principle in Man: it is that which Steiner usually refers to as the "etheric body," though he sometimes refers to it as the "life-body" or "formative-forces-body" (*Bildekräfteleib*). In some respects the term is an unfortunate one, as Steiner himself admits, and he is at some pains to point out that the word "etheric" has nothing to do with the hypothetical "ether" of physics.[4] Although the term "formative-forces-body" is the most graphic and in some ways the best, it is clumsy and un-English, and henceforth the term "etheric body" will be used. It must be admitted — perhaps emphasized — that the physical body alone is accessible to investigation by means of the bodily senses, and that the etheric body is accessible to investigation only to those who have developed the necessary higher organs of perception.[5]

The presence of etheric forces is manifested in the difference between the inorganic and the organic; an *organism* necessarily possesses an etheric body which lies at the base of all formative life — it organizes the matter of the mineral world and shapes it to specific purposes. A purely physical body has its form — a crystal, for example — through the action of the physical formative forces innate in the lifeless. A living body, however, does not receive its form through the action of these forces, because at the moment in which life has departed from it and it is given over to physical forces only, it disintegrates. The body of a human being becomes a corpse when etheric forces cease to be active in it; thus the etheric body preserves the physical body from dissolution at every moment during life. According to Steiner, the etheric body is responsible for the forces of growth and reproduction as well as for the powers of *memory* in the human being. It is the agent of healing when the physical body suffers damage or disease; it is the agent of preserving the shape, form and function of the bodily organs, which remain in spite of the continuous renewal of the matter which constitutes them. The etheric forces are those which preserve the species of living creatures, and provide their patterns of growth and propagation. The human etheric body, however, differs from that of plants and animals in that it is organized to serve the purposes of the thinking spirit also.

A third member of the human being recognized by spiritual science is the so-called "astral body" or "sentient-body." The latter term is in many ways to be preferred, but once again the unfortunate term "astral body" has persisted and is now commonly used in anthroposophical circles as a technical term. It should perhaps be mentioned that the same term is used indeterminately by quasi "occult-scientists" and spiritualists, thus generating considerable confusion and misunderstanding. However, the term "astral body" will be used henceforth, strictly as a technical Steinerian term within the semantic limits which he himself indicated. It is the vehicle of pain and pleasure, of impulse, craving, passion and the like — all of which are absent in creatures consisting only of physical and etheric bodies.[6] From this it would follow that minerals and plants are not in any respect sentient — they are incapable of having sensations or receiving sense-perceptions. The point is not whether a creature merely responds to an external stimulus, but whether such a stimulus is reflected in an *inner* process — in feeling.[7] In short, creatures which possess a nervous system also possess an astral body, and this includes not only Man but the whole of the animal kingdom.

The essential difference between animal and man is, according to Steiner, the fact that the human being possesses a fourth member — the "ego" or "I." The ego represents the factor of individualization, that which guarantees the uniqueness of every man, woman and child. The word "I" is itself unique in that no person can use it to designate another. In a manner

27

of speaking it represents the "higher self" in Man, and through it, declared Steiner, he is the crown of all earthly creation.[8] The special task of the ego is to purify and ennoble the other three members of Man's nature, and under its influence not only are his wishes and desires refined by its acting continuously on the astral body, and his life-habits, temperament and memory established by its acting on the etheric body, but the whole appearance and physiognomy, gestures and movements of his physical body are altered.[9]

Reincarnation and karma

Not only does this purifying and ennobling process continue throughout a single lifetime, but through many, as the ego evolves to higher and higher stages of development through successive lives or re-embodiments. In this connection it is undeniable that Steiner is in agreement with certain Oriental religious and philosophical tenets; indeed the twin concepts of reincarnation and *karma* or destiny are central to his spiritual-scientific system. Man's body and soul, he declares, yield themselves up to the ego in order to serve it, and in turn the "I" yields itself up to the spirit: the "I" lives in body and soul, but the spirit lives in the "I." What there is of spirit in the "I" is eternal; furthermore the "I" receives its nature and significance from that with which it is bound up. In so far as it lives in the physical body, it is subject to the laws of the mineral world; through its etheric body to the laws of propagation and growth; by virtue of the astral body it is subject to the laws of the soul world, and in so far as it receives the spiritual into itself it is subject to the laws of the spirit. That which the laws of mineral and of life construct comes into being and vanishes; but the spirit has nothing to do with becoming and perishing.[10] This argument, contentious as some may assert it to be, epitomizes Steiner's view of the realities of reincarnation. Essential to them is the doctrine of karma or self-created destiny, as remarked earlier, and this will now be dealt with from an anthroposophical point of view.

Steiner made it quite plain that there is nothing whatsoever arbitrary or fortuitous about the workings of human destiny; fate and fortune alike have no place — indeed it might be contended that no event of significance for the individual happens by mere chance. He was careful to point out that his use of the word *karma* precluded any fatalistic overtones: he stressed that it is the ego of a human being, during its pre-natal sojourn in the spiritual world, which prepares the opportunities for experiences in the earthly life before it, but can never decide in advance how it will use them. Thus every moment in earthly life is one in which the pre-ordained element is complemented by the new, willed element, whereby the individual may act in accordance with mere custom, convention or habit, or realize himself freely. In his book *Theosophy* Steiner discusses the questions of reincarnation and karma very thoroughly, and in it he asserts that after a deed has been accomplished through human agency, there is something in the world upon which an individual ego has stamped its character.[11] He goes on to pose the question: Might it not be that the results of a deed, on which the "I" has stamped its own nature, retain a tendency to return to the "I" just as an impression preserved in the memory revives in response to some external inducement? He concludes that through an action which the soul has performed, there follows the predisposition to perform another action which is the fruit of the first, and that the soul carries this as a necessity within itself until the latter action has come to pass. Thus, through a given action there has been imprinted upon the soul the necessity of carrying out the consequences of that action.[12] This lies at the basis of human destiny, and reflection will show how it is of necessity self-created. As an analogy, just as a person's actions on a given day depend on his actions the day or days before, and at the same time will largely determine his actions the day or days after, so it is with repeated earth-lives. A human being, in more ways than one, lives in a world of his own creation.

Rudolf Steiner held that one of the gravest prejudices of modern materialistic science consists in trying to explain the spiritual qualities of a human being by hereditary transmission from father, mother or other ancestors.[13] As physical entities he posits, we spring from physical parents and have the same shape as the whole human species; as spiritual entities we have our own shape, just as we have our own biography. Such a biography is not explicable through the biographies of our forebears, but only through the workings of our spiritual predispositions in the manner just outlined. Reflection will show that the twin concepts of reincarnation and karma are interlinked and mutually supportive of each other.

5 The Child's Body, Soul and Spirit

Our one and only help as teachers is that we learn to observe human beings: to observe the bodies of the children, the souls of the children and the spirits of the childen.

Birthlessness and deathlessness

Rudolf Steiner asserted that anthroposophy, by its inherent character and tendency, must have the task of providing a practical conception of the world — one that comprehends the nature and essence of human life.[1] He strove constantly to apply the results of his spiritual investigations to practical life, and to provide insights into the problems encountered in human existence. He was certainly no woolly-minded mystic issuing vague pronouncements about some indeterminate higher reality, divine or otherwise. It must always be borne in mind that he was trained as a scientist and employed scientific method in his spiritual researches, and he was acutely aware of his responsibilities in this direction. It was his rule never to speak about any matter, spiritual or otherwise, unless he was completely certain of his ground, and it is easy to overlook the fact that he was a scholar in his own right, who often delighted his friends and confounded his enemies by his breadth of learning.

Steiner was forty-one years of age when he made the difficult decision to declare publicly his great aim in life, which was "to found new methods of spiritual research on a scientific basis."[2] That he waited to do this until he was approaching middle age is typical of him, as he had to feel absolutely sure of seeing his way ahead. To those critics who scoffingly demanded empirical evidence of results of his researches he would point out that life itself provided evidence, given that people approached them without prejudice but with healthy judgement. He was perhaps aware that his spiritual-scientific system would appear to many to be somewhat self-enclosed, and rather too neat and tidy to be true; that many of his findings mutually supported one other, and that points of contact with ordinary science were few and tenuous. He was equally aware, however, that if thinkers took the trouble to study his ideas carefully and conscientiously, and above all without bias, he would gain supporters. He was equally scathing of spiritualism as of materialism, declaring that materialism understands nothing of matter and spiritualism nothing of spirit.[3] Steiner could perceive that materialistic science is enmeshed in its own self-enclosed system, and this he saw as the tragedy of modern times; he was tireless in pointing out that materialism is doomed not to understand matter precisely because matter is that in which the spirit is perpetually at work.[4]

It will be clear from the last chapter that Steiner spoke about the supersensible membership of the human being in quite concrete terms, as he did about the doctrines of reincarnation and karma — notions foreign to Western civilization and so often unacceptable simply because of this fact. It is scarcely necessary to point out, therefore, that he regarded every single child as unique, if for no other reason than that it had existed as a spiritual being prior to conception and birth as an individual in its own right. He looked upon the growth and development of the child as a process of gradual incarnation, as the descent of a spiritual entity into a material sheath fitted for existence in a world of matter. Parents in no sense whatever "create" their offspring, they are merely instrumental in providing a physical vehicle for the spiritual being seeking re-embodiment. Bearing in mind what has been said about destiny as being self-created, it would follow that in most cases children actually choose the parents they are born to, as there are invariably karmic links present.

It seems remarkable that the notion of pre-natal existence of the human "soul" seems to be so widely disregarded throughout the Western world, whereas its post-mortem existence is quite commonly accepted as belief or even fact. Belief in the *post mortem* immortality of the soul necessarily appeals to egotism in people, as Steiner pointed out.[5] Human beings, experiencing life in the ordinary sense and finding it sweet, not unnaturally wish it to continue in some form or other, and with some encouragement from religious interests, many people — from purely selfish motives, it would be safe to admit — subscribe to the notion of post-mortem immortality of the "soul" because they feel keenly the desirability of continuing living in some form or other. Yet, illogically enough, the vast majority of people who believe in the post-mortem immortality of the "soul" do not believe in its essential counterpart, the *pre-natal* immortality of the "soul." This is a particularly unfortunate delusion on the part of such people, for it can easily be refuted on philosophical and logical grounds. A "soul" or any other entity for that matter, cannot suddenly come into existence at a given point in time and then continue for eternity; an entity once granted the attributes of eternity must be understood to have possessed them eternally.

Steiner pointed out the lack of a suitable word in the language of civilized peoples for "birthlessness"; *immortality* is generally understood in the sense of "deathlessness." Equally lacking is a word approximating to "unbornness"; if the concept of immortality is to be taken seriously, "unbornness" and "birthlessness" are words fully deserving of validation.[6]

Life-epochs in childhood

Steiner divided the developmental process of growing up into seven-year periods, the most important of which, from an educational point of view are, as one might expect, the first two: from birth to seven years of age, and from thence to fourteen years of age. From many points of view the first period is the more important — certainly the more crucial. It should perhaps be mentioned at once that these "life-epochs" are only approximate, and that the first period lasts until the child loses its deciduous (so-called "milk") teeth, usually between its sixth and seventh birthdays, and the second period lasts from the second dentition to the onset of puberty at about the age of thirteen or fourteen, or sometimes earlier.

Before physical birth, the growing human being is totally enclosed by the physical body of the mother, and birth consists in the setting of the child free of its protective sheath, thus enabling the environment to work upon it directly. The child's senses open to the physical world, and the external world gains that influence in the human being which was previously exercised by the physical envelope of the mother-body. The immediate environment of the child after birth and for the first few years of its life is of paramount importance. The main reason for the crucial nature of this period is that, until the second dentition, body, soul and spirit of the child are in complete unity. In other words, the physical body of the child is enclosed, in effect, by an etheric envelope and an astral envelope; thus they constitute a certain unity, and this is an important consideration, as will become clear in due course.[7] For the time being, it should be mentioned that the second dentition is indicative of the liberation or "birth" of the etheric body, and that puberty marks the time when the child's astral body becomes free on all sides. The "birth" of the remaining member of the human being — the ego or "I" — takes place approximately seven years after puberty, at around the age of twenty or twenty-one, the traditional age for the commencement of true adulthood.

During the first seven years of life the forces of heredity are at work, but only, asserts Steiner, for this limited period. The reason he gives for this is that the etheric body is developing and moulding its own forces in preparation for its liberation, for its becoming independent, at the time of change of teeth. Until this event occurs one should not bring to bear on the etheric body those forces which are, for it, what the impressions of the physical environment are for the physical body. In educational terms, this means not calling on the child's powers of thinking and of memory to an excessive degree, and this aspect will be discussed fully later. After the second dentition, the child's etheric body is still under the influence of the astral body, which has not yet escaped from its protective sheath; this occurs at the time of puberty, when the etheric body completes a further stage in its development, culminating in the ability for the child to reproduce its kind.

Rudolf Steiner claimed that during the first seven years of a child's life one could see quite clearly at work the effects of its habits of life before birth or conception in its pre-earthly existence in the spiritual world.[8] His description is perhaps worth quoting in full:

> Yet if you know how to observe and note how each day, each week, each month, the indefinite features of the face become more definite, the awkward movements become less clumsy and the child gradually accustoms himself to his surroundings, then you will realise that it is the spirit from the pre-earthly world which is endeavouring to make the child's body more like itself. We shall understand why the child is as he is, if we observe him in this way; we shall understand that it is the descended spirit which is acting as we see it within the child's body.[9]

During the first seven years of a child's life, declared Steiner, its body, soul and spirit constitute a unity, and during this period more than any other that which affects one member necessarily affects the other two. This is the time when the child instinctively *imitates* that which goes on around; it believes, so to speak, in the morality of the world, and therefore believes that the world may be imitated. Thus the child lives in the past, and is to a great extent a revealer of the pre-natal past — not of the physical past, but of the past of soul and spirit.[10] The supreme task of the educator is to ensure as far as possible the harmonizing of the spirit and soul with the physical body.[11] For the first few years of life the parents or significant others are responsible for the child's education in the widest sense of the word, for its socialization and acculturation, and this consists, quite literally, in providing an environment worthy of imitation. This quite extraordinary predisposition for imitation, and the remarkable susceptibility to what goes on around the growing child at this time is of tremendous importance for its future development, physical, psychological and spiritual. Steiner asserted that the child feels its environment as an extension of itself, that there is no sense of differentiation between itself and the outside world: the child therefore senses its surroundings as "true" and grows into them with the conviction that the things it finds around it are as true as was its environment in the spiritual world, where everything was apparent in transparent clarity.[12] In fact, he said, nowhere in our observation of man and of nature are we confronted by spirit and soul so immediately as when we contemplate the manifestations of life in a tiny child.[13] Steiner often characterized the child at this period in its life as being "wholly sense-organ" and the educational implications of this will be fully discussed in due course.

As remarked above, from birth until approximately the seventh year the child is paramountly a being of body-soul-spirit in one; from the seventh to the fourteenth it is a being of body and soul with a separate nature of soul and spirit; and from puberty onwards the human being emerges in its threefold nature: a physical being, a being of soul, and a being of spirit.[14] At the change of teeth the senses, which permeate the whole being of the child, now come to the surface; they separate off from the rest of the organism and go their separate ways, as it were. This means that the soul and spirit are freed from the physical body and the child can develop its own inner nature.[15] The freeing of the etheric forces at about the seventh year means that they are available to serve the organism in a different way, and according to Steiner these forces become forces of soul, *the actual forces of mental representation* or ideation.[16] At about this age it becomes noticeable how the child is gradually able to form clear-cut concepts; whereas before they were only vague and indefinite, the actual formation of concepts is now possible.[17] Gradually, too, the child begins to differentiate between itself and its surroundings, a culminating point being reached at about the age of nine, an event to which Rudolf Steiner attributed considerable importance, and which will be dealt with later. The child, between its seventh and fourteenth years, seeks a natural authority to look up to, and this, too, is of tremendous pedagogical significance. Only after puberty, with the freeing or "birth" of the astral body, is the child ripe to apply its own judgement to the world, and this fact, too, is taken fully into account in the Waldorf system of education. Steiner declared the aim of this system to be the bringing up of children to be human beings strong and sound in body, free in soul and lucid in spirit.[18]

Aspects of our threefold nature

In his book *Von Seelenrätseln*, which was published in 1917, Rudolf Steiner saw fit to place on record the results of systematic spiritual investigation extending over a period of thirty years concerning the physical and psychic components of the human being.[19] He declared that *the body as a whole*, not merely the nervous activity impounded in it, is the physical basis of psychic life.[20] In other words, he saw the bodily organization of the human being, and the psychic organization also, as threefold: the nerve/senses system, located mainly in the head, serves Man's thinking processes; the rhythmic system, comprising heart and lungs, serves Man's feeling processes, and the metabolic/limb system, comprising the digestive organs and legs and arms, serves his willing processes. It should perhaps be pointed out at once that what Steiner meant by thinking, feeling and willing bears but faint resemblance to the cognitive, affective and conative attributes of the human being recognized by current psychological orthodoxy. Few modern scientists would concede that the actual seat of Man's life of feeling is located in the breast or that his will-impulses proceed from his digestive system and limbs, or even admit such notions as the basis of a working hypothesis, yet this is what Steiner asks one to do.

He does not offer "proof" in anatomical, physiological or neurological terms which have been arrived at empirically; rather does he adopt a phenomenological or symptomatological approach, as these would accord with his method of regarding Nature artistically as well as scientifically, the desirability of doing which he never tired of pointing out. He contended that what appears in science as the Idea is in art the Image, and that the surmounting of the sensible by the spirit is the goal of both art and science. Science, declared Steiner, surmounts the sensible through resolving it wholly into spirit; art through implanting spirit in it.[21] In this he agreed with Goethe, whom he quotes:

> I think science might be called the knowledge of the general, abstract knowledge; art, on the other hand, would be science applied to an action; science would be reason and art its mechanism, so that it might also be called practical science. Finally, therefore, science would be the theorem and art the problem.[22]

So it is both as artist and as scientist that Rudolf Steiner viewed the human being, and if his observations lack the icy, intellectual pedantry of orthodox empiricism, they must not be regarded as lacking the necessary rigour simply on that account. If his terms of reference appear to be more in the nature of characterizations than of definitions this does not necessarily render them less valid.

If, averred Rudolf Steiner, we speak as ordinary present-day physiology and biology do about the bodily-physical nature of the human being, we are then dealing with something which really is not present in the living human being at all. The whole bodily-physical nature is a result, is the work of, the soul-spiritual nature.[23] Steiner never tired of exhorting the teachers of the first Waldorf school to observe the children in their care, for the very reason that attributes of the spirit and soul of an individual are perceptibly manifest in that person's physical body. For this reason it is important to observe details of a child's physiognomy, its habitual gestures, gait, and suchlike, and equally important to be able to interpret one's observations correctly. Such matters will be fully discussed in a later chapter; for the moment, the notion that real knowledge of the spirit-soul nature of a human being is not possible without knowledge of the bodily-physical nature might be considered as a working hypothesis. Real knowledge of the bodily-physical nature is at the same time knowledge of the spirit-soul nature.[24] For most people such knowledge would have to be obtained by *indirect* means, mainly inferential, as *direct* observation of the supersensible members of the human being would be possible only to those who had developed the necessary ability. Steiner always stressed that such ability is possessed by every human being, albeit in dormant condition, but that supersensible perception is possible for those who accept the conditions necessary for it, and who undergo the rigorous training demanded.[25] To the question: How may spiritual vision be understood in the real and true sense? his reply was that one must learn to see all that appertains to the senses in a spiritual way, and look at the spiritual in a way that is akin to the senses.[26]

In order to obtain real knowledge of the human being, therefore, it is necessary not only to observe a person with scientific exactitude, but also with the eye of the artist. The abstract, theoretical mode of observation belonging to science, with its primary emphasis on the highest possible degree of objectivity, declared Steiner, can only lead to Man being regarded as a mere abstraction, a mechanism. Theoretical observation should pass over into artistic perception for an individual to be understood in his or her real being.[27] The artistic approach, he claimed, is the guide to the first stage of exact clairvoyance — that of

Imaginative knowledge.[28] Steiner was, needless to say, aware of the heretical nature of his insistence that an artistic approach to Man was not necessarily unscientific; as a scientist himself he knew the importance of objectivity, yet he persisted in his conviction that a true understanding of Man cannot be grasped by purely scientific modes of cognition. The human being is an artistic creation of Nature, he argued, and the moment we draw near to Man with the laws of Nature, we must pass over into the realm of art.[29]

Steiner, while in no way whatever attempting to deny or devalue the achievements of science, nevertheless deplored the tendency of the typical scientist to surrender himself to sequences of events and to giving himself up passively to the external world, and he called for a more active kind of thinking, and a greater degree of participation of an inwardly vital kind.[30] Scientific intellectuality, imbued and enlivened with inner forces of soul, together with artistic sense, could well lead over into the first stages of supersensible cognition. The difficulties inherent in taking such a step are of course formidable, not the least being the habits of thinking acquired by strict training in empirical methodology which every scientist undergoes. A "science of the supersensible," a science of the invisible, would seem to many to be a contradiction in terms. In the absence of visible evidence, spiritual science, faced with the formidable task of describing the supersensible, the non-sensible, in ordinary terms befitted to the perceptions of Man's bodily sense organs, is forced to use ordinary terms, albeit stipulatively. As mentioned earlier, Rudolf Steiner was inclined to prefer characterization rather than definition on the grounds that characterizations are "open-ended" and allow for the addition of further conceptual elements, whereas definitions are closed, rigid and final. It is important, he argued, that concepts should allow for growth in people's understanding, to reckon with their growing awareness of things around them as their comprehension is more and more enriched by life's experiences. Where the education of children is concerned, this principle is of paramount importance; the teacher should transmit a living apprehension of things, as definitions fetter the soul and stifle the spirit.[31]

One is not surprised, therefore, that Steiner used characterizations when describing the attributes of the human being as a being of body, soul and spirit. He saw each member of this trichotomy as itself trichotomous: the body he divided into head-system comprising mainly the nerve/senses system; chest-system, comprising mainly the rhythmically-functioning heart and lungs; and the metabolic/limbs system, comprising mainly the organs of digestion, the arms and legs. The soul he saw as possessing the attributes of thinking, feeling and willing, and those of sympathy and antipathy and oscillation between the two; the spirit he conceived in terms of consciousness: waking, dreaming and sleeping. The correspondences among all these factors are easily seen from the following table:

	Physical Expression	Psychical Expression	Spiritual Expression
Body	Nerves/Senses system	Thinking	Waking consciousness
Soul	Heart/Lungs system	(Antipathy) Feeling (Sympathy)	Dreaming consciousness
Spirit	Metabolic/Limbs system	Willing	Sleeping consciousness

It need hardly be pointed out that there is considerable overlapping among such systems, and that hard-and-fast boundaries simply do not exist; but these considerations do nothing to invalidate the Ideas present in them.[32] In the case of the bodily system, the sense of touch extends all over the body by virtue of the skin, and the network of nerves does the same, but it cannot be denied that the brain is located in the head, as well as the organs of sight, hearing, taste and smell. Hence Rudolf Steiner felt justified in designating the head-system as comprising *mainly* the nerves and senses. Similarly, the twofold functioning of the human soul can be seen to have fluid boundaries: firstly, from the aspect of body-and-soul, thinking can be said to be connected with the brain, as organ of consciousness, and thus with the head; feeling produces readily recognizable psychosomatic effects in the heart and lungs (for instance, increased pulse rate due to fear) though in other senses feelings affect both thinking and willing; secondly, from the aspect of spirit-and-soul, sympathy is seen as having affinities with willing and antipathy as having affinities with thinking, whereas the area of oscillation between the two can be deemed the area of feeling proper which influences a person's thinking or willing equally strongly. Viewing the body and soul from the spirit Steiner saw Man's waking consciousness as having connections with thinking and the head, his dreaming consciousness as having connections with feeling and the rhythmic system, and his sleeping consciousness or unconscious state as having connections with the will and the metabolic system and the limbs. At first sight this system of integrated systems may seem unnecessarily complicated, and anything but scientific, but further discussion of them from various points of view in later chapters may show otherwise.

The incarnation process

The preceding description of the human being from the point of view of the body, soul and spirit applies in the main to a mature person, an adult. The picture is considerably complicated when viewed against the background of the growing child, which, taken from the standpoint of spiritual science, is one of gradual incarnation of the human spirit. Indeed, Steiner declared that the whole task of education, conceived in the spiritual sense, is to bring the child's soul-spiritual nature into harmony with its corporeal nature.[33] From the point of view of ordinary pedagogy, the aim of the teacher should be to bring the child to the world of nature on the one hand, and to the world of spirit on the other.[34] Steiner deplored that the vast majority of people feel a lack of affinity with nature; they feel — as indeed they think and act — as if there were no connection between them and the rest of the universe. He never wearied of emphasizing that what takes place in Man is not a matter of indifference to the rest of nature, but rather the rest of nature reaches into Man, and what takes place in Man is simultaneously a cosmic process.[35] Each individual is a cosmic being as well as an earthly being; his or her life is inextricably bound up with the rhythmic processes of the universe, a notion which is clearly reflected in the importance placed in the practice of celebrating the passage of the seasons of the year in all Rudolf Steiner schools.

Steiner characterized the human head at birth to be "mainly body," and by this he meant that the head has reached perfection as far as its *bodily* nature is concerned. Put in another way, it means that the head bears the seal, the stamp, the imprint of the soul and spiritual elements, and this corresponds to Steiner's insistence that the material must always be regarded as being posterior to the spiritual: at all times and in all circumstances spirit is anterior to matter.[36] It is not without significance that throughout gestation the head develops, as it were, to the detriment of the rest of the body, and at birth is relatively perfect, as it grows proportionately less after birth than most other parts of the body. Because of this fact, avers Steiner, *in respect of the soul* the head is capable of the most complete development: in the head the *bodily* nature is most highly developed, but in it resides a dreaming soul and a spirit that is asleep.[37] In other words, at birth and for the first few years of its life the child's consciousness is dreamlike, not wide-awake and self-aware, as it becomes later. An important concomitant to this is that the child is an imitative being; it cannot do other than *imitate* what goes on in its environment — literally in an *unconscious* manner. Steiner characterizes this condition by saying that the child in spirit and soul, in its sleeping spirit and dreaming soul, is outside its head: it is with those around it. This goes on until approximately the seventh year or until the second dentition occurs, which event is an actual indication that the development of the head has reached its final stage.[38] At this time, too, it may be remembered, the etheric forces have completed the forming and moulding processes in the body and are now free to function in a soul-spiritual manner, and this shows itself in the child's acquisition of the powers and skills of ideation, of thinking. Thus, in effect, the head is engaged during early childhood in giving the child form and figure; in other words, a child does not grow *up*, it grows *down*.

True to pattern, Steiner argued that as the head during babyhood is solely body, the chest and rhythmic system comprises mainly body and soul, and the metabolic/limb system comprises body, soul and spirit. In terms of consciousness, this means that a baby is most "awake" in its limbs, less so in the chest, and least of all in the head; and ordinary observation confirms this. Conversely, the child has descended from the spiritual worlds with a virtually perfected spirit (asleep in the head), and a relatively perfected soul (dreaming in the head). The task of the educator, declared Steiner, is to develop that part of the child's spirit which is not yet perfect, and that part of the soul which is still less perfect.[39] In terms of pedagogy this means the education of the will (through the limbs), and partly educating the feeling life (through the rhythmic system). Direct education of the intellect or thinking life is virtually impossible; one cannot implant intelligence that is not there, one can only awaken those faculties already in the child, but sleeping. As the life of the intellect commences only with puberty and the birth of the astral body,[40] this means that between the second dentition and puberty the intellect can be reached *with impunity* only through the will and the feelings, and this is what Waldorf education sets out to do, as will be shown later.

Cognitive forces, powers of thinking and ideation become available for development at about the time of the change of teeth, and these obviously belong to the head system. As remarked just now, the intellect may only be reached, without detriment to the child, through the feelings and the will, which, it may be remembered, have their seat in the chest and in the limbs respectively. During the first seven years of life the will-nature is almost totally bound up with the limbs: the child has to learn to walk and talk, and there are many other motor skills to acquire; only gradually does it bring about co-ordination of action and intention. All this means that, during this time, forces of growth and development flow downwards from the head, while the will forces flow upwards from the limb/metabolic system, more particularly from the feet, and Rudolf Steiner emphasized that this is an anthroposophical truth of great significance for education.[41] Now at about the seventh year the downward-flowing forces from the head meet with the upward-flowing forces from the feet, and logically enough their meeting place is in the chest which encloses the rhythmic system. In psychic terms this means that the forces of thinking meet the forces of willing in the area of feeling, and during the next seven years, from the second dentition until puberty, these forces go through a stage of mutual adjustment, and this is of paramount importance from an educational point of view. This bringing of the child's thinking into a right relationship with its will does not come about of its own accord in the normal course of development, and in this, warns Steiner, it is possible to fail. It is the satisfactory union between Man's thinking and willing that forms the basis for his moral actions; it is because of this that he can become a moral being.[42]

The head forces flowing down from above, and the will forces flowing up from below meet, as it were, like two tidal waves in the chest, and flow through each other. These are marked in physiological terms by changes in the bodily organs at puberty; the upward-flowing will forces reaching the area of the throat culminate in changes in the larynx, and the downward flowing forces culminate in changes in the sexual organs. This coincides with the freeing or "birth" of the astral body, as observed in an earlier chapter. During the next seven years, from puberty until the age of twenty or twenty-one, the will-forces permeate the head with its powers of intellect and cognition, expressing themselves more particularly in the acquisition of true critical judgement; and the head-forces flow on into the limbs to permeate the will-forces, manifesting as practical morality, as love in action, as deeds motivated by altruism and idealism. As Rudolf Steiner once remarked, Man is more perfect on account of his limbs than on account of his head.[43] By this he meant that a person may well think rightly but act wrongly; but if a person acts rightly, this has been necessarily preceded by thinking rightly.

From these considerations it may be seen that, in pedagogical terms, the middle period of childhood, from seven to fourteen years of age, is a time when, above all, the *feeling* life should be involved, as the child is maturationally ripe for such an approach. It may be recalled that the soul-forces of sympathy and antipathy, having affinities with the other soul-qualities of thinking, feeling and willing, reside, as it were, in the chest, in the heart and lungs. It is perhaps worth noting that the twofoldness of the physical organs is reflected in the twofoldness of the psychic functions of sympathy and antipathy which lie at the basis of the life of feeling. It has been observed earlier that sympathy has affinities with the willing processes and that antipathy has affinities with thinking and cognition, and it may be said that the whole system of heart and blood circulation partakes more of the nature of metabolism and of will, while the lungs and breathing are connected rather with the head and the whole nerves/senses system. Obviously, the two physical organs are interconnected by their very functions apart from the fact that these functions themselves are both rhythmical in nature.

Rudolf Steiner pointed out that the rhythmical process of breathing is, in a certain sense, transmitted to the brain: as we breathe in we are continually pressing the cerebro-spinal fluid into the brain, and as we breathe out we press it back again into the body.[44] He maintained that there are subtle connections between the breathing processes and the nerves/senses system, and that harmony between these two is essential if the soul and spiritual elements of the child are to be satisfactorily incorporated into the physical. In fact, he declared, education consists in teaching the child to breathe rightly.[45] On another occasion he said that we can only understand the nerves/senses system aright if we are conscious of the fact that in the nerves/senses system laws really prevail which are not the physical-chemical laws of earthly matter; that Man, through his nerves/senses system lifts himself out of the laws of earthly materiality. In its formation the nerves/senses system is completely the result of his pre-earthly life. Hence, because in reality all the essential constitution of the nerves/senses system is lifted out of earthly materiality, it is able to develop on its own all its activity relating to soul and spirit.[46]

Rudolf Steiner was emphatic that the social problems of the twentieth century are mainly due to the reason that facts are confronting Man on a level to which he has not grown, that he lacks the necessary insight to solve such problems because he always confines himself to the externalities of the facts he faces. This is why people are "socially helpless."[47] There was a need, Steiner declared, for an educational system by which people could learn to learn, and to go on learning throughout their lives, and he claimed that the methods he propounded were designed to meet this need. What has become known as the Waldorf system of education, he contended, was the right and appropriate system for twentieth century Man. He had no desire whatever to introduce a "progressive" system of some kind based on abstract theories, or to initiate changes for their own sake. His ideas on education were, he claimed, based on realities, and such realities, moreover, that were impossible of detection by ordinary methods of observation and research. He made no attempt to conceal the fact that his pronouncements were based directly on the results of his spiritual researches, on direct insight into Reality. At the same time, he realised that his ideas would be opposed from many quarters and that they were open to abuse and ridicule. Nevertheless, he was confident that his ideas would appeal to people who were willing to consider them carefully, patiently, and above all without prejudice, and that they would gradually become more and more widely known.

Life in spiritual worlds

The social problems involved in education will be discussed later; it is necessary first of all to expound more of Steiner's ideas which go to form what might be termed the theoretical background to his pedagogical system, difficult and unusual as they may appear on first acquaintance. He never tired of stressing that the whole of contemporary civilization is founded on the egotism of humanity. This ranges from the desire to gratify one's own wishes to the inconvenience, even detriment, of other people, to the egotistical belief that life will somehow go on after death which has already been briefly discussed. Central to Waldorf pedagogy is the conviction that Man's life on Earth is a continuation, albeit in a different mode, of life in spiritual worlds. Steiner put forward the rather contentious notion that the task of teachers and educators is to carry on what has hitherto been done by higher spiritual beings.[48] Such beings cannot be approached direct, so to speak, and neither can there be any kind of pre-natal "education" as such. Some influences may possibly be transmitted by the mother of the child during the gestatory period, but only indirectly. If until the birth of her child the mother behaves in such a way that she brings to expression in herself what is morally and intellectually right, then of its own accord what the mother achieves in this prolonged self-education will pass over to the child.[49]

Not only has the child to learn to breathe rightly, as indicated earlier; it has to learn to accomplish the alternation between sleeping and waking in the way proper to Man.[50] Whereas an adult is able to work upon, to metamorphose, his waking experiences during sleep, and to carry the result of such spiritual labour back with him into waking life, the child is quite unable to do this in its early years, and it is a task of the teacher to enable it to do this. Furthermore, this enabling of the child to carry its experiences over facilitates reciprocal action, namely, the bringing back of power from the spiritual world which will help it to be a true human being in physical existence.[51] Rudolf Steiner averred that the very awareness a teacher has of such processes combats the purely personal thoughts he may have of a child, and this gives him an added sense of purpose and responsibility. Inner relationships between teacher and taught are thus more easily and firmly established to their mutual advantage. The rhythms of breathing, and of sleeping and waking, may thus be seen to be the means by which the teacher and educator facilitates the proper unity of the child's soul-spiritual nature and its bodily nature. Steiner was no believer in abstractions, but strove at all times to put the results of his spiritual investigations to practical use. His ideas are often difficult to come to terms with as he spoke so concretely of soul-spiritual phenomena; he manipulated ideas with ease and precision, and called upon his readers and hearers to do the same. Of necessity he used words more properly applicable to the world of sense to describe things and processes of a supersensible nature, and very often these words represent concepts that are already familiar in other contexts. Undoubtedly, he demanded a certain degree of mobility of thinking, of ability to handle concepts in unusual ways and in unusual settings as well as the necessary degree of goodwill to accept characterizations in place of definitions.

Mental imagery

As already discussed, one of the aims of Waldorf education is to foster the development of the child's abilities of thinking, feeling and willing. Thinking, the process of ideation or reflection, is characterized by its pictorial nature, its inclination and capacity for mental imagery. Steiner claimed that we are able to experience thought or mental imagery because the activity accomplished in the spiritual world before conception and birth is reflected by our bodily nature. Now the connections between thinking and antipathy have already been mentioned, and it must be clear that the kind of antipathy now being spoken of is of an unconscious nature — it is *not* a feeling of which we are aware. Steiner says that the "descending" individuality, no longer able to remain in the spiritual world and being brought down into the physical world, develops an antipathy for everything spiritual, and a result of this is that the spiritual pre-natal reality is mirrored, quite literally reflected, and mental imagery results. This reflective process, mirroring as it does cognitions raying in from the spiritual world of pre-natal existence, renders them weaker by virtue of the antipathetic element involved, with the result that *mere imagery, and not reality, is perceived.* Thinking is thus seen to be antipathetic in character.[52]

Having inferred that thinking belongs, so to speak, to the past, Rudolf Steiner suggested that its opposite quality of human nature, namely willing, belongs to the future. The nature of the will is enigmatic and notoriously difficult to define; it can scarcely be said to exist until an action has been performed, and by then it is already non-existent. Verbal definitions are of little real help, and psychologists, in desperation, have associated the willing faculty with either feeling or thinking according to inclination. Steiner invested the will with a nature that is spiritual, and as it has no real content he characterized it as being seed-like, the germinal essence of what will be soul-spiritual reality after death. He argued that a seed is something more than real, carrying within it the beginnings of what will appear later as reality, and that of such is the nature of the will. Thinking, therefore, is the mirrored image of pre-natal reality, while willing carries the seed, so to speak, of *post mortem* reality. Between these two faculties of human nature, claimed Steiner, is a boundary, represented by the human being clothed in a physical-material body who on the one hand "rejects" his pre-natal spiritual existence by producing the images of thought, and who on the other hand prevents the will-nature fulfilling itself by allowing it to be no more than seminal in character. This looking forward towards a *post mortem* reality is representative of the forces of sympathy, the urge to unite what lies in the future.[53]

The alternation between sympathy and antipathy which underlies the whole world of human feelings is thus expressed in what we experience in our soul life as the will for action and the life of ideas respectively. Forces of antipathy are present in the activity of thinking and ideation, and according to Steiner, if a sufficient degree of antipathy is brought to bear, a memory picture arises. Memory is thus due to an intensification of antipathy to an extent that ensures that the pictorial element, the objectifying element, is also correspondingly intensified. If this memory picture is in turn made the subject of further reflection consequent on a greater intensification of the antipathetic process, then there arises the concept.[54] Following the principle that everything pertaining to the soul is expressed and revealed in the body, it is not surprising that Steiner connected the whole processes of cognition, memory and concept formation with the nervous systems of the human being. He went so far as to assert that the brain and nervous system has nothing to do with the mental processes of cognition, but only with the *expression* of cognition in the physical organism.[55] In other words, the brain and nerve-sense system constitute the *organs* of consciousness; they do *not* initiate or give rise to consciousness in the way that the epiphenomenalist school of philosophy might argue.

Much in the same manner that memory arises from the intensification of antipathy, so the capacity for phantasy arises out of the heightening of sympathy, though this again is an unconscious process. If, said Steiner, phantasy becomes sufficiently strong that it permeates the whole nature of the human being right down into the senses, then there arises imagination, which in turn brings about sense pictures.[56] He pointed out that the senses of touch, taste and smell are closely bound up with the metabolic system, which appertains to the faculty of will, and this is indicative of the process as a whole. The bodily expression of the activity of willing, sympathy, phantasy and imagination is, according to Steiner, the blood, which he describes as being the functional polar opposite of the nerves. Thus, in a finely balanced working of the forces of sympathy and antipathy in us, expressed through the working of the blood and the nerves, we become aware of the two kinds of image-making processes, inner and outer. Sense-perceptions arise because the sympathetic tendency, the urge to unite with our surroundings is checked by the antipathetic tendencies of the nerves, which then gives rise to objectified sensations. Concept formation, on the other hand, is an inner process whereby the complete rejection of the idea by the forces of antipathy is prevented by the right degree of sympathy afforded by the blood.

Humankind's relationship with the world

In a sense, therefore, it can be said that the human being's relationship with the world is twofold; on the one side we confront nature in our thought life which is pictorial in character and is a kind of reflection of our pre-natal life; on the other side we come into touch with the world in all that is connected with the will, which has a germ character, and points to our life after death. Because of this, declared Steiner, there has arisen the mistaken belief in the twofold nature of Man.[57] Man is rarely conceived of as being threefold in nature, as there exists confusion concerning spirit and soul, which many people regard as being somehow a unity; other people use the terms interchangeably; but the great majority of people think of the human being in the dualistic sense as comprising body and soul, or body and spirit, or body and mind — all twofold concepts.

As for Man's twofold relationship to the world, Rudolf Steiner's own characterization of this is perhaps worth quoting in full:

> When I go into Nature I have the play of light and colour
> continually before me; in assimilating the light and its colours
> I am uniting myself with that part of Nature which is being

carried into the future; and when I return to my room and
think over what I have seen in Nature, and spin laws about it,
then I am concerning myself with that element in the world
which is perpetually dying. In Nature dying and becoming
are continuously flowing into one another. We are able to
comprehend the dying element because we bear within us the
reflection of our pre-natal life, and world of intellect, and
world of thought, whereby we can see in our mind's eye the
elements of death at the basis of Nature. And we are able
to see what will come of Nature in the future because we
confront Nature, not only with our intellect and thought, but
with that which is of a will-nature within ourselves.[58]

Were these two activities not as finely balanced as they are, namely
comprehension of the dying and apprehension of the becoming, Man
would not have the possibility of achieving freedom. Were he to confine
himself to the comprehension of the dying Nature, the moment he wanted
to call into free activity anything related to the future he would find it
impossible to do so. Were he to confine himself to the apprehension of
the becoming in Nature, he would find the urge to unite with it so strong
that his consciousness would be dulled, his will nullified, and free activity
impossible of achievement.

An anatomy of the human will

As mentioned earlier, feeling stands as a soul activity midway between
thinking and willing, and radiates its nature out in both directions. Feeling,
argued Steiner, is thinking which has not yet fully come into being, and it
is also will which has not yet come into being; it is thinking in reserve,
and willing in reserve.[59] He was fully aware of the difficulties attendant
on securing a firm grasp of what willing actually is. Most psychologists
regard it somewhat as an undifferentiated mass of conative elements
somehow appended to either faculties of thinking or of feeling. Steiner,
however, attempted a detailed analysis of the elements of will, and this
is propounded in the next paragraph. As mentioned earlier, thinking he
characterized as a "waking" activity because thinking occurs in the clear
light of consciousness; willing he characterized as "sleeping" because it is
largely an unconscious process, one of which we are not aware. As Waldorf
education lays great importance on the education of the feelings and the
will in the growing child, it is necessary to understand the theoretical
principles involved. There is no question of direct *training* of the feelings

47

or of the life of the will; in accordance with what has already been said about these soul-faculties such training would be impossible, as feelings have the nature of dream-consciousness and the will has the nature of deep sleep. In other words, they cannot be reached effectively by means of the intellect or the thinking faculties, and so cannot be "educated" directly. The means of doing so will be discussed in a later chapter.

If we want to study the will, said Steiner, we must first seek it in the sphere of *instinct*, and we must be aware that we find instinct in the forms of the physical bodies of the various animals.[60] All animals are superbly designed to serve their own particular instincts: the beaver is quite unlike the giraffe, which in turn is dissimilar from the kangaroo. Animal forms, their actual physical bodily configurations make manifest their life-styles, their instinctive propensities. It will be recalled that the physical body of Man and animal is permeated by the etheric body, and in a similar manner instinct is taken hold of by it with the result that the more inward faculty of *impulse* arises. As the human being possesses an astral body in common with the animals, and as this is the signature of consciousness, both instinct and impulse are lifted into consciousness and there arises *desire*. Feelings of desire are even more inward; moreover they are more variable in character than impulse. In line with spiritual-scientific principles, Man as well as the animals possess instincts, impulses and desires. Desires, when taken over by the ego of the human being become *motives*; animals may be said to have desires, but they cannot properly be said to have motives as they do not possess the ego-principle as does Man.

The will to progress

It was mentioned earlier (page 28) that the task of the ego is to ennoble and purify the lower members of Man's being — astral body, etheric body and physical body. According to spiritual science not only is the human soul a trinity, but the human spirit is also. Corresponding to the astral, etheric and physical bodies are the soul members (sentient soul, intellectual or mind soul, and consciousness soul); and the spiritual members (spirit-self, life-spirit and spirit-man). The following table will make these correspondences plain:

Spirit members	Spirit-self	Life-spirit	Spirit-man
Soul members	Sentient soul	Intellectual soul	Consciousness-soul
Corporeal members	Astral body	Etheric body	Physical body

Rudolf Steiner used these terms in a purely technical sense; words of some sort have to be used, and their unfamiliarity is complicated by the fact that they often incorporate yet other words with which one is conceptually familiar. Man is primarily a spiritual being; his nature is essentially spiritual. His soul members and corporeal members arise as the expression of spirit in matter; only the spirit is permanent — the soul members and corporeal members are transitory. The ego, functioning as a kind of co-ordinating medium, is the element in Man which *experiences* that which endures throughout his earthly existences. The ego lives in body and soul, but the spirit lives in the ego.[61]

The ennobling and purifying of the astral body enhances the qualitative development of the spirit-self, and there are similar correspondences between the etheric body and life-spirit and the physical body and spirit-man. The soul members are of less importance in this context; the sentient soul is virtually at one with the spirit-self; Man is most fully conscious of his physical body, hence the connection with the consciousness soul; he experiences his ego more particularly in his mental life, hence its special connection with the intellectual soul; and both have particular affinity with the spirit-self, as this is the spiritual member most accessible to the vast majority of human beings at Man's present stage of development.

To revert to the anatomy of the will: when the will is taken hold of by the spiritual member described as the spirit-self, something in the nature of a *wish* arises. The word is used here, not in its trivial sense of fleeting fancy or whim, but in the profoundly human sense that, having accomplished a certain task one *wishes* to have done it better. In terms of psychological systems Steiner's "wish" might be equated to Mead's "self-criticism" and to Argyle's "ego-ideal" in particular, in that everyone has the urge to revise upwards his or her ideal self.[62] The wish takes on a more concrete form, that of *intention*, when grasped by the life-spirit, and the even more concrete form of *resolution* as a result of the influence of the spirit-man. Wish, intention and resolution are often unconscious processes which accompany the accomplishment of a deed, but often they are quite conscious, as Argyle points out. Such, then, is the manner of Man's progress towards perfection.

A good deal of education, declared Steiner, is concerned with the freeing of feeling from the will.[63] In the young child feeling and willing are closely bound up with each other; ordinary observation confirms that with a child the act of will, the deed, follows swiftly on the feeling. Once feeling has been released from willing, the child is able to unite this released feeling with thinking and cognition to its advantage. Its thinking would then be fructified by feeling, rendering it less arid and abstract, with the result that its thoughts would tend to be more in accordance with reality, less theoretical and more able to evaluate life's experiences. The will faculty, having been released, can then be intensified into activities done out of enthusiasm and love — in effect, moral deeds.

6   The Four Temperaments

*There is indeed an intermediary between what is thus brought
over from earlier lives on earth and what is provided by
heredity. This intermediary has the more universal qualities
provided by family, nation and race, but is at the same time
capable of individualization. That which stands midway
between the line of heredity and the individuality is expressed in
the word "temperament".*

Cosmic and earthly children

Rudolf Steiner never tired of stressing the importance to everyone —
especially teachers — of the need for a detailed knowledge of human
nature. As individuals, by reason of our own nature and being, we are a
riddle to ourselves as well as to other people, and he pointed out that, in
the whole area of social intercourse, people's actions and reactions have
their base, not in *intellectual* understanding of oneself and one's fellow
human beings, but in a capacity for feeling and insight.[1] Human nature is
infinite in its complexity, and every individual is by very definition unique;
at the same time it must be said that people are subject to classification
and typification along general lines. Every teacher knows that, just as all
children are alike, they are nevertheless all different; each child represents
a riddle to be solved, a challenge to be met, and it is the teacher's plain duty
to strive towards as total an understanding as possible of each one of his or
her pupils. Steiner was emphatic on the need for a detailed knowledge of
the nature of the growing child. He wrote:

> Vague and general phrases — 'the harmonious development
> of all the powers and talents in the child,' and so forth —
> cannot provide the basis for a genuine art of education. Such
> an art of education can only be built up on a real knowledge
> of the human being. Not that these phrases are incorrect, but

51

that at bottom they are as useless as it would be to say of
a machine that all its parts must be brought harmoniously into
action. To work a machine you must approach it, not with
phrases and truisms, but with real and detailed knowledge.[2]

The well-known classification of people into the four basic temperaments
of tradition will be discussed later on in the chapter; for immediate
purposes Steiner's general classification of children into "cosmic" and
"earthly" types will be dealt with. The polarity of the human being as
"head-man" and "limb-man" has been discussed elsewhere from other points
of view; for present considerations they may be regarded as representing
"cosmic man" and "earthly man" respectively.[3] The human head with its
organization of brain and sense organs is concerned exclusively with *inner*
processes — thinking, ideation and the like — and as such is alienated from
the outer world inasmuch as it cannot work *directly* upon it. By contrast, a
person's limbs constitute the means of working directly on the *outer* world
by dint of exercising his or her will-processes, and as such become as
if merged with the objective world; because the human will, translated
into deed, necessarily has direct consequences for the world. The head
is concerned primarily with subjective processes; it cannot influence the
outer world otherwise than through the limbs. Any objection that a person
may influence other persons through the medium of ideas signifies little,
as material results of the application of such ideas in the external world
necessarily involves *action*, and this by definition involves the limbs —
somebody's limbs. Thus, only by translation of thought into deed can
the subjective metamorphose into the objective, can the inner become
the outer.

Steiner pointed out that the human head bears witness to life before
birth, to the spiritual world from which we have come; he maintained
that the head is formed and organized from the cosmos, from its function
of organ of nerve and sense to its spherical shape. On the other hand,
the human metabolic and limb systems are connected with the Earth and
its forces, including those of heredity and reproduction. For optimum
performance in our earthly environment, we are required to harmonize
as closely as possible our spiritual and corporeal natures, our cosmic and
earthly attributes, and this, as has been discussed from other points of
view, is very much the concern of teachers and educators.

Careful observation of children will determine whether they are
predominantly "cosmic" or "earthly." Children with particularly "round"
heads and who exhibit a certain lack of control over their limbs, invariably
belong to the cosmic type. Such children are often very able in the realm

of thoughts and ideas. Those children with small, perhaps narrow heads, and whose limbs are agile and movements quick and precise, belong to the earthly type. Such children are often given to brooding and pondering, and are generally slow to grasp ideas and handle concepts. Quite often the basic temperament of earthly children overlaps a tendency to melancholy, which may appear as subtle but unmistakable undertones of inner sadness. Such children, said Steiner, should be involved in extra activities of a rhythmical character, such as music and eurythmy; they may well exhibit little talent for such things, but the teacher should take the greatest pains to foster even the faintest sign of aptitude. As for cosmic children, teachers should take care not to unduly encourage or exploit their natural aptitude for thought and contemplation, in subjects such as history, geography and literature. They should concentrate rather on varying the children's mood of soul by arousing curiosity and anticipation, followed by satisfaction, or creating an atmosphere of tension, to be followed by relief and relaxation.[4] By use of such beneficial practices the spiritual and bodily attributes of the child are encouraged to develop harmoniously and not onesidely.

Qualities beyond heredity

Rudolf Steiner asserted that it is wrong to attempt to explain a person's spiritual qualities in terms of heredity. We are primarily spiritual beings, originating in spiritual worlds; only secondarily are we beings of matter and sense, yet these two poles of our nature become reconciled in our ordinary existence on Earth. If we accept that our corporeal nature has hereditary attributes provided by our parents, it should be reasonable to grant that our spiritual nature has as its precursor the individuality which evolves through repeated earthly lives. All that we as spiritual beings bring with us from previous incarnations are the underlying causes for our particular talents, tendencies of character and other "inborn" faculties which manifest themselves in our earthly life.[5] These attributes must somehow be integrated with hereditary characteristics of family, nation and race; our "cosmic" nature mentioned earlier must be brought into as close adjustment as possible with our "earthly" nature, the spiritual with the bodily. Steiner averred that what stands between the line of heredity and the individuality is expressed in the word *temperament*, that which brings about an adjustment between the eternal and the past.[6] Put another way, our temperament is the result of the interpenetration of our astral body and ego (representing the "cosmic" stream of soul and spirit) and of our physical and etheric bodies (representing the "earthly" stream of heredity).

53

When these two streams flow together at the birth of a human being, the four constituent members (ego, astral body, etheric body and physical body) intermingle in many different ways; the manner of interpenetration is such that one of the four members predominates, and gains control over the other three. It is this particular relationship between the dominant member and the others which gives each human being his or her temperament. If, said Steiner, the destiny of a person has strengthened the ego so that its forces predominate over those of the other three members, the temperament will be choleric. If the forces of the astral body are predominant, the temperament will be sanguine. If the etheric body impresses its inherent qualities upon the individual the temperament will be phlegmatic; and if the physical body with its laws works so strongly that the individuality cannot get rid of certain obstacles presented by its own nature, a melancholic temperament is the result.[7] It is, however, important to realise that these correspondences apply to older children and adults, and not so much to young children. Where children under ten years of age are concerned, the preponderance of the ego is indicated by a melancholic temperament; if the astral body preponderates a choleric temperament results; if the etheric body is predominant the child will have a sanguine temperament, and if the physical body is pre-eminent the result will be a phlegmatic temperament.[8]

It is important to realize that, of the four members of the human being, it is the etheric body which is the actual bearer of the temperament; it is the vehicle of memory and of lasting desires, inclinations and habits, and as such forms the basis of a person's character. Thus an individual's life-long basic behaviour patterns can be said to be rooted in the etheric body; changes are slow to manifest themselves, as character traits tend to be persistent — so constant are they that a person's behaviour in given circumstances may well be accurately predicted. The dense physical body, which in many ways might be regarded as "lower" than the etheric body, is even less susceptible to change; its conformation is relatively fixed, being subject only to the normal metamorphoses associated with maturation, health and disease, and suchlike. The physical body manifests the character and personality of a human being through being instrumental in direct action on his or her environment; it is that which actually "behaves", which registers responses to inner and outer needs and other stimuli.

The astral body, which might well be regarded as "higher" than the etheric body, could be said to be expressive of the personality. As such it is much more susceptible to change and development than the etheric body, which is the bearer of a person's more stable characteristics. Throughout the whole of our lives we learn, by dint of our mental processes, an extraordinary amount; our experiences include the absorption and development of concepts and ideas which are capable of producing great changes in us. Our emotional experiences, too, have a great bearing on our inner development as personalities. This is because the astral body is more subtle and delicate than the etheric body; its essential volatility enables more pronounced modifications or alterations to be made in it, which subsequently express themselves as personality changes.[9]

The fourth member of the human being, the ego, which is the entity that progresses through successive incarnations, expresses the individuality and, as previously mentioned, has the task of purifying and ennobling its three lower vehicles.[10] Most susceptible to its influences is the astral body, which is capable of influencing the etheric body with its attributes, which in its turn is capable of influencing the configuration and nature of the physical body. According to spiritual science, the ideas and feelings which transform the astral body during a long life will produce a marked change in the etheric body only in the next life. Similarly, it is the etheric body of one life which influences the physical body in the succeeding incarnation, which then manifests as innate tendencies to good or poor health as well as its basic conformation and constitution.[11]

Steiner was most emphatic that the teacher should always work with a child's basic temperament and never, in any circumstances, against it. He pointed out that it is worse than useless to try to foster the opposite qualities; that is to say, those qualities which are not "naturally" or temperamentally present. Any such attempt to produce a "balanced" personality would be futile and almost certainly harmful. For example, it would be as futile to try to get a melancholic child to "snap out of it" when it is feeling particularly depressed as it would be to "correct" a choleric child by a thrashing for being ebullient or aggressive. The child may be said to be, in a certain sense, a victim of its own temperament, and so teachers should go out of their way to help children to cope with it, as with a burden. On the other hand, they should devise ways and means of exploiting the child's temperament to its own advantage, both in class management technique and on the purely personal level. By sorting the children in their classes into groups according to temperament, and by treating each group in the appropriate manner, much can be achieved for the class as a whole as well as the individual child. Steiner maintained that it is more advantageous for both child and teacher for the pupils of similar temperament to be arranged in groups rather than be allowed to distribute themselves randomly. In this way, their temperamental tendencies are not, as might be expected, intensified and accentuated, but rather reduced and modified.[12] Thus the cholerics become tired of the boisterous behaviour of their neighbours, and tend to become more settled; the phlegmatics eventually become so bored with peace and quiet that they actually perk up and take an interest in what is going on; the sanguines, surrounded by the incessant chattering and distracting behaviour of their fellows, find relief in trying to concentrate more closely on the actual lesson; and the melancholics, sitting in silent self-contemplation, eventually find their own company so tiresome that they rouse themselves and take notice of what is happening around them.

Steiner recommended that the groups be so arranged that the cholerics and phlegmatics are kept apart by grouping the sanguines and melancholic between them. His reason for this was that just as the choleric and phlegmatic temperaments are polar opposites, so are the melancholic and sanguine. The groups also complement each other in that what one temperament lacks is found in another, and the teacher should make conscious use of these factors. For example, if teachers are dealing with subject-matter which calls for sharpness of perception and immediacy of response they will turn to the sanguine group; if their material calls for thoughtful reflection and the expression of considered opinions they will be conscious of the melancholics. For anything involving action or of an exciting nature, the choleric group is always ready and willing; on the other hand the phlegmatics, perhaps the most difficult group of all to deal with, must in their apathy and chronic inactivity be approached with outward indifference but inward sympathy, in that the teacher reflects their own behaviour and thereby stimulates responses. Where the teaching of arithmetic is concerned, Steiner pointed out that the adding process is related to the phlegmatic temperament, subtracting to the melancholic, multiplying to the sanguine, and dividing, working back to the dividend, to the choleric. If children are thus involved respectively in the workings of the four rules, interest is invariably aroused and maintained.[13]

By the way people express themselves, said Steiner, one should be able by observation to tell whether their perceptual powers are strong or weak, whether they live more intensely in their own inner world or the outer world, and whether they usually persevere at something and change but little, or show less perseverance and change a great deal. Such observations are helpful as they give further pointers concerning their temperamental tendencies. It should be remembered that an individual, while usually exhibiting general behaviour appropriate to one, or perhaps two temperaments, is in reality a combination of all four temperaments. Steiner offered the following chart as being helpful:

Melancholic
Attention not easily aroused,
strongly persevering.

Phlegmatic
Attention least easily aroused,
least strongly persevering.

Choleric
Attention most easily aroused,
most strongly persevering.

Sanguine
Attention easily aroused, little
strength of perseverance.

He pointed out that, in this chart, temperaments adjoining one another are most likely to admix; common mixtures are choleric/melancholic and phlegmatic/sanguine, whereas polar opposites are only rarely found. As for the dimension concerning a person's pre-occupation with his or her inner world or with the outer world, Rudolf Steiner once poked gentle fun at the psychologist Jung for making so much of what seems so obvious — his classification of people into introverts and extraverts, the reflective and the active types respectively.[14] It should be fairly apparent that melancholics and phlegmatics are introverted and cholerics and sanguines extraverted. Observation and experience will confirm that individuals with introverted temperaments generally exhibit *personality* difficulties, whereas individuals with extraverted temperaments generally exhibit *behavioural* difficulties.

The doctrine of the four temperaments is of course traditional, being easily traced back as far as Greek times. The choleric temperament was then associated with the element of fire, the sanguine temperament with air, the phlegmatic with water and the melancholic with the earthly element. Rudolf Steiner, as well as associating the temperaments with the four members of Man's being as delineated above, linked the choleric temperament to the function and activities of blood in the human body, the sanguine to those of the nerves, the phlegmatic to those of the glandular system, and the melancholic to those of the physical body *per se*. Such indications repay reflection and contemplation, as the result is a deeper understanding of that which underlies the temperaments themselves and their characteristic manifestations, and the corresponding behavioural phenomena. Furthermore, Steiner pointed out that until the age of puberty the overriding temperament of *all* children is the sanguine; that the overriding temperament of the adolescent and young adult is the choleric; that the long period of early middle, middle and late middle life is overlaid by the melancholic temperament, and that old age is characteristic of the phlegmatic.[15] Here again observation soon shows that, in the main, young people are extraverted just as older people are inclined to be introverted.

Steiner characterized a person's temperament as being, in a certain sense, the "physiognomy" of the individuality, saying that it is only when teachers understand the temperament of a child that they can find their way to its individuality, and so educate individually. The main recognition pointers for each of the four temperaments will now be given. Those with a mainly choleric temperament possess considerable ego-strength, and have thoughts and ideas that are intensely individual. They are typically people of action, forceful, determined and strong-willed, undeterred by obstacles in their chosen path. Often quick-tempered and somewhat aggressive in demeanour, they are generally optimistic in outlook and impetuous in behaviour. Choleric people are often short and stocky in build, with broad, square shoulders and short neck; they walk with firm, resolute steps, planting each foot deliberately, perhaps heavily, on the ground. The eyes are often dark and challenging, perhaps glinting with an inner light, and the gaze is sure and steady. Facial features are usually clear-cut, with chin or nose often prominent.

Sanguine people are inclined to vacillation: interests are quickly aroused but usually fade quickly as such individuals are easily distracted. Finding it difficult to concentrate, they are often easy-going and unreliable, and a certain superficiality is often in evidence. Being usually of a lively disposition they are generally a success in social matters and consequently often popular and well-liked. Sanguine people are often tall, slender and well-proportioned; their movements are quick and light, and they walk with a spring in their step. The facial features are usually regular, often handsome, expressive and mobile; blue eyes and fair colouring are often associated with the sanguine temperament.

Phlegmatic people are characterized by their strong sense of inner harmony and well-being. Consequently they are placid and self-contained, calm, patient and even-tempered; their imperturbability and passivity often give a general impression of laziness, which is their usual fault. They live, as it were, in their body fluids, and there seems to be insufficient interplay between their inner and outer life. Phlegmatics are often plump or portly in build, and their gait is usually clumsy and slouching, as if they cannot adapt their steps to the ground they are walking on. The facial features are often immobile, impassive and indeterminate; the eyes may well lack expression, being often dull and inward-looking.

Melancholics give the overwhelming impression of being unable to overcome the heaviness of their body, being weighed down as well by inner worries and anxieties. They are usually quiet and withdrawn, and of serious mien; they think deeply, spending much time brooding and pondering over real or imagined problems, and therefore appear moody and reserved. They walk with measured, steady steps which, however, lack the firmness characteristic of choleric people, and very often stoop, finding it difficult to keep the head erect. This is not helped by the fact that melancholics often have narrow or sloping shoulders, unlike, the phlegmatics who are often round-shouldered. The facial features usually reflect the body build, being long and narrow, and the eyes often carry a sad and dejected look.

Pedagogical aspects

Steiner warned teachers that children with extremely one-sided temperaments could present problems on the soul and spiritual levels, and these he characterized as follows:

Main temperament	Lesser danger	Greater danger
Choleric	Uncontrollable temper	Fanaticism, mania
Sanguine	Character instability	Lunacy, insanity
Phlegmatic	Extreme disinterest	Imbecility, idiocy
Melancholic	Extreme depression	Delusions, melancholia

However, he advised teachers that when they were faced with children who exhibited exaggerated temperamental characteristics, there were certain lines of approach that would work therapeutically. The excessively choleric child, for instance, should be guided by respect and esteem for authority. This does not mean that teachers should be domineering or authoritarian, but rather show the choleric child that they are, so to speak, on top of their job and are never at a loss for what to say or do. They must, at all costs, maintain their authority and semblance of value as a person in ways that are altogether genuine, so as to ensure the esteem and respect of the pupil. Furthermore, they should, tactfully and perhaps even surreptitiously, place obstacles and difficulties in the path of a choleric child; by following its temperamental inclinations to overcome such hindrances, the child expends its excessive force and energy, at the same time gaining respect for the hard facts of life which will inevitably come up.

Advising on how to deal with excessively sanguine children, Steiner contended that there is always *one* real and sincere interest for them, and that it is the teacher's duty to help discover what this is. It is important that sanguine children be led towards developing love for and dependence on a particular personality, and if this can be their teacher, so much the better. In addition, they should be introduced to many and diverse topics and activities in which a merely fleeting, transitory interest is justified. Not only does this practice assist in finding out a deep and lasting hobby or interest, it makes use of their temperamental characteristics in a therapeutic way.

In the case of the excessively phlegmatic child, Steiner warned that such a pupil is not easy to manage because of lethargy and indifference. The teacher should see to it, therefore, that such a child has constant social intercourse with other children, so that it may experience their interests and enthusiasms, and thereby learn and take notice of what goes on outside itself. Objects in themselves leave a phlegmatic quite indifferent — provided of course they are not edible objects — but the *interests* of others often communicate themselves strongly and lead to gradual awakening and enhanced consciousness of the outer world.

The extremely melancholic child often lives in a curious state of self-deception, in that it is usually of the opinion that its experiences are peculiar to itself. Such a child is apt to go out of its way to look for obstacles, difficulties, and things to worry about, and the teacher should never attempt to talk it out of its inner sorrows and afflictions, whether real or imaginary. By fostering the melancholic's natural tendency to shut itself up with its suffering, the teacher should make the child realize that there is indeed dreadful suffering in the *outer* world as well. It should be shown, by example or in literature, how steadfastly human beings experience and endure pain and dejection; on no account should the child be forced into merriment, or coaxed and cajoled by means of amusement. If teachers can show, seriously and solemnly, that they themselves have been put to the test in life, that they themselves have triumphed over adversity, so much the better. By learning of the pain and suffering present in the outside world, the melancholic child comes gradually to sympathize more with the sorrows and afflictions of others than with its own inner misery and unhappiness.[16]

As with the tradition of the temperaments, much has been written over the centuries about the so-called somatotypes, whereby attempts have been made to categorize human beings according to body build, and much energy and speculation have been expended. The literature is extensive, and the psychologist Eysenck, who has made a good job of reviewing it and collating the main findings, concluded that it is quite clear that body build is far from having simple and clearcut connections with temperament.[17]

There seems to be wide agreement that there are three main soma-totypes, which predictably correspond to people who are short and fat, tall and thin, and those whose build comes somewhere between the two extremes. Rudolf Steiner had no doubts that there are actually four somatotypes which, moreover, match quite nicely with the four temperaments. During a discussion with the teachers of the original Waldorf School in Stuttgart he characterized these four somatotypes as follows:

> The melancholic children are as a rule tall and slender; the sanguine are the most normal; those with the more protruding shoulders are the phlegmatic children, and those with a short, stout build so that the head almost sinks down into the body are the cholerics.[18]

He then drew caricatures of the four types on a blackboard, and these are now reproduced:

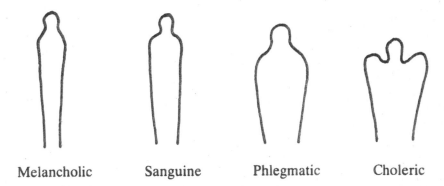

Melancholic   Sanguine   Phlegmatic   Choleric

With such infinite variety as is to be found in human beings, it should not be surprising that there exist confusion and misconceptions. Eysenck's conclusion should not really be surprising, according to Steiner's indications, as any given person is usually a mixture of at least two main temperaments, and this would render secondary considerations liable to mask any rule of thumb application of somatotype theories. There might, for instance, be a tendency to confuse the square, stocky build of the typical choleric with the heavy but rounded build of the phlegmatic; similarly, the two lighter builds of the sanguine and melancholic could easily be confused. Other clues and pointers as were given earlier are helpful in these respects. There could be no mistaking the purposeful stride of the choleric, whose characteristic gait can be recognized from a distance; a person of similar build with a shambling, indeterminate gait would almost certainly be a phlegmatic. As for the basic similarity between the sanguine and melancholic types: again the light, springy step of the former would contrast strongly with the steady plod of the latter; furthermore, the build of the sanguine person is usually well-proportioned and harmonious, whereas the melancholic is generally thin and wiry, with lanky limbs and narrow shoulders and hips.

Steiner gave many indications as to how to "read" the physiognomy of a person, especially that of the school-age child. For instance, the size and shape of the chin, and the degree of lower jaw underhang are worth noting in terms of determination and persistence towards whatever task is undertaken. The evenness or otherwise of the teeth as they grow through the jaws can often provide further clues: if the teeth of the upper jaw tend to grow crosswise or are grossly irregular, this often points to an inclination for the child to be confused in its thought processes; and if the teeth of the lower jaw are irregular this may well indicate confusion in the child's life of will. The texture of the skin and hair often provides clues as to personality: children with fine hair and thin, delicate and transparent skin are often over-sensitive, and can be petulant and tyrannical. On the other hand, children who have coarse hair and thick, tough skin are often insensitive and uncaring for people or property, and are inclined to be despotic.

The teacher's own temperament

As mentioned earlier a child is, in a manner of speaking, a victim of its own temperament; it is powerless to change it, and that is why Steiner emphasized that the teacher should work with temperament and not against it. However, it must not be overlooked that teachers, too, possess a basic temperament, and how they conduct themselves in front of the children is certainly not a matter of indifference. Teachers, said Steiner, should take pains to educate themselves to strive after self-knowledge, and to suppress any tendency to express extremes of temperament while they are with their pupils. Failure to do so can only result in harm to the children; not that this harm may become immediately apparent, but that it is likely to manifest *in later life* as disease and disorder. As discussed in an earlier chapter, errors in parental and pedagogical influences and treatments are almost certain to bear unwelcome fruit in later life, and the same principle applies if teachers mishandle their charges by giving way to their own temperament.

If, for instance, a choleric teacher behaves impetuously or violently towards the children, not only are they likely to suffer immediate fright and terror, but in later life they may well contract digestive and other metabolic disorders, and perhaps rheumatism and related diseases. If a phlegmatic teacher gives way to temperament, the children suffer a kind of psychic suffocation due to a lack of response from the teacher, whose basic indifference inhibits free exchange of thoughts and feelings, and when the pupils are older they are likely, as a result of this, to suffer from nervous disorders.

The melancholic teacher affects the children in such a way that their life of feeling is, so to speak, chilled; the pupils, instead of expressing their life of soul freely and invoking a like response, are instead obliged to constrain or conceal their emotions, and retire within themselves. Later in life, claimed Steiner, they are likely to suffer from irregularities of breathing and blood-circulation, heart trouble and allied complaints. In cases where the teacher is utterly sanguine the children may, in the short term, suffer from disorientation and lack of firm direction and guidance both on the educational and personal levels, and in the long term from listlessness and lack of vitality and zest for life, as well as lack of will-power and perseverance in face of difficulty.[19]

Needless to say, Rudolf Steiner regarded weaknesses of this kind in any teacher with severe disapproval. He considered it the plain duty of all teachers — especially Waldorf teachers — to attain to objective knowledge of human nature in general and themselves in particular. Not unnaturally, he expected actual or prospective Waldorf teachers to assist themselves in this by applying themselves to the study of anthroposophy, his system of spiritual science, and to take its indications, not in any sense as dogma, but as material for careful study. He claimed that it is a spiritual-scientific law that any one member of the being of Man is influenced by the *next higher member*, and that only under such influence can that member develop satisfactorily.[20] Clearly, considering the close personal relationship which usually exists between teacher and pupil, the implications of such a law are far-reaching indeed, serving to place even greater emphasis on the weight of responsibility carried by all parents, teachers, educators and significant others. Unfortunately, Steiner did little more than state the principles involved in this law, but it serves as material, not only for serious study, but for contemplative reflection and meditation. In practical terms, it means that it is the etheric body of the teacher which influences the physical body of the child, the teacher's astral body which influences the child's etheric body, the teacher's ego which influences the child's astral body, and the teacher's spirit-self — of which the teacher is not yet in the least conscious — which influences the child's ego. Education, observed Steiner, is indeed veiled in many mysteries.[21]

7 The Pre-School Years

*I should like to call your attention to the fact that our whole
Waldorf School education bears a remedial character. The
methods themselves of teaching and education aim at having a
healing effect on the child. That is to say, if the pedagogic
art is so arranged that the right thing is done at each stage of
the evolution of humanity in the child, then there is something
healing in the pedagogic treatment of children. If before
the change of teeth the child is treated as an imitative being in
the right way, if then authority takes its place in the right
way and prepares befittingly for the formation of judgement,
all this has an absolutely health-giving effect on the childish
organism.*

Head-knowledge and heart-knowledge

Steiner was insistent that where knowledge of Man is concerned, there
is no sense in talking of differences between theory and practice. A
knowledge of Man which cannot be applied directly to the practical
situations of life, but remains in the realm of abstractions, is quite literally
useless. Conversely, practical life which does not benefit from perceptive
insight into the nature of Man falls short of optimum results. Knowledge
of Nature can remain as theory; knowledge of Man cannot remain so.
With the intellect, Nature is but understood, and by means of it alone
true knowledge of Man is impossible.

Steiner always stressed that mere head-knowledge — and by this he
meant the content of ordinary natural-scientific knowledge — is unable
to attain a true understanding of the being and nature of Man. The
cold, logical processes of the intellect, the abstract nature of scientific
reasoning, leave nothing for the inner life; if the feelings or the will
are affected, it is only indirectly. If the heart is stirred, it is due to
its own inherent propensities, not to the qualities of the head. Small
wonder, argued Steiner, that social life is chaotic, because people have
tried in the past and still try to establish social theory with an instrument

that is least of all capable of knowing anything about the human being — his head.[1] The task of the future, he declared, is primarily that head-knowledge shall gradually be transformed into heart-knowledge, knowledge in which the whole human being can share. It is Man's nature that he can acquire head-knowledge rapidly and comparatively easily; children and young people take in many concepts and ideas during their years at school which they merely *learn* — in other words, acquire an intellectual understanding of them. For such head-knowledge to be transformed into heart-knowledge may well take up the rest of their lives; the young may be clever and intelligent, even learned, but wisdom is acquired only slowly during the course of life. Steiner once characterized this process as the development of the feeling-willing of the child into the feeling-thinking of the older person.[2] He pointed out that children, particularly young children, exhibit a close connection between willing and feeling: their actions invariably correspond to their feelings at the moment. On the other hand, older people's behaviour shows a strong connection between thinking and feeling; their actions are rarely impulsive, but a result of deliberate considerations involving both thoughts and emotions. An important aspect of education is the bringing about the proper release of feeling from willing, so that a person will be able to unite this released feeling with thinking as a mature individual, and so be better fitted for life. The more flexible one is in matters of concepts and ideas, the more mobile one's thinking, the more easily is head-knowledge transformed into heart-knowledge; and this is clearly taken into account in Steiner pedagogy.

In thinking the spirit of Man is active, yet it is not discernible. Intellect has only the *image* of spirit; mental processes reflect spiritual activity, yet in themselves they are essentially passive. This must be so, for if mind were active Man would not be able to understand the world; it is necessary for the intellect to be passive in order that the world may be understood through it. If it were active, Steiner pointed out, then it would continuously impinge upon the world and thereby alter it, so that a true reflection of reality would then be impossible.[3] Mind is the passive image of the spirit, and these are distinct one from another; they differ as much as one's personality differs from the reflection of oneself seen in a mirror.

An artistic view of reality

Man and Nature must be regarded artistically if the correctness of under-standing is to be transmuted into the truth of knowledge. The fundamental passivity of the intellect enables scientific study and observation to be exact; yet the ideas gained thereby are essentially inert, as unreal as the reflections of reality on which they are based. Rudolf Steiner, in the course of his lecturing career, referred on countless occasions to the notion that the world should be regarded as a work of art, and not merely as the manifestation of an interlocking scheme of natural laws. He maintained that, in order to attain to real knowledge of Nature and Man, the intellect must ally scientific understanding with artistic experience, applying the laws of logic as a discipline only.[4] He considered it absolutely essential that every teacher be an artist, and that all subject-matter of whatever kind, even the most abstract, be rendered into artistic experience before being placed before the children; and, moreover, that it be in a form most appropriate to their developmental stage. Steiner fully understood the difficulties that teachers are certain to encounter in attempting to apply this principle unfailingly in all circumstances; nevertheless he insisted that attempts should be made, however clumsy and seemingly inadequate and inartistic they may appear to be. Sincere efforts on the part of the teacher, he averred, would be met with corresponding sincerity and goodwill on the part of the children, and teachers should not be discouraged by apparent failure; as with all artistic activity practice tends to make perfect, and this principle applies here.

Steiner never tired of pointing out that spirit is supremely creative, is the very essence of productivity, is intrinsically active; and he stoutly contended that a person familiar with the tenets of spiritual science finds such tasks less difficult than one who is not.[5] Early attempts at transforming concepts, particularly scientific concepts, into artistic imagery may well present difficulties, but those teachers who identify themselves with their subject-matter and are earnest in their efforts, are more likely to communicate it effectively to their pupils than those who merely transmit watered-down scientific knowledge in intellectual form obtained from the latest textbook on the subject. As educators, declared Steiner, we should have the feeling: as far as you are a scientist only, you are in soul and spirit a monster. Not until you have transformed your psycho-spiritual-physical organism, when your knowledge takes on artistic form, will you become a human being.[6] Such a statement, bizarre as it may seem, gives some indication of the importance he attached to the fundamental attitudes of teachers towards their pupils, to the basic moods of soul deemed appropriate to the transmission of culture. It will be clear from other discussions how great Steiner considered the responsibilities of educators towards the children in their care; the realization of such responsibilities is grounded, not only in mere understanding of the tasks involved, but also in emotional commitment to them.

Rudolf Steiner often referred to infant children as being messengers from the spiritual world, and the reverence which he felt towards the individualities "descending" into the all-too-familiar world of matter communicated itself strongly to the teachers who accepted his educational philosophy. Just as the infant is, until the time of the second dentition, utterly devoted to its environment, wholly given up to it, so parents and teachers should endeavour to match this devotion with feelings of priestly reverence and corresponding attitudes of thought and action. In other words, they should provide, as mediators, that which is worthy of imitation by the child; if they recognize that in the child they are meeting with forces developed in the spiritual world before birth, feelings of deep reverence are invariably engendered which, declared Steiner, have an immeasurable formative influence upon the child. Just as the educator stands as a mediator of the material world, so the infant constitutes a role as mediator of the spiritual world, and the benefits accruing are entirely mutual.

Proportionate to the feelings of reverence fostered in this way arise feelings of enthusiasm for teaching, for preparing the child not only for its gradual adjustment to earthly conditions and circumstances, but for life as a social being compatible with individual freedom and self-development. Teachers, being conscious of their task of working for the future — not only for the future of their own pupils, but for the future of society at large — find that their enthusiasm is thereby amply sustained. Steiner suggested that if teachers were aware that preparation for the future of the child extended not only through earthly life but continued to influence it in the spiritual worlds after death, their enthusiasm for their calling would be less likely than ever to wane.[7]

Another feeling which Steiner stressed should be ever-present in the souls of all teachers is the feeling of protection towards their pupils, especially during the kindergarten and class teacher periods. They should try to ensure that the children in their care grow *slowly* into the world; they should strive to protect them from excessively powerful influences of all kinds which are potentially damaging to the emerging individual. By this is meant that influences of whatever kind of origin, *if they are too strong*, are likely to harm the growing child. Just as, in its infancy, the child needs milk in the ordinary sense, so at later stages in life it needs "soul milk" and "spiritual milk."

These three feelings — reverence, enthusiasm, and the feeling of protection — were regarded by Steiner as the three fundamental forces in education which constituted a kind of "artistic-scientific" formula for all teachers and educators.[8] Cultivation of these three feelings, he insisted, form the groundwork of the teacher's art, for, as will have been made clear from different viewpoints, he regarded teaching as an art and not a science.

The period of child development from birth until approximately the seventh year is widely recognized as being critical, for the child's experiences during this time leave impressions that are often permanent; mistakes and omissions made during this period may never thereafter be rectified or made good. It is a time of intense activity within the child, when it learns, among other things, the basic skills of walking, speaking and thinking, all tremendous achievements in themselves.

Spiritual laws in development

As mentioned earlier, from a spiritual-scientific point of view child education consists mainly in integrating the soul-spiritual members with the corporeal members, and from the theoretical considerations already discussed it may be seen that the whole process is extremely complex. Rudolf Steiner maintained that there is a spiritual law which, when expressed in terms of human development, means that various bodily, psychic or spiritual faculties operative during certain periods in life undergo changes, metamorphoses, and re-appear later during other periods as quite different in character.[9] In this respect he brought people's attention to the fact that Man exists in time as well as space; he is a temporal being as well as a spatial being. Orthodox natural scientists confine their investigations of Man mainly to his organism as it exists in space. Spiritual-scientific methodology claims to achieve an understanding of human beings in the element of time also.[10] Human spirit and soul members, hidden as they are from direct investigation by the ordinary senses and sense-instruments, are nevertheless inter-related also through the medium of time, but these inter-relationships may only be apprehended by means of spiritual cognition, supersensible research. Just as the human being's physical organs bear spatial relationships to each other, so his or her supersensible organs bear temporal relationships to each other. Steiner gave numerous examples of how causes present in the psychological environment during early childhood reappear in later life as effects in the physical organism. It is possible, he claimed, that circulatory disorders of the rhythmic system during a person's fortieth or fiftieth year may be due directly to the fact that the person concerned was subjected to the unbridled choleric temperament of a teacher during early school years. Such facts, little known and understood as they are now, will be better understood in the future. There will come a time, declared Steiner, when someone may write a thesis for a doctor's degree in which it is shown that a case of diabetes occurring at the age of forty may be traced back to the harmful effects of the wrong kind of play in the patient's third or fourth year.[12]

As already mentioned, the child during the period from birth to the change of teeth at about the age of seven is an imitative being. Instruction by way of direct appeal to the intellect is impossible: reason, logical argument, abstract theories are all lost on the child. The human being in its infancy is, as Steiner so often described it, one great sense-organ; it puts up no barriers whatever to its environment — it simply surrenders itself utterly and completely to every act, gesture, thought, emotion; it is devoted to its surroundings in a manner which can only be described as absolute; nothing, absolutely nothing in its environment fails to make an impact on the childish organism. For this reason the child's parents and significant others bear a tremendous responsibility to it, as do the child's teachers. According to spiritual science the child's body, soul and spirit are united until the time of the second dentition, and in consequence that which affects one member must affect all, though the effects may not appear until much later in life. We must see to it, urged Steiner, that our actions in the presence of young children contain a moral quality, that we do no actions which they should not imitate, that we think no thoughts which should not have entry to their souls; we must not allow ourselves to think any impure, ugly or angry thoughts when we are with them.[13] Children, he claimed, really can perceive the morality which underlies every look and gesture of the people around them, though this may not be possible for those who are older.

Impressions on the child's physiology

It was said earlier that the young child is a creature of will; it is active in its limbs, for in imitating its environment its movements are direct expressions of will. And it is the will, active in the physical body, that has the task of awakening the dreaming soul and sleeping spirit of our earlier discussions. In the first place, in the case of the new-born baby, said Steiner, it is milk which works on the sleeping spirit and awakens it, pointing out that in animal as well as in Man the production of milk has an inner connection with the limbs.[14] It is perhaps not without significance that the forces contained in milk reach the head via the metabolic system, which is connected with the soul-force of will. The child is "awake" in its limbs, and the gestures and actions it imitates, consciously and unconsciously, work their way into the whole organism. An example of the precise and delicate manner in which this process takes place is in the child's' acquisition of the mechanics of speech: not only does it acquire the vocabulary it hears, but the very intonation of the words, even the accent, be it regional or otherwise, is picked up, to be reproduced in an uncannily similar way.

The child is awake in its limbs, and its limbs are connected with the faculty of will, which has close affinities with sympathy, that which expresses itself as the urge to unite with the entity attracted by it, and this, in ordinary language, is the expression of love. The baby is deeply devoted to the human beings in its environment in the most profoundly religious sense; the love it has for its parents and significant others is thus, in a manner of speaking, automatically generated and channelled in their direction. The child, in a certain sense, has no choice as to whom it loves — but love it will. It is more than likely, however, that the child will have karmic relationships with such people, in which case the love is reciprocated to the undoubted advantage of the child and to the great satisfaction of parental instincts. In its loving surrender to those in its immediate environment the child receives impressions which are unhindered and unaffected by any discriminating or critical faculty, as at this age it of course possesses none; consequently the impressions, uncensored as they are, work all the more powerfully. The word "impression," said Steiner, is to be taken in the most literal sense: the outer happenings "imprint" themselves into the formation of the finest ramifications of the vascular system.

Thus the very health of the child for the rest of its life is largely determined by what goes on in its environment during its early years, certainly the first five. It is not fully realized, claimed Steiner, how good and evil in a person are expressed in gestures, which are perceived by the child and taken into its very organism, into its unconscious reaches.[15] Edmunds graphically describes the child as "imbibing" the world, whereas the adult merely reacts to it; just because a child does not understand what goes on around it does not mean that it fails to perceive it and be affected by it.[16]

In learning to walk the child is of course learning a motor skill, and it is easy to overlook the fact that the hands and arms which are employed in a motor sense during the crawling period are used for grasping and clutching when the child has learned to walk sufficiently well, and this enables it to employ its forces of will to a greater degree. Steiner often pointed out that, in general, the tremendous effort required of the child to raise itself upright is underestimated, and that the ability to orientate itself in space and propel itself through it is of far greater significance than is commonly realized. Man's spine is vertical, is perpendicular to the surface of the earth, unlike that of animals, and Rudolf Steiner claimed that when the child is learning to walk and to attain the equilibrium of its own organism within the cosmos it unconsciously incorporates into its being statics and dynamics, and that in a more complicated way than the cleverest mathematician could conceive. At the same time, however, this process, far from being abstract and mechanical, is wholly permeated with spirit and living morality; therefore Man, with his perpendicular spine, is a moral being; the animal, with its horizontal spine, is incapable of moral deeds. A person's fate, declared Steiner, may be read in the way they stand and walk.[17]

After the infant has learned to walk with confidence and skill, the hands and arms are freed for the purposes of assisting the child to explore its environment and to help in the gratification of its needs, desires and impulses. In other words, they assume their proper role as servants of the inward life and become ever more dexterous and skilful in acting, not only in the gratification of its own needs, but also the needs of its fellow human beings. The legs and feet, however, are not called upon to develop skills and dexterity, and their function is wholly a lower one, serving bodily movement and concerning themselves with *bodily* equilibrium. The hands and arms, however, having been liberated from exclusively serving the body, now are instrumental in enabling the child to find its psychic equilibrium by serving the needs of the soul.

Absorption of language

Very little is known about the acquisition of the ability to speak in the young child. The linguist Chomsky points out that the child acquires language without explicit instruction, and furthermore at an age when it is not capable of complex intellectual achievements in many other domains, and that this achievement is relatively independent of intelligence or the particular course of experience.[18] Another linguist, Slobin, admits that science does not yet have an adequate theory of language acquisition.[19] Rudolf Steiner provided the answer in a single word: *imitation*. But, as has already been seen, what he meant by imitation is something vastly different from the ordinarily accepted meaning of the term. The manner in which all sense impressions in the child's environment are literally imprinted on, one might almost say inscribed in, its organism has already been discussed; but it must not be forgotten that, from a spiritual-scientific point of view, the childish organism until the second dentition comprises body, soul and spirit as a *unity*, and this has far-reaching implications, most of which are either not known to, or not acceptable to, orthodox materialistic science.

An indication that the child is living, as it were, outside its body, that it is not fully incarnated, is the fact that it does not refer to itself as "I" until about the age of three; it invariably refers to itself by the name, whether given or pet name, by which it hears itself being referred to by people in its environment. Its identification with its surroundings is complete; it lacks the ability to differentiate itself from the world around it; it regards that which it finds around it as an extension of itself. Taking this and the foregoing as a postulation, it is conceivable that the child, by dint of its capacity for absorption, takes in not only the words and "surface structure" of language and syntax, but the "deep structure" as well, and all this in a living way. By perceiving language directly, without the need to understand it or intellectualize about it, its potency is enhanced; there are no barriers to impede its ingestion. As Harwood points out, the manner of a child's learning — by absorption — is the precise opposite to the way in which an adult learns, which is through conscious study and reflection, and concentrated application of intelligence and other powers of cognition.[20]

It has already been mentioned that activity, limb activity, is an expression of the will, and Rudolf Steiner pointed out many times that *repeated action* strengthens the will, a notion that will be returned to later in connection with practical pedagogy. Ordinary observation will confirm that children often talk — inconsequentially, it is true — but they do chatter and verbalize when they are playing, and such "playing" invariably involves the serious attributes of "work." This interlocking of speech and action, or synpraxis, seems to be mutually supportive; the child's manipulative actions are supported by its vocal actions, and the constant practice by repetition of both activities may well result in a kind of reciprocal process which benefits both verbal and manipulative skills. The sleeping spirit in the head, as Rudolf Steiner said, may only with impunity be reached via the will, the limbs; and this sleeping spirit is seen to awaken to a degree commensurate with the development of the motor and verbal skills. This process in turn might well be regarded as reciprocal; it certainly accords with observation.

Generally speaking, having learned to walk and to talk, the child learns gradually to think; and the ability to think, declared Steiner, develops from speech.[21] He said that, as a baby needed a loving environment if it was to walk properly, a truthful environment enabled it to speak properly. In common with most educationists, he deplored the practice of speaking "baby-talk" to young children, holding the view that it could be positively harmful. Above all, he urged that the thinking of people in the child's environment should be clear and precise; muddled thinking and inconclusive habits of speaking evoke reciprocal responses from the child, which at the same time leave their mark on its bodily constitution only to re-appear later as digestive disorders and the like.

Thinking is consequent to speaking because it involves conceptualizing, and this process is impossible until the child has acquired sufficient skill at verbalizing. It cannot express its thoughts until it can handle concepts, and concepts are wrought in words and confined within semantic limits. Needless to say, the conceptualizing skills of young children are very limited indeed, and their intellectual powers are therefore correspondingly limited. As mentioned earlier, thinking proper does not commence until the second dentition, when with the freeing of the etheric forces and the genesis of true memory, the child is ready for school. Certainly before the age of five the child's memory is, to say the least, unreliable; it is unorganized and haphazard, pictorial rather than conceptual. Ordered memory processes coincide with the child's ability to think in an ordered fashion, namely when the organism indicates its readiness for this by the appearance of the permanent teeth.

The three activities of walking, speaking and thinking which the child develops during the first seven years of life are acquired, generally speaking, by virtue of the intensity of its disposition to imitate that which goes on in its surroundings. The child pays heed to what people *do*, and such deeds as gestures are literally incorporated into its organism through the agency of the etheric body whose formative forces are actively engaged in moulding and shaping the physical body. During the time between the second dentition and puberty the child is mainly concerned with speech and the forces connected with its generation and production. This concern shows itself in several ways, which will be discussed in the chapters dealing with practical pedagogy, but its greatest importance lies in the fact that during this period the child pays heed to what people *say*, and herein lies the key to the principle of authority which underlies the educational principles of the Waldorf method during the years from seven to fourteen. The gradual unfolding of the child's rudimentary powers of thinking during the last few years before the second dentition has its reflection in the development of true critical judgement during the seven or so years from puberty until the birth of the ego at the twentieth or twenty-first year, when the youth becomes adult.[22] As so often discernible in spiritual science, such correspondences are real as well as apparent, and not indicative of some kind of spurious "proof" of rhythmic sequences or evidence of some quasi-recapitulatory theory. Abstractions were always repugnant to

Steiner; his "theories" were without exception based on direct insight into the supersensible and not a mere thought-spinning.

In the kindergarten

The pre-school years, the kindergarten period, are the most important of all in the education of the child, said Steiner.[23] With the emphasis he put on the importance of gesture and the child's remarkable imitative capacity, this is not very surprising. His insistence on the cultivation of self-control and of the high moral principles deemed to be necessary, or at least highly desirable was, not unnaturally, very daunting to Waldorf teachers, but Steiner as usual stressed the positive aspects. He suggested that the sense of added responsibility towards the children in their care would not only make them better and more enthusiastic teachers, but would fill them with feelings of charitable love for humankind in general.

During these years, every opportunity should be taken to instil into the child feelings of gratitude to the higher worlds, or God, or Providence, or some such transcendent principle, for all that with which Man is favoured. Children should learn, in the widest sense of the word, to pray, to experience feelings of awe and wonder for the silent expanse of the night sky full of stars, or for the serene majesty of mountains. This would be in accord with the profoundly religious attitude which permeates, albeit unconsciously, the being of the child during its early years. It is inherent in the very nature of gratitude to grow, and if cultivated as a fundamental mood of the soul it ripens into a harvest of social responsibility and concern for the world as the home of all humankind.

It is primarily the duty of the Waldorf kindergarten or nursery class teacher to provide suitable opportunities for the children to imitate her. If she wants the children to do something, she should do it herself and allow them to copy her. Her feelings of delight on seeing a butterfly, or of disgust at a deliberate act of spite, will be copied just as surely as the act of sitting down will induce the children to sit down with her. Any teaching as such, in the sense of appealing to reason or the intellect is, it need hardly be said, strictly avoided. Any "work" as such is confined to imitating what is done by grown-ups in ordinary life — sweeping, sewing, cooking, hammering, gathering leaves or wood, and suchlike. Cleverly designed toys intended for the development of a child's manual or motor skills are shunned, as are artificially devised contrivances to assist in the formulation of concepts, or direct teaching. "Work" is, of course, play to the child, and far removed from the purpose and usefulness with which the adult invests work. It is, said Rudolf Steiner, only the formal side of adult activity that is imitated by the child, not the material side; the "work" of a child is rarely useful, as no definite purpose is pursued. Whereas an adult's work is determined from without, the child's urge to work and play comes from within, as part of the impulse towards self-unfolding. It is the task of all schools gradually to lead the child over from play to work, and the basis of this should be the imitation of the real work that adults do.[24] Education proper for Waldorf school pupils commences at the time of the change of teeth, and that is in Class 1, when they are seven years of age.

Many educationists have pointed out that any form of education of the young human being constitutes interference with it, that education is not "natural" in the sense that it is artificially devised and designed to serve the best interests of the society in which it is growing up. Children born in primitive communities need a different kind of education from those born into cultures which are more sophisticated and highly organized; an economy based on subsistence production does not demand the same skills as those required to sustain a technological society. Whether the "noble savage" is more satisfied with his lot than the technologist with his, is a debatable point; as far as western civilization is concerned, the children born into it are generally educated in a manner deemed to be desirable or necessary for its progress. Progress towards what? is a very different question which is not our immediate concern.

Rudolf Steiner characterized education as attacks on the health of the child,[25] but at the same time he claimed, as mentioned earlier, that Waldorf pedagogy is therapeutic in its effects, that it mitigates the harmful consequences of having to subject the child to the claims of civilization. Thanks to the tremendous resilience of human beings and our inexhaustible capacity for adaptation to prevailing circumstances, not to mention our great resourcefulness and inventiveness, we continue to avert terminal disaster and current catastrophe in our onward progress, which in the twentieth century seems to be confined to the side-stepping of one crisis, only to be confronted by another. Whatever the type of society, whether pre-industrial or technological, with the type of education it demands it gets the type of education it deserves, and this theme will be returned to later when the sociology of education is discussed.

Although the original Waldorf School did not possess a kindergarten, nursery education or pre-school activities are now part of most Steiner schools for normal children. Ideally, of course, there is no substitute for the caring home, which is able to provide in abundance the love and security which the infant needs. However, if society condones the necessity for some mothers to work outside the home, nursery schools undoubtedly have their place. Whatever befalls the child during the socialization process, it is by definition inflicted by society, and it is society which must bear the responsibility.

Kindergarten work, declared Steiner, should consist simply and solely of the external imitation of the external picture of what grown-up people do.[26] In other words, it should be a mere copy of work and not the work itself, which is obviously beyond the capabilities of children in their infancy. Activities that have been contrived merely to "occupy" the children, or those with some indeterminate "educational" element in them should be suspect if they have no obvious connection with real life. Similarly, "creative" toys which have been ingeniously thought out in order to stimulate rudimentary reasoning or practise manual dexterity *for its own sake* should also be suspect. From a spiritual-scientific point of view the emphasis should be on action, the actual deed performed by the limbs — in other words the exercise of the *will*. It may be recalled from previous discussions that the infant is awake only in its limb/metabolic system, whilst dreaming in its feeling and asleep in its thinking. It is just as pointless to appeal to a child's aesthetic sense at this time as it is to appeal to its powers of reasoning, and any coercive attempts to do so are harmful in the long term. Rhymes and songs involving action of some kind are therefore preferred by the kindergarten teacher, together with simple fairy stories of a highly pictorial content, most likely traditional tales which have their setting in the children's cultural *milieu*. Some of these may be chosen for acting out, particularly those with seasonal themes, which are then performed at the appropriate time in an atmosphere of festival, sometimes before a small, sympathetic audience. The child is ready for schooling proper only when it is in the process of shedding its milk teeth, which usually occurs during the sixth or seventh year.

8   The Class Teacher Years

And in truth from the soul-spiritual point of view, my dear friends, if I fail in my teaching and educational connection with the child between the ages of seven and fourteen to live as an authority by his side, from a soul-spiritual point of view, would be the equivalent of robbing him of two fingers, or in certain cases a whole arm, so thus physically handicapped it could not lead a full bodily life. I rob this child of something which his whole nature desires if I rob him of the experience of having people around him who in their upbringing and education are to him real authorities.

The best years of our lives?

The period from the age of seven to that of fourteen covers the time between infancy and adolescence and is the most truly characteristic of childhood proper. Freed from excessive dependence on parents and others and not yet burdened by the complexities of puberty, the child lives out what are truly the happiest days of its life. It has — or should have — no responsibilities beyond the most trivial of every-day duties, nothing but the gloriously secure feeling that everything has been taken care of by others, that the world is there to explore and enjoy. With equal scorn for the baby and its baby ways and the adult with his grown-up ways, the child at this age does indeed feel king of its own castle.

   This is the age, said Steiner, when children long for the sway of authority from the innermost depths of their beings.[1] What Mummy or Daddy says, and especially what Teacher says, is invested with an authority which seems disturbingly total; they stand as guardians and interpreters between the children and the outside world, moderating its harshness and cruelty, regulating its joys and sorrows, enhancing its beauties and charms. The child is thus cocooned from the world, insulated from its direct impact, from its raw influences. In this the child is fortunate, for it is no longer confined to a small social circle such as the typical family provides, to the environment it has imbibed since birth. Horizons widen gradually, from home to school and beyond, but it is never lost.

By the age of six and a half or seven the tendency to copy, the irresistible urge to imitate, has diminished because the head-forces have flowed downwards, and having completed their task of moulding the physical body provided by the forces of heredity, are now free to serve the faculties of ideation and memory. These new powers result from the freeing of the etheric body, and until now have been modelling the physical body; the astral body is not yet freed, and this, together with the fact that the sleeping head has been roused to a dreaming condition by the will activities of the limbs during their motor development, means that the chest and rhythmic system are now the focus of soul-spiritual activity, and this in turn means that the faculty of *feeling* now constitutes the proper avenue of approach to the child's being.

The influence of art

Again it need hardly be said that *direct* means of somehow "educating" or training the feelings is not implied. Rudolf Steiner said that just as *conscious* repetition works on the will-nature of the child, *unconscious* repetition works on the feeling nature, strange as this may seem.[2] By these means the willing nature and the feeling nature of the child are aroused, awakened, but the child's being is left inviolate. There can be no question of implanting some kind of *content*, however nobly conceived or morally devised, into the child in order to influence its feeling, however much people may think to the contrary. If, however, such a practice is regardlessly pushed on with, the result will probably be that the child will grow up to be weak, nervous and vacillating. The child between seven and fourteen, declared Steiner, is an aesthete, and we must therefore take care that it experiences pleasure in what is good and displeasure in what is bad; this is the best way for it to develop a sense of morality.[3] This is a truly efficacious approach — to appeal directly to the child's feelings of sympathy and antipathy, soul faculties which, if the spiritual scientific pattern be followed, belong rightly to this period of childhood. Just as willing dominated the first period, when the child was in sympathy with its surroundings and viewing them subjectively, and as after puberty the thinking faculty will be strongly appealed to, and the child will be, in more senses than one, antipathetic to its environment and regarding it objectively, so the middle period belongs rightly to feeling, to the oscillation between sympathy and antipathy that constitutes the feeling life of the human being.

Just now Steiner was quoted as calling the child of this period an aesthete, and as the whole sphere of artistic creation is the proper study for aesthetics, this gives the clue to that branch of human culture to which the child has maturational affinities at this time — that of art. Just as, as has already been discussed, a religious mood permeates the every attitude of the child from birth to the change of teeth, an artistic perception of the world is unconsciously sought and cultivated by the child from the second dentition to puberty; and after this time the adolescent, with rapidly developing intellectual powers and objectifying approach to the world, is by nature a scientist. Thus, claimed Steiner, are the three main fields of human endeavour reflected in the three ages of childhood, which together span the first two decades of the life of Man. The first period of the child's life, he said, is spent with the unconscious assumption: the world is moral. The second period is spent with the unconscious assumption: the world is beautiful; and only with adolescence dawns the possibility of discovering: the world is true. It would follow from this that education of a truly scientific character, in the sense of systematizing facts and marshalling them in support of theories and postulations, should be left until after puberty, and this is indeed the case in Waldorf schools, as will be seen later.

If the middle period of childhood belongs rightly to the sphere of art, then it would follow that the teacher should be an artist, and this is what Steiner constantly emphasized that the teacher dealing with this age of children should be. Naturally, he did not mean that all teachers should be trained artists, though he did say that all teachers should have artistic training of the most varied kinds — in the areas of painting, drawing, modelling, music, drama, speech and song, eurythmy — and this notion is made clear in Chapter 3 (see p. 20). Art, rightly conceived, is basically to do with the pictorial element, with imagery: the plastic arts have to do with the visual sense, and the musical arts with the aural sense. For instance, painting appeals to the outer vision, poetry to the inner vision, but both are essentially pictorial in character.

Steiner pointed out that until the sixteenth century there was not really that sharp distinction between an intellectual and artistic comprehension of the world, and as symptomatic of this he drew attention to the fact that even the Scholastics strove consciously to make use of a certain architectural art in the plans of their books, going beyond the more obviously artistic device of illuminating initial letters.[4] Furthermore, it should not be overlooked that both art and science were until then both subordinated to religion; both were developed in the service of theology, the medieval Queen of the Sciences. In the Middle Ages, too, the seven liberal arts were the basis of all education: the trivium, comprising grammar, rhetoric and logic, and the quadrivium, comprising arithmetic, music, geometry and astronomy. Although some of these arts have since become abstract sciences, their active cultivation during medieval times would tend to signify that the artistic approach that Steiner advocated possessed a hoary and altogether worthy ancestry. Now, in the twentieth century, religion, art and science have diverged into very different paths: religion, starved of art and denied by science, has atrophied; art, bereft of emotional content, has become a facsimile of the intellectualisms and abstractions of the scientific ethos; science, and materialistic science at that, now dominates the cultural scene. It is ruled by Doubting Thomases who must see, hear, touch, taste or smell — or deny.

Art of whatever genre appeals to the heart, to the feelings, to the individual human being's sympathies and antipathies, however grounded. Feelings of pleasure and displeasure play themselves out in the life of the soul; some are rational, others are irrational. It is always easier to find feelings for our reasons than reasons for our feelings, and this points to the spiritual scientific fact that we are not fully awake in our breasts as we are in our heads: we are dreaming in our feeling life, and this is why it is often very difficult to rationalize about it. A further connection, tenuous as it may seem, is that dreaming is essentially pictorial in character, as is art; we dream in images, and we day-dream also in images.

Rudolf Steiner said on many occasions that art is the great rouser of the intellect, the powers of cognition and ideation. He was emphatic that every effort should be made to awaken the intellect rightly through the will; and this can only be done by passing over to intellectual education by way of artistic education.[5] Now it may be recalled that the human faculty of thinking, according to spiritual science, has affinities with antipathy, memory and conceptualization; willing, on the other hand, has connections with sympathy and the powers of phantasy and imagination, and that these connections were considered to be justified. Art, as argued just now, has its basis in imagery; it is essentially pictorial, and it can be seen from the scheme below that it is allied to phantasy, which can fairly be called the enlivener of imagination, that which contains more of the will-element.

Cognition	Willing
Antipathy	Sympathy
Memory	Phantasy
Concept	Imagination

It should be understood that the term phantasy as here used is employed strictly in the sense of image-making ability, and not to do with that which is fantastic in the sense of unreality, of extravagant escapist visions. The image-making ability that is allied to the cognitive element is concerned with conceptualizing and memory-pictures, which are dependent mainly on the nervous system including the brain; they arise because of the antipathetic, objectifying nature of thinking.

Steiner pointed out that poverty and wealth of imagination as seen in children are often less discernible in activities directly connected with imagination than they are in the development of memory, which has, nevertheless, a very close relationship to imagination, as indicated just now. At one extreme are those children who possess strong powers of imagination and phantasy, whose life of ideas is so strong that concepts and images acquired by the memory do not remain stable; when perceived in the act of remembering they re-appear in a changed form. At the other extreme are those children whose imaginative powers are poor, and whose memories are equally poor; their memory-pictures remain fixed, and they find difficulty in bringing them into consciousness. Between these two extremes is found the majority of children whose memory images are perceived unchanged, in the form in which they were remembered. Steiner recommended that children who tend to be poor in memory and imagination be given opportunities for developing their powers of observation; they should be required to listen carefully to what is said in class, and encouraged to read as much as possible. Those children who show tendencies in the opposite direction, whose minds work so rapidly that their ceaseless flow of ideas is almost a torment to them, should be encouraged to do more than the average requirement of writing; they should also be given opportunities for painting and modelling — indeed any activity or exercise that brings them into movement. Such children should be encouraged to learn to play a musical instrument, and during eurythmy lessons should be given exercises involving consonants which for the most part should be done when they are standing still. Children of the opposite type, those who are rich in imagination and memory and the life of ideas generally should be encouraged to sing, and when partaking in eurythmy lessons should be given exercises involving the vowels as well as those entailing much bodily movement, such as running and stepping.[6]

Such detailed indications as these signify just how Rudolf Steiner regarded the human being as a whole; Man's soul-spiritual nature is not in some way located only in the head; attributes such as memory and imagination are not, in his scheme, merely psychological — purely psychological — in character or essence. He never tired of emphasizing that Man is a unity in the very strictest of senses; the human being is not primarily a body with mental attributes any more than primarily a being of mind with bodily attributes. Such a dualistic way of thinking, he often said, has had in the past and still has the most insidious consequences for western civilization. Man as a being of body, soul and spirit, is a trichotomy and not a dichotomy. Confusion arises because his bodily nature is plain to see and is fairly easily definable, whereas his nature of soul-and-spirit cannot be so readily determined, not to say differentiated. It is certainly not difficult to understand why materialism has secured such a grip on modern ways of thinking; on the other hand adherents of spiritualism (posited here as the direct antithesis of materialism), though in the minority, attract a modicum of sympathy but little real support.

Steiner's system of spiritual science argues that both materialism and spiritualism are fallacious; both doctrines are, from their own particular standpoints, *correct*, but neither is *true*. The truth concerning the nature of the human being can only be arrived at by one who possesses not only sensible perception but supersensible perception also. The simple logic contained in such a statement is so patently obvious as to be in danger of being regarded as simplistic and therefore suspect. That which is material and sensible may only be perceived by that which is itself material and sensible; that which is immaterial and supersensible may only be perceived by that which is itself immaterial and supersensible. This does not preclude the possibility of sensible phenomena being interpreted in supersensible terms, or supersensible phenomena being interpreted in sensible terms; that this possibility exists is evidenced by the tenets of both materialism and spiritualism, and the possibility of further confusion arises. But the fact remains that that which is material-physical may only be perceived by organs of sense, and that which is soul-spiritual may only be perceived by supersensible organs. Man's bodily nature is equipped with developed organs of sense; his soul-spiritual nature is equipped with supersensible organs which have not been developed. Rudolf Steiner claimed to be able to perceive the supersensible; at the same time he claimed that the possibility for doing this lay within the reach of all human beings.

Intellectualism and materialism

Most modern orthodox educational methods are intellectualistic both in their conception and methodology, and herein lies the recipe for the spread of materialism. Many people, while deploring the devastating effects of materialism in modern society and culture, feel helpless in its grip; having received an education which chiefly recognizes intellectual values and achievements as paramount, they are thereby predisposed and conditioned to regard the cultivation of the intellect as the primary aim of education. By implication, such people are also predisposed to thinking materialistically, and so the condition becomes self-perpetuating. Remedies for the deleterious effects of materialism, themselves arrived at by intellectual exercise, are by definition abstract, and hence necessarily removed from reality. The tragedy lies in the fact that whereas materialism is able to diagnose its ills, it is powerless to apply the remedy, and the same is of course true of intellectualism.

Memory and phantasy

Rudolf Steiner maintained that there was a certain hidden relationship between the forces of life-development in human beings and their powers of memory and phantasy. If during childhood the memory is excessively stimulated the child has a tendency within certain limits to grow tall and thin; if its powers of phantasy are over-stimulated the child's growth may well be retarded.[7] There are, as pointed out earlier, typical children of phantasy, those who transform everything in their minds, and those on the other hand who are typically children of memory, those who easily notice and remember things. Thus, by 1919 at least, and probably much earlier, Steiner had anticipated educational psychology in that children could be roughly classified into convergent thinkers and divergent thinkers, the children of memory and the children of phantasy respectively. Obviously, it is no more advantageous, in the strictly educational sense, to deal with children of one type or the other. Research tends to suggest, however, that convergent thinkers, the children of memory, do better at examinations,[8] but the latter merely represents an external device that happens to work in their favour. In fact, Steiner declared, it is the task of the teacher, as far as possible, to regulate the development of the powers of memory and the powers of phantasy in the children in their care, so that they may grow up into more balanced human beings. And here we touch on something that is absolutely central to Waldorf education — the class teacher system, by which the same teacher stays with a class whilst the pupils progress from the age of seven to that of fourteen, from Class 1 right through to Class 8. The main reason for this is to enable the class teacher to watch over the physical, psychological and spiritual development of the children in the class for eight years, thus affording the maximum degree of continuity of pupil-teacher contact. Attempting to achieve the right balance between memory and phantasy is part of the class teacher's task and this, declared Steiner, is why it is so important for class teachers to keep the same children throughout the period between the change of teeth and puberty, and why it is such a "mad arrangement" to pass the children on to another teacher every year, as in common practice.[9]

The importance of the artistic approach to education proper to this period cannot be emphasized enough. It is impossible, said Steiner, to abuse it through over-use; it is impossible for the child to suffer from a surfeit of art. He insisted often that a child is not ready for knowledge, in its raw and undigested form, so to speak, until *after* puberty, and that the child between seven and fourteen has a deep need for artistic beauty that will serve head, heart and will. During the primary school years and far beyond them the whole teaching should be warmed through and fired by the artistic element. Certainly before puberty everything must be steeped in beauty, urged Steiner, and in later years beauty must rule as interpreter of truth. Those human beings who have not learned to walk in the ways of beauty, and through beauty to capture truth, will never come to the full adult maturity so necessary for meeting the challenges of life.[10] An artistic education promotes a kind of thinking that is active, alive; intellectual thinking is passive, dealing as it does with dead concepts and inert ideas. Thus an artistic education is at the same time an education of the will, and the will is thereby empowered to stir thinking into activity. In Waldorf schools passivity is avoided at all costs. It is rare indeed to see ready-made visual aids, for instance; aids are generally created — made, devised, constructed by the teachers themselves often in co-operation with their class. Similarly, apparatus such as film projectors, television sets, radios, record players, and suchlike are rarely used. Such devices necessarily thwart inner activity, active thinking; they have a paralysing effect on the will, as may be readily deduced from previous arguments.

Before the change of teeth the child has the faculty of grasping the world with its whole being, as has been explained earlier, and there remains with the child, even when it is older, an unconscious or semi-conscious urge to experience the world in other ways than the intellectual. The tendency nowadays is to channel everything that proceeds from Nature through Man's head, said Steiner, and the rest of his organism stays dull and unconscious; there remains, nevertheless, the childish urge to experience the world with its whole being, and this urge should be satisfied.[11] If the child is subjected to teaching that is abstract and of a scientifically conceived character, namely, education which appeals directly to intellectual understanding, it remains cut off from the personality of the teacher, from the soul of the teacher. As a scientist one cannot allow elements of soul to modify or colour one's deliberations; science is not an individual affair: it strives for uniformity of textbook-like character. The approach, in other words, is factual, meticulously exact, closely defined, precise to a degree; little room is left for individual interpretation — the personality is entirely excluded. This may be admirable for a teaching methodology *after* puberty, but not before, when the approach to Nature and the universe should be essentially artistic; this, as argued just now, has the tendency to enliven the thinking abilities, to activate and vitalize them, and the child's intellectual faculties are thus kept fresh and lively, able to bring vigour and zeal to the rigours of scientific methodology, in which the human individuality plays no part.

On the other hand, in the realm of the artistic each human being is a different individual in his own right; uniformity of feeling is practically impossible to achieve, even if this were desirable. As argued earlier, art is the sphere appropriate to sympathy and antipathy, and reactions to artistic creations of whatever kind are unquestionably individual — no-one expects otherwise. Now just because of this there can come about an individual relationship between the child and the teacher who is alive and active artistically, as Steiner explained.[12] And this possibility, which in actual practice becomes a probability or still more likely a certainty, lies at the root of Waldorf educational practice during the years between the second dentition and puberty — the principle of the teacher's *authority*.

Authority and respect

The authority of the class teacher during the lower school period, from Classes 1 to 8 in all Steiner schools, is fostered in every way. This does not mean, it need scarcely be said, that *authoritarian* methods are employed by class teachers; rather does the competent teacher strive to be *authoritative* in the best sense of the word. This is made possible by the very methods of teaching that are employed during this period — those based firmly on the artistic approach. Within the artistic atmosphere created between teacher and pupil there usually develops that relationship between leader and led which favours or inclines towards the leader who can do things artistically, and the child, for this reason, feels that it would itself like to do what the teacher does. Thus, said Rudolf Steiner, no opposition is aroused because the child feels that it would be counter-productive and would work back destructively on its own interests.[13] As might be expected, there are other beneficial aspects to such a relationship: for example the child, which has a natural yearning for authority anyway, looks up to the teacher as a model, and this adds to the teacher's sense of responsibility and perhaps efficiency as a pedagogue. This is particularly the case during the child's seventh, eighth and ninth years when, said Steiner, the child still retains the tendency to imitate, as it has not fully dissociated itself from the outside world.

The child, in this middle period, seeks to comprehend the world, not by attempting to assimilate facts in conceptual form, but by socializing with other human beings and learning *through* them. Concepts exist within strictly delineated boundaries; they are necessarily limited, inclining more to the quantitative than the qualitative. Human individuality, on the other hand, is expressed qualitatively, in intensities of feeling, and this is precisely what the child yearns for at this time. In other words, the living artistry of the teacher provides the basis for authority, and the fundamental needs of the child at this time are met from a single source.

It is at about this age that the child first truly learns to separate itself off from its environment, when it divines for the first time its existence as an independent personality. This feeling of individuality is a foreshadowing of the birth of the ego which is to follow a whole decade or so later. Steiner described it as a passing from consciousness to self-consciousness. And this enhancing of the objectifying faculty, primitive and undeveloped as it is, brings the child to see its teacher in a slightly less rosy light than before. During the seventh, eighth and ninth years the teacher has enjoyed unchallenged authority of a more natural kind, especially if established firmly as interpreter of the outside world. Between the ninth and tenth years there arises in the child's consciousness a feeling of unease and uncertainty that questions, in a vague and indeterminate way, the body of teaching that the teacher has passed on so confidently and self-assuredly. The pupil realizes that all it has received in the way of education has come from the teacher, but the question arises: where did the teacher get knowledge and skills from? These and other doubts and uncertainties come crowding in. Moreover, the child feels a vague sense of insecurity on account of its new-found feeling of identity and, again in a dim and instinctive fashion, it formulates the question: who am I?[14] It often happens at this time, too, that the child approaches its teacher with some personal problem or learning difficulty, and very much depends on the manner in which the teacher handles the situation. In any case, when pupils are in their ninth year, the teacher must be watchful for signs of crisis, and must be ready to act accordingly, and must also bear in mind that quite often children present a "front" problem which masks a much deeper disturbance. The teacher needs to be sufficiently observant and perspicacious to notice when this is the case. If the teacher is able to preserve authority while responding to the child's difficulties with warmth, sincerity and truth, then much will have been gained in the pupil/teacher relationship. Above all, the child should see that the teacher can be relied on to support it in a loving and understanding way, and possesses a certain changeless human quality which is unaltered and unalterable.

Somehow, teachers must succeed in giving the impression that there are depths within themselves yet to be plumbed by their pupils, and if all goes well they will maintain their natural authority. If they do not succeed in this, they may be tempted to *assert* their authority by external means, and this would be disastrous.[15] If teachers have to resort to authoritarianism in order to hold their class, by threat of punishment or sanctions of some kind, they have lost the natural kind of authority that inspires trust and confidence, and which makes for a happy and industrious classroom.

At about the tenth year, too, concurrently with its sense of new-found identity, the child's hidden talents and predispositions start to emerge energetically, and if these are not always compatible with what is planned, the teacher must resist the temptation to disregard them, or worse still check or even crush them; this would be disastrous, as it could lead to all kinds of resentments, misgivings and doubts which would undermine the teacher's natural authority.

At about this age, too, there often occurs an upsurge of "naughtiness," and the teacher must be on guard to treat this with humour and understanding; at all costs teachers must avoid authoritarian methods. The tenth, eleventh and twelfth years should be those when the authority of the teacher is well grounded and well regarded, for at the age of twelve or so begins to dawn the critical faculties which will come to birth at puberty. The child will feel more and more strongly that it should somehow exert its own independent power of judgement, and this should be allowed for by the Waldorf teacher just as it is allowed for in the Waldorf curriculum.

The activating impulse in the child between the ages of seven and fourteen is, according to Steiner, the virtue of love. Just as the course of moral development of the child before the change of teeth expresses itself as gratitude, so love is active in the whole human organism as a quality of soul before it comes to physical expression at puberty.[16] On his visits to the original Waldorf School in Stuttgart, Steiner would always ask, in ringing tones: "Do you love your teachers?" and the answer was always: "Yes!"

Love for the opposite sex at puberty, which is at the same time an expression of *universal love for humanity*, must be free of authority. Until puberty the child demands love egotistically, and devotes itself lovingly to that authority and feels pleasure in doing so. The love expressed by the child during the class teacher years is of course Platonic, unalloyed as it is by sexual considerations; the angelic purity of affection shown by the pre-pubescent child, its manifest frankness and artlessness, its sheer exuberance and *joie de vivre* render it singularly attractive, albeit in a somewhat nostalgic way. This period of life is indeed paradisical, and not for nothing frequently regarded as the best years. Steiner mentioned on one occasion that it is in the character of the astral body to lead us back to these years,[17] and its affinities with this period may be readily perceived. Teachers should try to give children beautiful memories of their school years for they serve as rejuvenating influences throughout the rest of their lives.

The boundless energy and seeming tirelessness of the child during this second period is reflected in the tirelessness of the rhythmic system, the regular beat of the heart and in the complementary activity of in-breathing and out-breathing. Steiner often pointed out that this connection was real as well as apparent, and that if teaching pays overall heed to the rhythmic principle it is all the more effective in every way. Certainly this principle is applied to Waldorf pedagogy in very practical ways, as will be seen later; the rhythmical activity of sleeping and waking may not appear to be of significance where educational method is concerned, yet this is also made use of. Steiner maintained that the child should learn in ways that will not make it tired, and this means appealing directly to the rhythmic system and its correlates on the soul and spiritual levels. Teaching that is imbued with artistic quality actually works back upon the physical organism and makes the child's breathing and circulation more healthy, not only during actual childhood but throughout the whole of life.[18]

Occupation with intellectual pursuits, brainwork, is tiring, as is any physical activity; artistic, creative activity on the other hand is refreshing and *recuperative* in its effects. Physical activity of any kind, declared Steiner, produces a craving in the organism for artistic activity, and this principle is also applied in practical terms in Waldorf education.[19] In spiritual work the activity of the body is excessive; in bodily work, on the other hand, the activity of the spirit is excessive.[20] Artistic activity seeks to hold the balance between the two, and therefore the teaching should entail this. Spiritual work, as far as the body is concerned, is brainwork, intellectual work, cognitive activity, *thinking*; bodily work obviously entails physical exertion, limb activity, *willing*, though it matters not a little what kind of exertion this is; it should above all be purposeful bodily activity, namely, that which is done in accordance with the demands of the environment. Physical exertion which satisfies the demands of the body, for instance playing games or performing gymnastic exercises, gives rise to an excessive desire for sleep, and should be kept within moderate bounds.

It is easier to teach intellectually rather than artistically because with the latter the intellectual content has to be worked through with the feelings and presented as pictorially as possible, without having recourse to conceptual thinking. It is, furthermore, quite impossible to overdo the artistic presentation of lesson material because the child will begin to intellectualize such material independently to its own needs. This means that its intellectual growth is in no way forced or stimulated to an excessive degree, and moreover its conceptual thinking is rendered more mobile and more vital; the child will proceed at its own pace and this means, in effect, that the whole class of children is proceeding at the rate best suited to each single member. Progress is thus appropriate to the abilities of the individual, and if the teacher is sufficiently observant and sensitive to the pupils' needs, there should be ample opportunities for rectifying any mistakes, making good any deficiencies and modifying any excesses in good time.

Rudolf Steiner roundly condemned the kind of learning by rote which was fashionable in the majority of European elementary schools during the last quarter of the nineteenth century and the first quarter of the twentieth century. The ability to reel off the dates of wars and other important historical events, and geographical facts such as the longest and shortest rivers of various countries, the highest mountains, and the location and present population of major cities is, he argued, acquired only to the great detriment of the child. Nowadays the futility of this kind of learning by heart, of rehearsing lessons, is widely recognized and is no longer practised; the cluttering up of the memory with useless facts and irrelevant encyclopaedic-type knowledge is now rightly regarded as a waste of time and effort. There exists, however, a tendency for the learning of number bonds and tables to be neglected in favour of calculating machines and similar devices, and for the correct spelling of words to be regarded as secondary in importance to meaning and content. The failure of teachers to insist upon a reasonable degree of structured conformation in the areas of literacy and numeracy might well lead to an inner slackness on the part of the child. Children feel secure in a structured environment, and the insistence upon certain standards of conventional behaviour, whether social or educational, gives support that is at the same time both inner and outer.

The involvement of feelings

Any educational process constitutes an interference with the freedom of the individual, but this is at the same time regarded as socially acceptable, even desirable. Education involves learning, and learning, by definition, involves the committal to memory of conceptual material of varying complexity. The memorization of certain items such as names, addresses, telephone numbers, timetables and suchlike which possess no inherent meaning-content is little more than a mechanical process, a physical process. When, however, mental processes involving understanding and conceptualizing are connected with memory, the spiritual nature of Man is also involved. What is acquired in this way must be led over into the bodily nature and become a physical process. Steiner's ideas concerning memory-processes have an important bearing on one of the main tenets of Waldorf methodology — the involvement of the child's *feelings* in all aspects of teaching. He argued that the comparison between memory and perception is, from a certain point of view, real as well as apparent.[21] An act of perception must take place before concepts can be formed; normally such perceptive activity is directed *outwards*, towards the outer world; an act of remembering also involves perceptive activity, but this time it is directed *inwards*. In other words, the function of memory involves the perception of concepts rather than the perception of objects. When we remember, declared Steiner, we are perceiving something that is going on inside us, just as at other times we perceive things that are outside us.[22] He averred that the processes which eventually lead to memory take place in the same region of the soul in which the life of *feeling* is present; that the life of feeling, with its joys and sorrows, its tensions and relaxations, is the bearer of that which is permanent in the conceptual life. It is for this reason that Steiner insisted that the teacher should never remain in the realm of the purely intellectual, but to see that teaching is accompanied by feeling, that it is permeated by the artistic element. Concepts acquired in this manner remain, as it were, *alive* and capable of further development and metamorphosis, particularly if related concepts have also been acquired in the same manner. The life of feeling is mobile and subject to the workings of sympathy and antipathy, and this leaves open the possibility for concepts acquired by means of it themselves to be mobile and extendable. Such concepts therefore, having been worked over in this way, are not necessarily perceived by the memory-processes in their original form; it is more than likely that they have been modified by the influences of on-going experiences affecting the soul-life, that is, the feeling life, which have been channelled in their direction.

On the other hand, concepts which have been acquired in an intellectual manner suffer a deficiency of the feeling-element which is necessary to ensure the mobility of such concepts, and their ability to grow and develop. Such concepts are, as it were, *dead*, and remain so; they remain inert, lacking the multi-ordinate quality which allows of extension and metamorphosis; hence, when perceived — or rather, in such cases re-perceived — by the memory-processes they are unlikely to be very different in form from when they were initially perceived by the senses and conceptualized by the intellect. Again and again in his lectures to teachers Rudolf Steiner emphasized the importance of transmitting concepts to the children that are capable of growth; otherwise people, as they grow older, still retain concepts in the form in which they were initially given, and this has the effect of hampering the mobility of thinking and restricting its range and penetration. Not only this, but grown-up people, using childish concepts, find it difficult to apply them to the circumstances of adult life, so that their thinking often becomes confused and ineffectual. Moreover, such people also find it difficult to learn, to extend and develop their range of concepts, tending to become impervious to cultural influences; unable to extend themselves intellectually by means of spiritual activity, they find themselves confined to expressing themselves in physical activity of all kinds, sports, games and similar trivial pursuits.

As discussed elsewhere, it is much easier for the teacher to proffer material in intellectual form, by mere narration or practical demonstration, than it is to permeate it with warmth and feeling and to clothe it in artistic imagery. Feelings of joy or sadness may well arise from the teaching material itself, but even when dealing with such dry subjects as physics or geometry, urged Steiner, the teacher should still try to stimulate in some way the pupils' life of feeling.[23] The feelings that are aroused need not always be of a purely emotive character; the teacher should learn how to use expectation and fulfilment as an effective teaching technique, and how to induce tension and its subsequent relaxation in dealing with the children. Steiner urged teachers not to underestimate the value and usefulness, in teaching, of the unknown or half-known, as their influence on the children's life of feeling is of immense significance. If the children are told that some time in the near future a certain subject or topic is to be dealt with in class, powerful feelings of expectation are aroused, and keen interest stimulated, with the result that the children become curious and inquisitive, and are therefore in a receptive frame of mind when the actual teaching takes place. Similarly, all kinds of rhythmic activities can be made use of by the teacher to stir the feelings: comic and tragic elements wherever they may be found; positive and negative aspects of certain questions; concord and discord, forgetting and remembering, attraction and repulsion, loving and hating, as well as the inducement of tension and relaxation, anticipation and fulfilment mentioned just now. In addition to all this, the teacher should strive at all times to connect the teaching material with people; this technique in itself is almost sufficient to ensure the interest of the pupils; when things are related to human beings the children's feelings are most easily aroused, and this in itself should give rise to effective teaching. Needless to say, the responsibilities of teachers are very great in that they are guiding the children's feelings and thoughts for good or ill; such guidance is, however, necessary, as has been argued elsewhere. Children have to be educated and their freedom interfered with; it is therefore the duty of the teacher to minimise the ill effects of such interference.

Feeling versus abstraction

The acquisition of abstract knowledge in intellectual form does not — cannot — stir the feelings. A child may be enthusiastic about science, for example, but the knowledge that water boils at 100° Centigrade or 212° Fahrenheit bypasses its feelings entirely. Both figures represent abstractions, and in themselves are virtually meaningless and are nothing to get enthusiastic about. The majestic beauty of the star-scattered sky may well prompt typically human responses in terms of feeling, and a child may be gripped by intense curiosity concerning the stars, a feeling which motivates it to learn all that it can about astronomy; but the actual laws governing the movements of stars and planets do nothing in themselves to stir the feelings. In cases such as these, teachers should perhaps stir the feelings indirectly, by connecting the abstractions of physics and astronomy with the human being. For instance, if temperature is being dealt with, teachers could bring in ideas concerning frostbite and fever; if astronomy is being dealt with, they could bring in reverential feelings on the one hand, and the seasonal joys of skating and snowballing, swimming and sunbathing on the other. Teachers must use their inventiveness even if this means bringing together seemingly incongruous elements. Why not, asked Steiner, while studying the elasticity of materials, lead over to the phenomenon of vomiting?[24]

The undesirability of appealing directly to the intellect of the child before puberty has already been discussed from the spiritual-scientific point of view, but the rationale behind the reluctance to teach the children to read *before* the age of eight or nine was not specifically dealt with. It may be recalled that, at about the age of nine the child develops or acquires a heightened sense of selfhood; it feels more of an individuality. It feels less sympathetic — in the technical sense — towards its surroundings, it feels less at one with them. Conversely, it feels more antipathetic to its environment, and this it is which helps to induce the enhanced self-consciousness; the child is capable of greater powers of objectification and therefore a sharpened capacity for the intellectual process of apprehending concepts. It would follow, therefore, that it is most appropriate for the child to learn to read at the age of eight or nine, and Steiner frequently reiterated this.

9 Imagination in Childhood

*If one wants to come to terms with practical life, it is far
better to allow full play to the child's ever mobile and living
imaginative powers than to foster intellectual capacities which
encourage the atomistic nature of present-day thinking. The
child's imagination represents the very forces which have just
freed themselves from performing similar creative work within
the physical formation of its brain. It is for this reason that one
must avoid, as far as this is possible, forcing these powers of
imagination into rigid and finished forms.*

Interpreting nature in images

In the years before the child's ninth birthday the teacher should concentrate
on bringing into consciousness what remains as unconscious impulses in the
organism. This entails working in images, in pictures, both in the telling
of stories and in the artistic activities of painting, drawing and modelling
on the one hand, and by stimulating the inherent musical forces on the
other. These two artistic streams then mutually complement each other
and support each other. In this way, by working with what is *within* the
child, by engaging the feelings and the will in appropriate ways, its best
interests are served. One should not impose things from *without* until this
time without first moulding them into artistic shape, and this includes all
subject-material at however elementary a level, and conceptual matter of
every kind. Thus the artistic approach may be seen to be at the same time
a highly suitable one. Teachers are called upon, in the Waldorf system, to
give full rein to their imaginative powers while at the same time ensuring
that what they teach the children is in some way connected with real life.

We can comprehend nature, said Rudolf Steiner, only if we know that
it is an image for something else; for instance, the human head is not
spherical in order to resemble a head of cabbage, but rather to resemble
the form of a celestial body! The whole of nature is pictorial and teachers
must find their way into this imagery.[1] Scientific or factual explanations of
even everyday happenings in nature are not suitable for children between

seven and nine; ways must be found of presenting them, not in conceptual form, but clothed in artistic imagery. The teacher should not hesitate to use anthropomorphisms; clouds, plants, insects, animals should talk to each other, have mothers and fathers, brothers and sisters, and so on. It is because of their strong element of phantasy, and because they often conceal a traditional folk-wisdom, that fairy tales are very much the stock-in-trade of the Class 1 class teacher in a Waldorf school. The tales should for preference correspond to the *Märchen* of the German-speaking peoples, stories of universal appeal which move in a realm which is not subject to the laws of the natural world, and indefinite with respect to time and locality. Often, before the hero achieves his goal or reward he must overcome a series of obstacles or solve a number of problems, and frequently his adventures feature encounters with supernatural and miraculous powers.[2]

Modern children's stories which involve toy cars, trains and suchlike in a twentieth century setting are not really suitable. It must be remembered that the child of seven or eight does not possess the wide-awake consciousness of the adult. Its consciousness is much more dreamy, and the pictures presented to its imagination in story form should be in the nature of dream-pictures from the world of make-believe. The outside world still needs to be interpreted to a child of this age, and interpretations should be clothed in the form most suitable, namely artistic.

It is often advantageous for teachers to make up their own stories to tell the children, stories which may carry a hidden message for one or more members of the class. Children are expected to be rascally from time to time, but more serious breaches of propriety are often best dealt with by telling a story which contains a suitable moral, provided the teacher exercises the greatest care in altering characters, setting, circumstances and so on; at all costs they must not be detected in such machinations!

Obviously, any kind of moral message contained in fairy tales, folk tales or stories of the teacher's own devising must in no circumstances be "explained" to the children; cautionary tales should be told and left at that. As mentioned just now, the pictorial character of such stories, the imagery in which any concepts are clothed, corresponds to the diminished consciousness of the life of dreams. What is taken in then works powerfully on the feelings and the will, and the intellect will assimilate only what it is capable of; it is not coerced, impelled, dragooned into making rationalizations or judgements. In this way the whole being of the child is stimulated, not just the head, and it is good for understanding and realization to dawn on the child later, sometimes much later, perhaps when the child is far removed from school and its activities.

The role of the class teacher

In all this, as mentioned before, the responsibilities of teachers are onerous, particularly so for Waldorf trained teachers who have been taught that what they are to their children and what they do with them in terms of pedagogy and didactics affect not only their faculties of soul and spirit, but even their bodily constitution. Rudolf Steiner put it this way during a lecture to Swiss teachers at Berne in April 1924:

> If you take up educational work knowing that what affects
> the young child will continue through the whole of life as
> happiness or unhappiness, sickness or health, then at first this
> knowledge may seem a burden on your souls; but it will
> also spur you on to develop forces and capacities, and above
> all an attitude of mind as a teacher, strong enough to sow
> "seeds of the soul" in the young child which will only blossom
> later in life, perhaps even in old age. This is the knowledge
> of man which anthroposophy sets forth as the basis of the
> art of education.[3]

These remarks apply mostly to teachers of the class teacher period in Waldorf schools whose pupils range from seven to fourteen years of age, though more particularly to those dealing with children under twelve years. Steiner expected all class teachers to get to know each individual child intimately, and strongly recommended that they let the whole group of their children with all their peculiarities pass before them in meditation every morning. By this means teachers gradually develop an inward perception of each child's mind and soul, which will enable them to see at once what is going on in their class. Such a meditative review of the children need not take long, perhaps ten to fifteen minutes.[4]

It is clear from the foregoing that Rudolf Steiner expected much of the teachers in Waldorf schools; he exhorted them to be at all times utterly conscious of what they were doing, and why, and the likely result to stem from their actions. He reminded them to be persons of initiative in general and in detail; that they should never be slack, that they should, so to speak, spiritualize their classroom techniques and procedures and never take the lazy way out by teaching from textbooks and offering subject-matter in conceptual form. Furthermore, he expected teachers to take a keen interest in current affairs, local, national and international, as well as social problems of all kinds as they manifest in communities and individuals, particularly those affecting their pupils and their parents. He always emphasized that all teaching should in some way or other be connected with real life, with what actually goes on in the everyday world.

Steiner stressed that teachers must be individuals who never strike a bargain with untruth, that they must be profoundly and inwardly true; if not, then falsehoods of all kinds could insidiously infiltrate teaching content and method with pernicious results. He said that a sure sign that teachers are proficient in the art of pedagogy is that they have not become pedants, that they should have a lively, fresh disposition of soul, and above all a sense of humour. This means keeping alive one's powers of imagination and phantasy and not allowing oneself to deal in dry abstractions and purely intellectual ideas. His closing words to the two lecture courses he gave to the teachers of the original Waldorf School in Stuttgart in September 1919 included most of the exhortations outlined in this and the preceding paragraph.[5] He gave a meditation then which has been adopted by many Waldorf teachers; it runs:

> Imbue thyself with the power of phantasy;
> Have courage for the truth;
> Sharpen thy feeling for responsibility of soul.

That a parent, teacher or significant other constitutes a human pattern for the growing child Steiner was of course well aware, and he stressed time and time again that what the teacher is as a person is far more important than what he or she knows as an academic. What passes from teacher to pupil by word of mouth is easily matched in importance by what passes as subtle influences from soul to soul. It has already been discussed how the faculty of willing, expressed as sympathy towards the environment, contains within it the seeds of future action; it may be remembered that love is another expression of the will, symptomatized by the urge to flow over and unite with whatever is the object concerned. The education of the will is just as important as the education of the feelings and intellect, and it is therefore important for teachers to assist the sympathetic propensities already present in their pupils by appealing to their will, and this is best achieved, said Steiner, by the cultivation of teachers' own sympathy with the children. In other words, teachers must love their pupils in the very best sense of the word. Now they are, at the same time, called upon to understand their pupils, and this involves the intellectual activities of objective thinking, which in turn is a manifestation of the forces of antipathy. It is by applying the opposite forces of sympathy and antipathy in their dealings with the children that teachers become aware of their sympathetic and antipathetic tendencies, and it is their knowledge of these which enables them to educate their charges aright.

A truly child-centred curriculum

In the light of the continuing debate among educationists concerning the subject-centred curriculum and the child-centred curriculum, it is clear that Rudolf Steiner was a staunch advocate of the latter. He argued that it should no longer be thought that subjects exist in order to be taught as subjects. On the contrary, arithmetic, geography and all the rest should be taught in such a way as to facilitate the right development of the children's faculties of thinking, feeling and willing.[6] All instruction should be made use of as a means of educating; all handing down of the content of human knowledge should entail its manipulation in order to develop human abilities. And all this supports the theoretical notions discussed earlier concerning the bringing into harmony of the child's spirit and soul with its body.

From all these considerations it may be better appreciated that the class teacher system is essential to Waldorf pedagogy. Perhaps the primary reason is that class teachers are enabled to develop an intimate and lasting relationship with each child in their care, and are allowed to maintain continuity of teaching in method and content. It is important for the feeling life of the children if they are told something on the authority of the teacher which is accepted on trust at the time, but only understood much later. It is good, too, if the teacher is able to refer to something which was told to the pupils years before at a rudimentary level, and now is able to expand and elaborate. In this way, the rhythmic element which is so important in this middle period of childhood is practically employed. Class teachers will deal with the teaching of writing, reading and arithmetic, painting and elementary music, geography, history and the natural sciences insofar as they are dealt with in the lower school — in short, all general subjects. Specialist teachers are, however, employed in the teaching of specialist subjects such as eurythmy, religion, foreign languages and perhaps handwork.

Class teachers take their class every morning without fail for perhaps half the morning hours, amounting to two hours or so, and this is referred to in Waldorf schools as the "main lesson." It is during these main lesson periods that all general subjects are taught on what might be called a "course principle"; in other words, teachers deal with one subject every morning for maybe four, five or six weeks, or perhaps only two or three as they see fit. Thus during one term there may be only three or four subjects that are dealt with, but these are dealt with very thoroughly. Naturally, the whole two hours of main lesson are not devoted exclusively to the one subject; as might be expected from what has been discussed earlier, all kinds of artistic activities take place in support of the main lesson subject. There may well be singing, the playing of elementary musical instruments, learning poems, acting out stories or incidents, a trip out of doors, practical handwork, painting, drawing or modelling. Class teachers take great care to balance their teaching so that no one faculty is exercised disproportionately: action, bodily movement or limb movement serves the will; artistic activity of all kinds serves the feeling; and the intellect is left to absorb what is appropriate to each individual member of the class, according to inner need. The approach is thus seen to be truly inter-disciplinary, in so far as the various subjects are manipulated in order to serve the development of the growing child. This helps to preserve the wholeness of experience and the sense of the inter-relatedness of knowledge; subject barriers are simply non-existent, and artificial frontiers are crossed and re-crossed without hesitation or compunction.

In all this the effects on the teachers themselves must not be overlooked. The mutually supportive systems of class teacher and main lesson present them with greater challenges than those faced by their counterparts in orthodox schools, in that their horizons are often wider, their artistic skills perhaps more manifold; moreover, they are called upon to be inwardly and outwardly creative and adaptable to fresh stages of maturity in their pupils. Lastly, their work with the children along these lines helps them to develop their professional skills and to gain in experience, which in turn may well benefit their colleagues and thereby other children.

The main argument against the class teacher system is the risk of personal incompatibility between teacher and pupil, but this would invariably be more apparent than real. Most teachers possess sufficient professional skill and commitment to temper their personal attitudes, and children are not usually persistent in their antagonisms. In Waldorf schools the eight-year association between class teachers and their pupils is usually exceptionally happy and fruitful, and often extends into the upper school years and even after they have left. Quite often, too, lasting friendships spring up among class teachers and the children's parents, who meet socially at parent-teacher meetings and school festivals. As might be expected, Steiner encouraged all teachers to take a keen personal and professional interest in the social and family backgrounds of their pupils, not only to facilitate better understanding but so as to enlist the co-operation of the parents in any remedial, therapeutic, or hygienic measures considered necessary or advisable. Most Waldorf schools employ a medical doctor trained in anthroposophical medicine, who may be consulted by teachers or parents. As quoted earlier, Steiner exhorted all teachers to observe not only the bodily health and functioning of each child in their class, but also manifestations of soul and spirit aberrations, for example excessive melancholy, kleptomania and suchlike.

The spoken word

Whereas before the age of seven or so children pay most attention to what people *do*, from then until puberty they pay most attention to what people *say*, and this is symptomatic of their inner yearning for authority. It is far better, at this stage, to simply tell a child certain things in a kindly, loving way than to offer scientifically-conceived or other "proofs." If the child persists in its questions, it is still more preferable to give an interpretive kind of explanation rather than a direct one, with the advice that understanding will come when it is older.

There are many other reasons why the spoken word is so important during this period, some of which are very practical. Steiner insisted that teachers *tell* stories to the children, and not *read* them. They should go to the trouble of mastering the details of whatever fairy stories, folk-tales, legends or fables and making them their own, immersing themselves in the pictorial element always present in such narrative material. When they tell the class a story there is nothing coming between them; direct contact is maintained between teacher and children — a subtle matter but an important one. Furthermore, teachers should take the greatest care in the telling of the story, to speak clearly and musically and without resort to exaggerated gestures or over-dramatizations. They should make sure that they keep long vowels long, short ones short, and to articulate consonantal sounds with clarity, so that the children hear each word, so to speak, in plastic outline. Accurate listening is itself a good training in accurate observation as well as close attention to detail, and this leads to better spelling and sentence construction by the children.[7] Moreover, teachers should not speak in a dry, prosaic way, but should strive towards the musical-poetical by uttering full-sounding tones and having regard for the melodic and rhythmic elements; they thus appeal to the unconscious musical nature of the child referred to earlier. Children who spell badly often have little ear for music, and consequently lack an ear for what is correctly spoken; or it may be that they have been brought up in a family or environment where people speak indistinctly or in a slovenly manner, and so are actually constituted to speak indistinctly and spell inaccurately themselves.

Furthermore, close attention to what a teacher says in itself enhances its authority: constant reference to names and processes have all the more impact on the children if they develop the habit of listening carefully. The telling of something by the teacher cannot be equated with the children reading that something in a book, if for no other reasons than inconsistencies in vocabulary and conceptual ability in the different pupils. The teacher, preserving a greater degree of contact with the children, facilitates a more living relationship and better feedback. It is important that the children should have keen regard for *living* authority, not only in people rather than in inanimate books, but also in language as it is used by grown-ups, and not by rigid application of any abstract grammatical rules; in other words, grammar should be referred to as a system serving the use of language rather than dogmatically governing it in a rigid, uncompromising way. At the same time, due regard should be instilled for orthography and style and other linguistic conventions that have been settled on by our forefathers, as this is important from a social standpoint; respect, and perhaps even reverence should be accorded what our ancestors have achieved before us. This attitude, too, tends to strengthen the natural authority that children feel for adults; it helps to sensitize the children to authority rather than submit them to external coercive measures, perhaps by tyrannizing over them with threats of punishment or other sanctions, even physical violence. Steiner insisted time and time again that the child's response to authority must be an inner process, a voluntary submission; no teacher should adopt a domineering manner and authoritarian measures to prop up their authority over the children. In other words, the teacher should *be* an authority rather than wield it as something apart, and should be an authority *with* the children rather than an authority *over* them.

Learning versus play

It follows from the foregoing that the so-called "play way" is regarded as deplorable and unworthy of child nature. This does not mean that learning should not be an enjoyable experience for the children; but it should, said Steiner, be enjoyment of a higher, human kind, and not mere "animal" enjoyment.[8] By this he meant that teachers should call forth feelings of sympathy and antipathy as forces of soul, and never lose sight of that living artistry which is the manifestation of these soul forces. It is easy to allow teaching to slip from this level down to that which is paltry and commonplace, trivial and hedonistic. Mere training in dexterity by means of ingenious toys, and games artifically devised for the purpose of teaching have no place in schools. That learning is play, declared Steiner, is the very best possible educational principle for ensuring that nothing at all is learnt.[9] A good deal of learning involves toil and woe, and the best and noblest thing in the acquisition of knowledge is the feeling that it is difficult, that it costs effort to get hold of things.[10] The inherent danger in methods involving play is that it tends to give children the impression that life is more or less a game; one day they will find that it is not. Connections with real-life situations should be maintained in teaching, but it must not be forgotten that the class teacher is standing as mediator between the child and the outside world; their role is protective as well as interpretive. It is rare that things need to be explained to young children in abstract scientific terms; as discussed earlier, conceptual information is stiff, rigidly delineated. Similarly so-called "visual aids" of necessity depict static conditions, not dynamic ones; the immobile picture is as fixed in its nature as the immobile concept, and both should be avoided. "Moving" pictures in the form of cinema and television and video with its images consisting of dots, are a lie as far as the organism is concerned; the pictures do not actually move, of course — they merely appear to move; each image is just as fixed as in a "still" picture. Better by far, according to Waldorf educational philosophy, is the conjuring up in the children's imagination of vivid pictures of their own making; the creativeness of the teacher in inventing suitable imagery is then matched by the creative efforts made by the pupils. Pictures are thus enlivened, vitalized, and any accompanying concepts are likewise alive and mobile, ready to be amplified and added to at some future time.

Creative work and the will

With the intellect, said Rudolf Steiner, Nature is but *understood*; only by artistic feeling is Nature made *living experience*. The child who is brought up to understanding ripens to *ability* if such understanding is imbued with life; but the child who is brought up to art will ripen to *creative work*. In their abilities, in their faculties, people merely express themselves; in creative work they are able to grow by their faculties.[11] A child who is brought to model or paint, however clumsily, stimulates soul qualities; they awaken and stir of themselves with repeated artistic activity. When introduced to the musical-poetical forms of art the child feels as if its very soul is being taken hold of by a kindred entity, which indeed it is, and communication between soul and soul is rendered possible.

The impulse for activity, the urge to *do* something, lies at the basis of human nature, in the adult as in the child. The external world demands of the adult finished work, and it is often harsh in its demands. Evolving human nature in the child demands an appropriate activity which, when rightly introduced and guided, forms an initial seed of future work. In its play the child is earnest and sincere in its activity, and this is a manifestation of the universal human urge for deeds referred to just now. Education bridges the gap between the need to be active in play in the child and the need to be active in work in the adult. Pedagogy must be able to preserve the serious attitude of mind, the earnest enjoyment of the child at play, and metamorphose it into the right attitude to work when at school so that it is maintained into the working life of the adult. In Steiner's own words it is the ideal of all educational and teaching practice to awaken in the child the impulse to learn with the same earnestness of application with which, so long as play is the sole content of the inner life, it plays.[12]

The great virtue of artistic activity during a child's school years is that the urge to create is maintained, and inventive, adaptable and versatile faculties are correspondingly maintained and enhanced. Steiner contended that one-sided development of the intellect gives rise to the opposite of the creative urge, namely laziness, indolence. Artistic activity stimulates the will, which in turn stimulates the intellect, thus combatting the tendency towards inactivity and idleness. Unfortunately the effect is likely to be cumulative, in that indolence and inner laziness opposes thinking, and if the will forces have suffered paralysis by dint of one-sided stimulation of the purely intellectual powers a kind of chronic listlessness may well ensue, an inner passivity which thus feeds on itself.

An important aspect of the artistic activity that is so much a part of Waldorf education is the experience of colour by the children in their early school years. They are not at first encouraged to paint any particular thing in a representational sense; the main idea is to teach them to deal freely and spontaneously with the element of colour itself, to experience it aesthetically. Steiner insisted that the children should not use blocks of colour commonly found in paint-boxes, but should paint from a jar or mug containing liquid colour, water-colour dissolved in water, and that the paper be damp so that no hard edges appear in the form of definite lines. The teacher should quite deliberately guide the children in their painting lessons, so that they experience colour harmonies and disharmonies as looking more beautiful together or less beautiful together. For example, primitive experiences may be gained by putting a patch of blue next to a patch of yellow, and then a green patch next to a yellow patch and pointing out that the former arrangement perhaps appears more beautiful than the latter. Similarly, exercises involving the juxtaposition of green and red patches and green and yellow patches and so on, may be carried out. Experience of musical tones may also enable the children to hear the more beautiful harmonies of concordant notes and the less beautiful harmonies of discordant notes.[13] It is obviously impossible to explain to an eight year old child *why* blue should look more beautiful next to yellow than green does, or why this chord sounds discordant and that chord concordant, and it is very doubtful indeed whether the child would be interested in explanations. The important thing is that the pupil should engage in activity which does not involve comprehension, understanding, cognitive processes — in short, intellectual activity. Experiences which make a *direct* impact on the whole human being and do not appeal to understanding alone, should be brought to the child.

Just as feeling lies midway between thinking and willing, so the education of the feelings lies midway between the education of the thinking and willing faculties. In this respect it is helpful to recall the states of consciousness which correspond to these three soul faculties: adults are awake in their thinking (head system), dreaming in their feeling (rhythmic system), and asleep in their will (limbs-metabolic system). In children between the second dentition and puberty, however, the upward-surging will forces are, in a certain respect, in conflict with the downward-flowing head forces, and the arena for this encounter is the breast and rhythmic system, which is the bodily foundation for the feelings.

It may now be better appreciated why Steiner emphasized that the education of the feelings is so important at this time, for the thinking and willing faculties are organized in such a way as to be particularly open and susceptible to influences from the feeling life. Activities which involve comprehension, immediate understanding, appeal to the child's thinking and perception, to the powers of knowledge acquisition; those which make a direct impact on the child's whole being, that which is intuitively interpreted in terms of the overall aesthetic impression experienced inwardly appeal to the child's feeling; and those activities which involve rhythm, measure, and repetitive actions of all kinds, including learning by rote — those things which either possess no intrinsic meaning or which cannot be understood at the time — influence the child's will. Steiner made it quite plain that the teacher should, indeed, *must* make adequate provision for activities that train the will.

He characterized the will as being asleep, and so no direct training of a child's will is possible; to try to make a child use its will would be like admonishing it to be very good in its sleep, in order to bring goodness into its life when it wakes again in the morning.[14] Sheer repetition, the doing of the same thing over and over again, that which is the essence of habit or custom — this is the basis of will training. A strong and healthy will must have its support in the well-developed forms of the physical body, which in turn, it may be recalled, depend on the formative action of the etheric body; and that which makes the strongest impression on the etheric body emanates from profoundly religious experience, which may be described as feelings and thoughts by which people divine their relationship to some transcendent Reality.[15] A human being's character is closely associated with the will-forces and their expression as deeds, and if a person is not to experience excessive tendencies towards divisiveness, uncertainty and vacillation, they must, as a child, have absorbed such religious impulses.

Feeling, as standing midway between thinking and willing, is able to influence both; it forms a bridge between the two. Steiner characterized feeling as will in the becoming, or will that has not yet become; the two are closely connected, and it may readily be seen that action invariably follows the impulse of feeling that arises in the soul. Spontaneous action characterizes deeds that are performed unthinkingly, without premeditation or forethought, acts of impulse. Now in such acts thinking is, as it were, only minimally present; the person does not, so to speak, "stop to think." In a manner of speaking, therefore, such acts are unconscious acts inasmuch as the presence of the faculty of thinking is far outweighed by the twin presence in the organism of feeling and willing, as impulse and action.

In order to have a good influence on the feeling nature of the child, the teacher should introduce actions that have constantly to be repeated; moreover, such repetition should be essentially unconscious. If the child is led to do something which will awaken its feeling for what is right, and it does this repeatedly until such an action becomes habitual in similar circumstances, this is good for the development of feeling.[16] It is conceivable that the reverse procedure obtains, namely that a person, when confronted by given circumstances would therefore be inclined to perform the action most morally and aesthetically appropriate.

Strengthening the will

Fully conscious repetition cultivates the true will impulse, for it enhances the power of resolution, of determination. For this reason Steiner recommended that teachers deliberately set out to strengthen the will-forces of their pupils by this means. Children should be given various tasks which they then do day after day for perhaps a year or more; typical examples would be fetching and returning the class register, tending potted plants or flowers in the classroom, keeping shelves and cupboards tidy, and similar daily jobs. A secondary advantage is that the authority of the teacher is thereby strengthened; furthermore, the social atmosphere in the classroom is improved. Performance of such tasks on a regular basis makes the children inwardly firm and strong, as the powers of determination which are dormant in the subconscious are aroused by the conscious repetition of such actions. Practice of all kinds, especially practice involving limb movements, such as those performed in the playing of a musical instrument, also has a beneficial effect on the will. Artistic activities of whatever kind have the same effect, as they are enjoyed afresh each time, and so strengthen the will even more.

It is clear that the education of the feelings and the will is dependent on factors that have little to do with intellectual activities. The child is *not* required to understand every notion or idea that is presented to it; it is not expected to be able to "grasp" meanings or otherwise employ the cognitive faculties. If a notion is presented in conceptual form and is immediately understood by the child, thereafter to be retained in the memory, then it has no effect on the feeling or will natures; they have been by-passed and remain unexercised. It is only when such a notion is presented again and again that it tends to affect the dreaming feeling and the sleeping will. When a notion is presented to the child in such a manner that the meaning is immediately clear, there is little left to be gained by repetition, and boredom is liable to set in. If ideas are presented to the child which are not fully understood at the time, the matter is very different; the child, consciously or unconsciously looks forward to the time when understanding will dawn, and this keeps its interest fresh and anticipation alive. Meanwhile, of course, the child's knowledge and experience of the world in general is increasing, until it is sufficient to allow of unaided comprehension; explanations by teachers or others may then not be necessary. This particular kind of "discovery method" met with Rudolf Steiner's full approval.

Integrating the whole personality

Subject-material taught in such a way as to engage the feelings and the will of the pupils is more efficiently retained in the memory. As discussed earlier, memory expresses itself in imagery, in pictures, and it would follow that the more vivid and lively the input, the more vivid and lively the output in the form of memory-pictures. The activities involving repetition, practice and habit are essentially will-activities, and these necessarily build up the powers of memory. All teachers seek to arouse interest in the children concerning their teaching material, and Steiner argued that the greater the interest, the more pupils' will-natures are stimulated and the more easily memory-pictures are recalled to consciousness.[17] This sequence, it need hardly be pointed out, makes for more efficient learning by the children. Steiner gave three golden rules for the development of memory: concepts load the memory; the perceptibly artistic builds it up; activities of will strengthen it and make it firm.[18] A good example of the application of these principles in the training of the feelings and the will is the morning verse written by Rudolf Steiner for children in the lower classes of Waldorf schools.

It might be argued that, since bodily activity has a stimulating effect on the will, physical exercises of all kinds could have the same effect. This is only so to a limited extent; the natural playing and romping of the young child, that which gives joy in movement, is health-giving in every way to *thinking* as well as feeling. In many sports and games, the rules dictate movements of the body in which there is little or no feeling or thinking, but mostly instinctual reactions to the behaviour of a moving ball. In such activities, the human ego is negated in favour of arbitrary and external sanctions in the form of the rules of the game. Gymnastics will be discussed later when it will be compared and contrasted with the art of movement originated by Rudolf Steiner, namely eurythmy. For the present it may be said that he was not alone in condemning the Swedish and similar types of drill which were popular before the Second World War as being, from a physiological point of view, sheer barbarism.

Purposeful movements, on the other hand, are desirable from many points of view; for example, in order to help children in their thinking, getting them to run in follow-my-leader formation into and out of right and left spiral patterns is recommended.[19] This should obviously be performed in a hall or playground, but exercises may also be done in the classroom. A typical one which Steiner claimed would help in promoting mobility of thinking and imagination involves the children in touching their own bodies according to rapid instructions from the teacher who might say: "Touch your right eye with your left hand! Touch your right eye with your right hand! Touch your left ear with your right hand! Touch your left ear with your left hand!" and similar variations. More complicated movements requiring greater concentration may also be ordered: "Describe a circle with your right hand round the left! Describe a circle round your left hand with your right! Faster now! Faster and faster! Now move the middle finger of your right hand very quickly! Now the thumb! Now the little finger!" and so on. Such exercises require a fair degree of alertness and concentration, and Steiner said that if children do such exercises when they are eight years old they will learn to think realistically and wisely when grown up. Intellectual exercises specifically designed to promote the cognitive powers of "intelligence" may well work in the short term, but in the long term they induce intellectual laziness and weariness in face of problems that demand clear thinking.[20]

For individual children who lack powers of concentration Steiner recommended getting them to imagine a series of events or systems backwards and forwards, for example: tree — root, trunk, branch, leaf, blossom, fruit; man — head, chest, stomach, leg, foot. Such exercises should be followed by talking to the child about the need to concentrate.[21]

In order to promote general dexterity, and in particular to help children who write poorly formed letters and figures, the teacher should get them to hold a pencil between their toes and draw simple forms such as circles, semi-circles, triangles, star-forms and the like. This kind of exercise, and getting the children to pick articles up with their toes, is more helpful than attempting *direct* improvements in handwriting by setting exercises involving the movement of the hand itself.[22] Steiner encouraged the teachers of the first Waldorf School to teach the children to write artistically, which is best achieved by engaging the eyes actively in co-ordination with the hand in the forming of the letters, rather than writing from the wrist in a mechanical fashion. In this way the connection with the artistic element contained in drawing is preserved, which helps to prevent handwriting from deteriorating into mechanical scribble.

Grammar as thinking, feeling, willing

During Class 1, when the children are in their seventh year, the teacher should ensure that the children speak clearly and well, and that the foundations for correct writing are laid. Steiner recommended that in order to teach pronunciation well, examples should be taken which are based on the element of language itself and not on the thought content. Certain combinations of vowels, diphthongs and consonants should be chosen without regard for word sense but for precise articulation. Examples of these words and their settings devised by him for practice by the teachers of the original Waldorf School may be found in *Discussions with Teachers* (see bibliography). No grammar is taught as such, though the children should be able to distinguish between an activity (verb) and object (noun). Obviously, children have an unconscious knowledge of grammar which has been obtained purely by imitation, and there is little point, from a spiritual-scientific point of view, in attempting to make such knowledge conscious until about the ninth year, when, it may be remembered, they become truly ego-conscious. The child does not really discriminate between itself and its surroundings until about this age, and an echo of this childish way of thinking, said Steiner, is contained in the so-called subjectless sentences. Such sentences correspond to that feeling in the young child when it still feels itself as one with the surrounding world, when the distinction has not yet arisen between the ego and the outer world. When our forebears said, for instance, "it is raining," they must have felt more as part of nature than apart from it, and the semantic value of "it" needed no further precision. This kind of expression, retained in modern usage, is redolent of the subjective experience of the world that the young child feels. A similar type of correspondence with the natural world is expressed, for instance, when we refer to our own vision as being "cloudy" or "misty" rather than simply "unclear" or "indistinct," which are purely abstract terms.

When an infant says its first meaningful words — Mummy or Daddy, for example — such words are not merely nouns, as they signify to a grammar-conscious adult; they also serve the child as verbs, for the child is, in effect, *uttering sentences*, sentences which are similar to the subject-less sentences discussed just now. In saying the single word "Mummy" the child is expressing in a living way the *activity* that its mother conveys to it.[23] Steiner pointed out that learning to speak is the enlivening of an outer activity, and that substantives come later, as recent research in linguistics confirms.[24]

The fundamentals of elementary grammar should gradually and in a natural way be brought to the consciousness of the child, and it is useful in this connection for the teacher to realize that the three main parts of speech, namely verb, noun and adjective, have close affinities to the three human faculties of willing, thinking and feeling respectively. It is fairly obvious that the verb is connected with action, deed; it is the "doing word." Through all that is expressed in nouns we become conscious of our independence as human beings; we disassociate ourselves from the outside world in learning to describe things by the use of nouns. When the object is defined qualitatively we use adjectives to describe it; we associate ourselves with the object, the noun, within the terms defined by its qualities.[25] The qualities we associate with the object may in themselves be either objective or subjective by nature. A given chair may be upholstered in red cloth; the attribute red is a universal, and this quality may not be gainsaid; it is objective by nature. I may like the chair because I like the colour; you may not like the chair because you do not like the colour; it may be seen, therefore, that this qualitative element resides not in the chair but in ourselves, and is thus subjective by nature. It should be clear from this argument that the adjectival element may be associated with the human faculty of feeling.

Rudolf Steiner's paradigm concerning the soul qualities expressed as sympathy and antipathy may also be usefully applied here. From all that has been said about his use of these terms in a technical sense it should be clear that the verb has sympathetic associations; not only is there the well-established connection with willing, but the individual when performing an act permanently associates himself with it, flows over into it, unites with it — this must be so by definition, and karmic factors may well be incurred, as mentioned earlier (see p. 28). The antipathetic processes involved in the act of naming objects may also be recognized; the self disassociates from the not-self and thereby objectifies it. Adam named all things and creatures of Earth and thereby experienced self-consciousness. The processes of oscillation between sympathy and antipathy may be recognized in the work of the adjective. When applied to our example of the red chair, the universal red, in that it is a universal in the philosophical sense, is representative of the objective element, the antipathetic element. The fact that we call the chair red already carries within it attributes of *naming*, of further refinement of the objectification process. Whether or not we like the chair already signifies activity; the emotions or feelings are stirred and the process is alive, is vital, and therefore has affinities with the sympathetic element.

Steiner pointed out, too, that our listening, particularly to verbs, is in reality always a participation. When I use a verb, he said, for example in "Someone writes," I do not only associate myself with the individual of whom I use the verb, but I participate in the action of his physical body; I perform it with him, my ego does it with him. My ego joins in the gesture of a physical body when I use a verb.[26] Although at this point he went on to explain how speech eurythmy gives expression to a form of listening, the indications he gave are nicely reflected in the independent working out of similar ideas by the linguist Britton.[27] The ability to listen to another person is a social skill of considerable importance. The kind of listening in order to have one's say in turn is not real listening at all; genuine listening is not a passive thing, but an active following of what the other person is saying, or attempting to say. What Steiner pointed out in 1909 has been reiterated since by several thinkers, including in particular the American educationists Ohlsen and Patterson.[28] One should be able, by consciously practising and cultivating active listening, to hear through the words into the soul of the other person, and before making reply, warned Steiner, one should be careful to consider another's opinions, feelings, and even their prejudices. Behind Steiner's concern can be seen the reasons why he insisted on teachers *telling* stories to their pupils in order to enhance their listening powers, and why he emphasized that concepts should be imbued with life, should be really alive. He stressed that we simply cannot experience other people with dead concepts. We can comprehend them only if we meet them in such a way that they become for us an experience which takes hold of us inwardly, which is something for our own inner being. It is very often the case that we do not really find another human being, but always ourselves.[29] Such considerations have important implications for social intercourse; the highest possible degree of empathy should be cultivated and striven for, so that in our listening we may better understand the other person, such that we do not pass one another by. A reason for Steiner's exhortations for the teachers to make sure to educate the child's will so that it grows up with inner firmness and self-reliance, and not weak and vacillating, is surely to be found here. If someone has too little will-force, and has not sufficient strength of character or ego-strength, they are reluctant to enter into another person's thoughts and experiences because they are afraid of losing themselves in doing so. Such people fail to listen properly on the first count, and on the second they consciously or unconsciously reject whatever they find in the other person which does not harmonize with their own idiosyncrasies. Thus do certain pedagogical principles and practices manifest as social habits.

10 A Creative, Artistic Approach to the Curriculum

*An artistic sense in the educator and the teacher carries soul
into the school. It will give joy in earnestness, and strength of
character in joy. With the intellect, Nature is but understood.
Only by artistic feeling is it made living experience. The
child who is brought up to understanding ripens to* ability *if
understanding is imbued with life; but the child who is brought
up to Art will ripen to* creative work.

Motivation for life-long learning

Rudolf Steiner put great emphasis on the importance of the very first
lesson on the first day for the new Class 1. The children, he said, should be
told why they have come to school, and that they should appreciate why.
They should be told that one day they too will be grown up and expected
to be able to do things which the "big people" can do already, and this
idea should be worked through and illustrated from many standpoints.
Important too is the arousal in the children of a feeling of respect, even of
reverence, for what previous generations have achieved, for the work done
by their fathers, and grandfathers, and their ancestors before them.[1] Time
and care should be taken to instil into the souls of the children that they
have come to school to learn to play their part, too, when they are grown
up. The teacher should not hesitate to speak of ideals to the children which
they will not understand, but which they will probably recall later, possibly
years later, on the prompting of the same class teacher who seizes on an apt
moment for doing so.

It is of great importance, said Steiner, during the first few days at
school, to draw the attention of the children to the fact that they have
two hands. This may seem ridiculously obvious, but the object of doing
so is to awaken in the consciousness of the children that no other creature
on Earth possesses hands apart from humans, who use them to perform

useful work, for themselves and for others. As mentioned earlier, human beings are gifted with the ability to use their limbs, and particularly their hands and arms, to perform moral deeds in the service of mankind. This may seem to be a notion that is beyond the comprehension of a child of six or seven years of age, but Steiner stressed time and time again that the teacher should never be afraid of putting ideas to the children that they will only fully understand much later, when they are older. The acceptance by the children on trust of what the teacher tells them, on the strength of the teacher's authority, only to have the truth dawn on them of its own accord much later, has a powerful effect on the feelings. It is not at all necessary for the children to understand everything they are told then and there, especially where human ideals are concerned. Such things work on powerfully in the dreaming soul and sleeping spirit, to manifest later as ethical feelings and moral deeds, and the responsibility of the teacher in this regard is heavy indeed.

A dynamic approach to writing and reading

Until the change of teeth the whole being of the child has been a unity — body, soul and spirit have been as one. At this time, however, the soul-spiritual forces that have been flowing downwards from the head into the rest of the organism as an organizing principle are somewhat released, to serve the child as powers of ideation, of thinking. Until this time the keynote has been that of action, and this is held; at the same time the organizing, formative forces are encouraged to come to expression in the limbs, particularly the hands and arms, to be employed in the movements involved in painting and drawing. In this fashion the artistic approach is maintained and developed to serve the acquisition of the basic skills of writing and reading. In the effort of acquiring the skill of forming the different letters of the alphabet the whole body is brought into action, not merely hand and eye. Children are actively engaged in running the forms of the letters on the classroom floor, or perhaps tracing them in the air; sometimes they arrange their trunk and limbs to form letters with their whole bodies — X, Y and R for example. Class teachers are expected to use their own artistic imagination in order to present to the children as pictorially and actively as possible the forms of the letters. Writing arose out of copying the outside world, from picture-writing and hieroglyphics, gradually becoming more and more abstract and stylized as civilization progressed. In the same manner, though not because of any slavish application of the recapitulation theory, the letters of the alphabet are first represented by the teacher pictorially in the painting or drawing of pictures. The teacher might tell a story about a cave, and draw a picture showing the mouth of the cave as a stylized capital C; similarly M may easily be adapted from the shape of the mouth, W from the gesture of waves or water, and so on. In this way the children are led over artistically, pictorially, imaginatively, from the gesture to the abstract letter; they are not suddenly confronted with the letter as a finished product and then encouraged to memorize its shape. Consonants are represented pictorially by objects that exist in the outside world, but vowels, which represent the inner soul content, are best indicated by gestures, or perhaps imaginative drawings connected with the experience of feeling. It is the teachers' task to use their powers of phantasy in the teaching of the letter forms; what they must remember is that they must be careful to explain the consonants by drawings of external objects, but never the vowels.

Words and the letters that comprise them are highly intellectualized abstractions with which the being of the child has no connection whatever, and Steiner never wearied of pointing out that everything that is brought to the child between seven and fourteen should be thoroughly immersed in the pictorial element. The head, with its now dreaming spirit, may best be awakened by the limbs, which involves the will element, and the rhythmic system, which involves the feeling element; combine the two artistically and optimum results in terms of education of the whole human being should result. Movement of the limbs has more affinity with the being of the child at this time than perception and observation, and this is why in Waldorf schools writing is taught before reading. Reading is essentially a mental act, a one-sided activity involving eye movements and little else. Steiner particularly deplored the practice of children picking ready-made cut-out or printed letters from a heap and constructing words with them.[2] In such a practice only the intellectual powers are being called on; there is nothing for the feelings to engage in and nothing for the limbs to do to satisfy the inner impulse for will activity.

Working from the whole to the parts

The principle of *going from the whole to the part* is well established in Waldorf pedagogy, and this is applied, as might be expected, to the practice of writing and reading. Speech is primary and all forms of written communication are secondary, and just as the child speaks whole words in whole sentences, so the analytic principle is preferred to the synthetic.

Ideally, a whole sentence, however short, should be introduced to the child in its spoken form and then its written form. If the child has been taught the shapes of the letters together with their corresponding sounds as outlined above, not only as initial letters but as constituent letters also, it will experience them not as mere externalities but as the coming to expression in reading and writing of its own breath. Complete words and sentences should be written down and the child impressed with the whole word picture *before* passing on to the individual constituent letters, which can then be arrived at by analysis, and their particular sounds practised. Rudolf Steiner claimed that a tendency towards analysis is inherent in Man's nature, and only when this longing in the child for analytic activity is satisfied should the teacher apply the reverse activity — that of synthesis.[3] In other words, once having taught the child the various letter forms and their sounds from the analysis of many words and by dint of much practice and repetition, the teacher should attempt the synthesizing process, that of making up words from the constituent letters; in short, learning to spell.

All that is expressed in writing and reading is determined by convention and has arisen within the realm of physical activity. The very forms of the letters are important, not to mention the order in which they are decreed to appear in order to render them meaningful to a third party also schooled in the same convention. Teaching the child arithmetic, said Steiner, is quite another thing; the figures as forms are not the most important feature of any number, it is the *reality* that lives in the figure-forms. Arithmetic, and indeed the whole sphere of mathematics, engages more of Man's soul-spiritual activity than do writing and reading, as reflection will show. When artistic activities are engaged in, such as painting, drawing, music and so on, it is the soul and spirit that are, as it were, being taught. A rational and balanced plan of study, therefore, should include all three impulses: the super-physical in the artistic activity, the semi-super-physical in arithmetic and the entirely physical in reading and writing; and just this combination, averred Steiner, will bring about the harmonizing of the individual.[4]

Rudolf Steiner always maintained that the principle of going from the whole to the parts was a good one when applied to practical pedagogy, and this usually meant working from real life and not abstractions. A wood when seen from a distance appears as a unity irrespective of the number of trees that comprises it; similarly every number, irrespective of the number of units comprising it, also represents a unity. The child must obviously learn to count before being introduced to the various arithmetical procedures from as many sides as possible. Counting generally starts with mere naming, for instance, by means of nursery songs and such

115

like, and the conventional method of proceeding by the addition of single units need not be strictly adhered to. As well as this the teacher could adopt the principle of going from the whole to the parts and divide a certain length into 2, 3, 4, 5 and so on, as indicated in the following diagram:

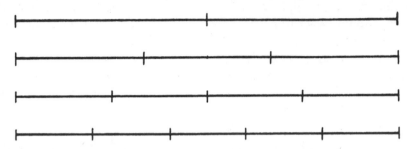

Similarly, a teacher could make use of the unitary nature of the hands and feet and go on to explain their composite nature; they could discuss with the children how the hand is a unit in its own right, irrespective of the fact that it is comprised of fingers and thumb, knuckles and auxiliary bones. Counting on the fingers, and toes for that matter, is the primitive method and should be actively encouraged. Steiner held that we count subconsciously on our fingers in any case, and not in a purely mental way; he argued that it is the body that counts, that the head merely observes what is reflected into it by the bodily nature. He condemned the abacus and similar counting and calculating aids as being too abstract, and as having too coercive an effect on the child's intellectual powers which is at the same time damaging; such apparatus has a place in office and factory, but not in school.[5]

Learning arithmetic

The four rules of addition and multiplication, substraction and division should be introduced as and when appropriate, and not in any preconceived or "logical" order. The principle of going from the whole to the parts should be followed; for instance in the Waldorf method the teacher starts with the sum first and then goes on to the addenda. The sum is of course the whole, and the addenda may be varied in order to emphasise that although they may be changed the sum may not. Thus a sum of 24 potatoes may be shown to comprise a single heap which can be divided into 4 smaller heaps containing 9, 7, 5 and 3 items or 4 smaller heaps containing 6 each, or any other combination right down to 24 single units. The "adding back" always leads to the sum, the whole, which remains constant. After practice in this, ordinary processes of addition may be introduced, as indeed they must when the rule of multiplication is dealt with, as it is nothing more than repeated addition of the same number or quantity.

When subtracting procedures are being dealt with, Steiner recommended starting with the minuend and remainder and having to find the subtrahend, which he described as doing subtraction in a living way; conversely, starting with the minuend and subtrahend and working out the remainder is a dead process. In real life it happens much more often that a person knows what they originally had and knows what is left over after using or losing some of the commodity. This method may be continued into the multiplication process by presenting the whole, the product, and asking how many times a certain quantity is contained in this product. Multiplication and division processes are reciprocal and can with advantage be introduced together; if the principle of proceeding from the whole to the parts is held firmly in mind, and if real-life situations are presented to the children as examples, little damage is done. Steiner emphasized that by insisting on proceeding from the living whole to the separate parts the reality underlying all arithmetical calculations is touched on, namely, the setting in vibration of the etheric body, the body of formative forces, which needs such a stimulus at this time.[6] The important thing is to go from reality, not from thought; for example $3+3+4=10$ beans starts with thought; the reality, in this case the 10 beans, is arrived at secondarily. Putting things together in order to arrive at a sum, a whole, is, declared Steiner, abstract and intellectualistic, and instead of the children being bright and lively, under such teaching they become apathetic; the calculating machine is a proof of how difficult it is to make the teaching of arithmetic perceptually evident.[7]

At first sight there may not seem to be much connection between the treatment of numbers and moral ideas that may be engendered in the child, but Steiner insisted that there is. When a child has acquired the habit of adding things together its disposition tends to become grasping and acquisitive as a result. In proceeding from the whole to the parts, not only with the addition process but with the other arithmetical processes as well, the child will tend less towards acquisitiveness but, on the contrary, more towards considerateness and moderation: in short, goodness.[8] Such a child will be less materialistic, and more generous in thought and deed towards other people when it grows up.

Unlike some other subjects on the Waldorf schools curriculum, arithmetic and geometry are taught throughout the whole of childhood, and this is because they harmonize with every part of Man's being. Not only do they have a stimulating effect on the formative forces, as described above, but they give many opportunities for analytic and synthetic activities, as in the case of reading, writing and spelling already mentioned. These have correspondences with the feelings of sympathy and antipathy which operate at the soul level: sympathy, as discussed earlier, has connotations of flowing over into, of unifying with, a given object; antipathy has connotations of differentiation, objectification. It would follow, therefore, that sympathy finds its echo in the synthetic tendency, whereas antipathy corresponds to the analytic activity. These alternating activities, which represent that which is rhythmic in character, therefore find expression on the soul-spiritual level as well as the corporeal level, and operate in a harmonizing way, bestowing healthy influences and a sense of wellbeing on the children.

Some characteristics associated with etheric forces in general, namely growth, rhythmical repetition and metamorphosis, are seen clearly at work during the period between the shedding of the child's teeth and the onset of puberty. These characteristics emerge in the principles of Form Drawing, and their application in teaching the formation of the letters in both printed and cursive writing, geometry, and "pure line" drawing in general. Such exercises contribute significantly towards the development of a lively imagination and mobility in thinking. The etheric body continues its activity *during sleep*, working over and perfecting day-time impressions, and Steiner indicated that, as mentioned just now, working to the principle of going from the whole to the parts is particularly compatible with this activity. A true teacher, he declared, is not only concerned with the waking life but also with what takes place during sleep.[9]

From Form Drawing to geometry

During Class 1, a start is usually made with the rudiments of geometry, and here again the approach is artistic and pictorial; abstractions such as the drawing of constructions are too intellectual for a child of seven or so. A start is made, therefore, which is based on inner perception, so to speak, and not outer perception; for example, a strong sense of symmetry is stimulated and developed in the children by means of simple drawing exercises. The teacher draws a figure on the blackboard, adds a straight line and indicates the beginning of the matching symmetrical line, as in the figures opposite.

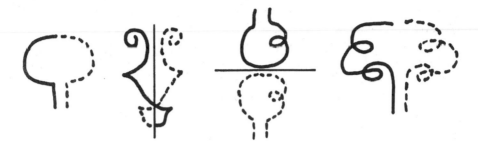

The children realize that the figures are not wholly complete, and the inner urge is awakened to finish that which is not yet complete. Then, depending on the inventiveness of the teacher, other more and more complicated exercises are embarked upon, compatible with the abilities of the children which are assessed by their individual performance. The figures below are those Steiner himself drew for the benefit of his audience of British teachers during a conference at Ilkley in August 1923:

The main idea is to awaken a sense of space in the children and how correspondences may be juxtaposed spatially. All drawing is done freehand, and the patterns gradually lead over to more and more intricate and delicate forms, including those that exhibit "a-symmetrical symmetry" in the manner of those shown above. Geometrical constructions requiring the use of instruments are left until much later; for the time being the purely artistic approach is adopted.

Learning from the arts and music

Rudolf Steiner pointed out that everything that approaches Man artistically falls into two streams — the stream of the plastically formative and the stream of the musically poetical.[10] To the first belongs all art that is presented pictorially, in painting or drawing, sculpture and architectural forms. To the second belongs not only music proper, with its harmonies, melodies and rhythms, but everything connected with speech when employed to express the dramatic and poetic. All plastically formative art tends to *individualize* people: not only are paintings, drawings and so on highly personal creations of the individual artist, they may, in general, only be viewed by small numbers of people at a time. This is due mainly to the fact that they are creations in space; such works of art possess spatial qualities which of necessity circumscribe their form and content. On the other hand, all poetic and musical art furthers social intercourse: although such works may have been conceived and shaped in solitude, they may be enjoyed by many people simultaneously. Furthermore, they come to expression through time, reaching the audience through the sense of hearing rather than the visual sense. Although the plastic and musical arts are, in a sense, polar opposites, they may nevertheless be combined to serve certain art forms, for instance, opera and eurythmy.

It may be recalled that at the time of the second dentition the plastic-formative forces that have been acting mainly in the head flow down into the chest, meeting there all that proceeds from the breath rhythm and the rhythm of the heart and circulatory system. The child is at this time particularly well equipped, so to speak, and particularly well suited for everything that comes its way in the form of art, whether plastic or musical. It is as though the child's whole physiology demands artistic satisfaction, and it is the duty of the teacher to meet it.

Steiner maintained that in Man's expression of the plastic-formative arts — drawing, painting, modelling — he produces out of his own nature the forms which he finds again in the outer world.[11] In artistic activity of this kind it is not keeping to the model that matters; what is most important is that artists develop a sense of form from out of their own nature. What is represented in a typical work of art of this kind, in a drawing or a painting, is indeed outer nature, elements of the outside world which surround us in our waking state, and the spatial qualities inherent in the manifestation of the outside world to us. The exhortation to a child to "draw what you see" may appear to be heeded, yet it is well known that children, especially young children, tend to draw what they *know* of their experiences of the world, and this would seem to support Steiner's contention that human beings produce forms out of their own nature. For example, the typical drawing a young child makes of its parents is of a disproportionately large head from which rudimentary stick-like limbs protrude — the trunk is not represented. This may not be surprising when it is recalled that the infant, until the shedding of the milk teeth, is itself pre-occupied with its head forces; it produces the head-form from out of itself. Naturally, as the child grows older, the outer world is represented more and more according to forms apparent in it, yet the earlier tendencies remain. For instance, lines are drawn as they are seen and manifested to us, yet they do not actually exist in nature; rather are they abstractions which border on the untrue.

On the one hand, therefore, it may be said that the plastic-formative arts have affinities with the outer world; on the other hand, the musically poetical arts are essentially an expression of the inner world, Man's soul-spiritual nature. In music and speech — which is permeated with musical qualities — is represented what is experienced in the human soul. There is no question of copying the outside world in a naturalistic way; spatial qualities are impossible of being expressed in temporal terms. In paintings and drawings the outer world is represented as experienced by Man in his waking consciousness; in music and poetry the inner world is represented by Man in his dreaming consciousness. The outer world is material, objective, determinate, explicit; the inner world is immaterial, subjective, indeterminate, implicit. Rudolf Steiner pointed out that Man experiences increasing and decreasing tensions, expectations and disappointments, inner conditions of soul which express themselves in the most manifold pictures in dreaming. These experiences correspond to those of musical melodies with their *crescendi* and *diminuendi*, and to the tenuous and indefinable qualities recognizable in all true poetry. The child acquires the skills of speech when it is not fully conscious; it is imbibed when the soul is dreaming and the spirit asleep; learning to speak comes forth from the unconscious. The dreamlike consciousness of the child at this time finds comparison with the melodic elements of music with their affinities to the life of soul. Such melodies give experiences of a world in which the human being is not fully conscious, and they impinge upon our daily waking life like reminiscences. In order to mitigate materialistic influences and get beyond them, Steiner said that it was just this unconscious element which prevails in dreams and above all in the melodies of music which must be taken up into the art of education.[12]

From the seventh to the tenth year the child wants to experience everything that comes to it through inner measure and rhythm which corresponds to its own rhythmic activity of breathing and heartbeat. In its very organism it yearns for music. From about the ninth to the twelfth year the sense for melody is developed, and the child no longer has the same need to produce rhythm in its own inner nature, but rather regards it as external to itself.[13] Steiner claimed that the whole being of Man is permeated with and representative of the musical element, and he elaborated this on many occasions; just as Man experiences the inherent nature of music, so the forms of his body are shaped out of music itself.[14] Speech and music come together in the act of singing, and as the child acquired speech in an unconscious way, the ability to sing is also acquired unconsciously: there is no question of knowing musical theory, as melody, harmony and rhythm are built into the very anatomy and physiology of the human being, coming to expression in song and the metrical rhythms of poetry and verse. The forces which have come to expression in the human form are musical in character and have affinities with the astral body, which, it will be remembered, gradually becomes emancipated during the period between the change of teeth and puberty. It is therefore important to assist this process by getting the children to sing, and if possible to play a musical instrument of however simple design, such as a bamboo pipe or home-made lyre. Steiner pointed out that harmony stirs the human breast — and feelings — directly; melody is more consciously perceived as tonal expression of musical ideas and is therefore connected with the head; when harmony extends into the region of the limbs and the activity of the will it expresses itself as rhythm, beat.[15]

In the realm of speech, music expresses itself not only as song but in the rhythms of poetry and verse in recitation, for poetry should ideally be uttered aloud, not read silently. Steiner argued that poetical activity lives in the fashioning of the language, not in the content but in the measure, in the rhythm and in the preservation of the rhyme, and that this is at the same time musical activity.[16] He deplored any tendency to stress the thought content of a poem, insisting that a good recitation is one which particularly emphasizes the musical element.[17] What he also deplored was the "interpretation" of poems by the teacher, the detailed explanation or paraphrasing of a poem line by line or even word by word. Such a practice nullifies the artistic impact of a poem, reducing it to the level of mere prose; explanations deemed necessary for the understanding of a particular poem should be made in the course of general teaching, so that when the poem is recited no further calls on the intellect are necessary, leaving the artistic element untouched.

The development of speech and the musical elements connected with it is maturationally appropriate to the child between seven and fourteen. During this period, too, the feelings of the child are cultivated by the application of artistic methods of teaching which appeal directly to its feelings of sympathy and antipathy. Steiner pointed out that the actual production of speech is a breast-activity, and that it is more closely associated with sympathy and antipathy than may be immediately apparent. The thought content of speech is rendered comprehensible by the anti-pathetic activity of the head, which according to spiritual-scientific tenets, it may be remembered, is its proper role. The feeling content of speech finds immediate sympathetic expression in the tone of voice whereby the individual experiences the tendency to unite with what flows towards him or her from without, or for that matter from within. Hence the involuntary interjection or cry of surprise or astonishment at a sudden outward experience and the vocal expression of joy or grief which seems to rise unbidden to the lips.

The very sounds of speech also indicate the workings of sympathy and antipathy in Man, and this observation of Steiner's may be readily confirmed by ordinary experience. All vowels, he said, express inner soul-emotions experiences in sympathy with things; for example O is connected with astonishment, OO with fear and alarm, A (as AH) with wonder and so on.[18] Consonants, on the other hand, represent Man's antipathy to external objects which often expresses itself in an imitative way, as in onomatopoeic words. The tendency is one of warding off, of dissassociation from, the outer world. Obviously, speech comprises the combination of vowels and consonants, of feelings of sympathy and antipathy in their overt and covert forms. It is worth noting that consonants necessarily employ tongue, lips and palate and are essentially antipathetic actions; vowels, on the other hand flow out unobstructed and are supremely sympathetic. Steiner pointed out that in the degree in which speech consists of vowels, it contains something musical, but in the degree in which it contains consonants, it contains something plastic and formative. Thus it expresses a real synthesis, a real fusion of the two main streams of artistic activity, the musical and the plastic-formative.[19]

What is education for?

The idea that a child is something like an empty vessel into which knowledge must be poured is abhorrent to increasing numbers of educa-tionists. The question: What should a person *know*? is slowly giving place to the question: What should a person *be*? The image of the schoolboy creeping like a snail unwillingly to school, there to be crammed with facts, most of which are irrelevant, is being replaced by that of the pupil who finds school an exciting place to be in. Rudolf Steiner asked the two questions above of his audience of teachers in Dornach during a lecture course held at Christmas 1921, and they represent the traditional subject-centred approach and the "progressive" child-centred approach to education in general. That there must be some kind of curriculum there is no doubt, but thereafter opinions differ. Obviously, teachers must teach *something*, and as far as Waldorf teachers are concerned, Steiner gave them a detailed exposition of child development according to spiritual science and a curriculum designed to support it, so that the rationale is rendered largely self-evident. It was, however, his habit to throw off aphoristic remarks, leaving his audience to reflect on them in the light of the general principles of Waldorf pedagogy; he always required active thinking of his audiences. Casual readers of his lecture courses on education might well be discouraged, as his frames of reference are so different from those of orthodox pedagogy. His systems and models are not at all easy to become familiar with and therefore are not likely to be persevered with; his policy of not attempting to explain his educational philosophy in any other than his own terminology, and his apparent aplomb, have deterred many readers. However, Steiner had excellent reasons for conducting his lecture courses as he did, and it must be remembered that most of them were addressed to earnest enquirers, the majority of whom were already familiar with his system of spiritual science.

The Waldorf curriculum for children under nine has already been outlined; it consists mainly of practice in the basic skills of writing, reading and number along the lines explained, together with the usual artistic activities already referred to. Subject-matter as such is conspicuously absent, as there is little point in teaching it; it may be remembered that, according to spiritual science, the child is not fully self-conscious until the age of nine or so. It regards itself somewhat as part of the outside world, as an extension of it, and is therefore unable to distinguish itself from its environment as an adult can. Steiner rejected the animistic theories which were as popular in his day as they are now, and came out strongly in favour of encouraging the child's innate tendencies towards anthropomorphism; he emphasised that it is good for children to feel at one with the universe and to treat it and everything in it as part of its own family, so that its whole environment is living and articulate. The loving relationships which are part of the home atmosphere should be extended to take in the things of Nature — animals, flowers and plants, insects, wind, rain, snow, clouds, sun, moon and stars — all created things; and at the same time feelings of gratitude should be encouraged and stimulated for all that with which Man is favoured. Thanksgiving should not be confined to the season of harvest, but should be cultivated as a fundamental mood of the soul the whole year round. Such feelings may easily be conveyed in the form of stories, poems and prayers which appeal to the imagination and powers of phantasy; direct precepts of all kinds should of course be strictly avoided. If gratitude and love have been unfolded in the child before the age of ten, said Steiner, foundations have been laid for the development of a true sense and understanding of duty in later life.[20] Such feelings of responsibility obviously carry implications for the social life, and lead on to attitudes of caring and fellow-feeling concerning people and property.

Active language skills

Before the age of nine or ten most language teaching should lay greater emphasis on oral rather than written work. Writing and reading skills should of course be practised, but the accent is on the telling of stories by the class teacher and their re-telling by the pupils. The children should also be encouraged to tell the class of their own experiences, or something they themselves want to talk about. In this way, said Steiner, mistakes which are made can be pointed out in a natural and friendly way, and the necessary guidance given for the children to develop the habits of educated conversation.[21] With the awakening of ego-consciousness at about this time, the child is able to differentiate between itself and the outside world, and with this comes the enhanced ability to discriminate between things and to objectify things. Now is the time to teach the laws of grammar, as this assists in the development of the new self-consciousness. With the child's new-found sense of independence the time is now ripe for the introduction of the rules of grammar objectively; hitherto its use of language has been instinctive, and many rules unconsciously absorbed, and the bringing of these rules into full consciousness is one of the healthiest ways of developing the human understanding.[22]

Between the ages of ten and twelve, narrative descriptions of what the children have seen and heard and accounts of actual experiences should be the main sources of inspiration for written work. The recounting of incidents that have occurred, accurate reporting, should be encouraged; otherwise, declared Steiner, they will not be able to play their proper parts in social life.[23] If factual reporting is practised and indeed insisted upon by the teacher, this has the effect of obliging the *truth* to be manifested, and not all kinds of inventions. This point should not be laboured by the teacher, but the children should become more and more accustomed to dealing with that which is in accordance with fact and with reality, and this not only enables them to see various situations objectively and more in accordance with their inherent truth, but they will be enabled better to detect untruth wherever it appears. In other words, untruths and half-truths are quite apparent to those whose discriminatory powers are well developed, whereas people who regard things subjectively fall prey to biassed news reporting in the mass media, to say nothing of advertising material devised by copy writers trained in the school of depth-psychology. As quoted elsewhere, Rudolf Steiner earnestly exhorted teachers to "have courage for the truth," and this message can be passed on to the children by means of sheer methodology, by practices inherent in the pedagogy itself.

Accurate reporting of events is by definition a truthful description of actions, of deeds, and this ensures that the faculty of will is engaged in the process. The spinning out of thoughts and ideas by means of the intellectual faculty is not so suitable for children below the age of twelve, and Steiner emphasised that so-called "free composition" should not be done until about the thirteenth or fourteenth year.[24] By this age the pupils' powers of objectification should be sufficiently strong to enable them to keep fact and fiction apart, and to prevent mere invention from becoming mistaken for reality. The time for mixing fact and fantasy ended at the age of nine, before which age the child's inner and outer worlds are inextricably mixed and when it views everything in a purely subjective light. But with puberty only a few years away, twelve-year-olds are already becoming mature enough to exercise their critical powers, and their developing sense of judgement should enable them to discuss ideas objectively, to see things from various points of view and argue accordingly.

It is about this age, too, that syntax should be dealt with as far as deemed necessary by the teacher, as this is a purely objective linguistic element. In order to balance this intellectual exercise the teacher should introduce artistic considerations in terms of style and the uses of metaphor, simile, hyperbole and suchlike.

Steiner declared that what must be strictly avoided is allowance for the children to write compositions about anything that the teacher has not first talked over with them in great detail, so that the subject is always thoroughly familiar to them. The teacher, as an authority with the children, should first speak about the subject or topic to be written about, and the children should produce their essays under the influence of what the teacher has said. This principle should hold until the children are approaching puberty; they should not write down just what occurs to them, but should always feel that a certain mood has been aroused through having discussed the subject with the teacher, and that this mood must be preserved in the writing of the essay.[25]

To the objection that this practice is likely to stifle the imagination, the inventiveness, of the children in the writing of stories, plays, verse and suchlike which demands the free play of phantasy, it must be said that very little *truly original* work is ever produced by children before the age of puberty. It is invariably the case that children *reproduce* what they have previously heard or read, and close observation will confirm this. What has the semblance of original work is often nothing more than remembered or half-remembered incidents from life or from children's books, comics, magazines, radio, television or video. What is often hailed as originality in children's work is all too often indicative of the precise opposite: it merely *appears* to be original because of the re-arrangement of anecdotes, descriptions or snippets of information which the children have previously encountered. Moreover, what manifests *to adults* as original work is very often the result of lack of expertise in language usage on the part of the child; the seemingly original turn of phrase is invariably due, not to imaginative use of language by the child, but to lack of skill in verbal expression. It is in the very nature of the child, at least until the age of ten, to imitate, to copy; to expect anything from a child of below this age which is not a reproduction of what has been previously seen or heard is to expect the impossible.

Characterization versus concept

With the tenth year the child begins to feel more self-contained and self-assertive, and now is the time to dwell on distinctions in the outer world. With its enhanced sense of self the child needs guidance in the direction of its perceptions of the outside world as it feels more and more disassociated from it. Teaching about the environment and natural history should until now have been clothed in fairy tale and fable, chiefly narrative and descriptive in character. Now, however, the teacher should dwell on distinguishing features of things, on characteristics that lead to discrimination and objectivity. The teaching of natural history at this time should start with Man himself, and his pre-eminent position in the realm of Earthly creation. The feeling should be engendered in the pupils that Man is a synthesis of all three natural kingdoms, and it need hardly be said that this should be made implicit in all teaching in artistic and imaginative characterizations.

The attention of the children should be drawn to the human form in its outer aspects: the principal division of the physical shape into head, trunk and limbs should be pointed out and their main functions described. Steiner suggested that teachers point out the spherical shape of the head, thus appealing to the artistic element; then going on to describe the trunk and its main organs, and the limbs as appendages to the trunk. The essential difference in function of the legs and feet and the hands and arms should be dwelt on in some detail, and in imaginative ways which appeal to the feelings, teachers should discuss the selfish nature of the feet and the unselfish nature of the hands, which may be used to perform work for the benefit of others.[26]

Having dealt with the human form, teachers should go on to the animal kingdom, pointing out that animals vary in their conformation according to habitat and eating habits. They should give the clear impression that the lower animals have features that characterize the human head, such creatures as the cuttlefish, molluscs and primitive creatures of like nature whose softer organic parts are encased by shell-like formations in a way similar to the human skull which, with its bony cup-like form, encloses the soft tissue of the brain.

Next, the children's attention should be turned to the fishes, reptiles and other creatures with vestigial limbs but with highly developed spinal characteristics. Comparison should be made, not in any pedantic or scientific sense but in pictorial ways, with the chest system of the human being with its rib-cage which encloses the rhythmic system. Attention should be drawn to the manner in which the head-systems of fishes and similar creatures are merely extensions of the main bodily conformation and are not really separate at all, as in Man. Such creatures, too, have stunted limb-formations, the means of locomotion being afforded by the spine's rhythmical movements; in human beings our spine enables us to stand upright, thus allowing freedom to our fore-limbs, our hands and arms.

When the higher animals are dealt with, teachers should point out the great variety of functional habits where the limbs and metabolic systems are concerned. The essential differences between the herbivore and carnivore should be described, as well as the various ways in which the higher animals have adapted themselves to their environments. Obvious examples are the camel, the lion, the bear, the hippopotamus, the elephant, the giraffe, and the fox; in each case their one-sided development of one or more features of conformation and life habits should be discussed with the children. Moreover, the various soul qualities which are traditionally associated with animals should also feature in stories and poems; obvious examples are the bravery of the lion, the greediness of the pig, the stubbornness of the donkey, the timidity of the lamb, the cunning of the fox, the patience of the ox, the curiosity of the cat, the faithfulness of the dog and the obedience of the horse. The great diversity of animal life in terms of bodily conformation and adaptation to their natural surroundings by means of one-sided development of certain organs or limbs should be emphasized. At the same time the children should be introduced to the idea that Man is representative of a kind of amalgam of all animals on a higher plane; by adopting a symptomatological and artistic approach, the human being as body and soul should be characterized as a synthesis of animal characteristics. In human beings, however, everything is balanced and harmonious; our organs and limbs show no one-sided development in response to environmental factors. We are undoubtedly related to the animals, but at the same time we are raised above them because each individual person is the bearer of a spirit-filled ego, and this is indicative of the essential difference between the animal and human kingdoms.

Steiner claimed that grasping a living conception of Man's relationship to the animal world effects an exceptional strengthening of the child's will. The programme just briefly outlined should be gradually worked upon during the pupils' tenth, eleventh and twelfth years, returning to the being of Man from time to time for comparisons to be made. The external feature of human beings which grants them utter supremacy over the animals, what in a manner of speaking makes them perfect, is their limbs. The differentiation of our limbs into legs and feet, arms and hands, should be stressed again and again, and the strong feeling awakened in the children that we are thus rendered capable of serving others as well as ourselves. Hence the moral aspect is fostered — not directly or explicitly, but in all kinds of imaginative ways, by means of the living artistry of the teacher.[27] Such expositions of the human being's connections with the animal creation lead on in a very effective way from the fairy tales and fables of the first few school years. If the teacher has formerly told the children stories in which animals behave like people, the artistic and symptomatic division of Man into the entire animal kingdom follows quite naturally.

Where the plant kingdom is concerned, Steiner stressed that its connection with the Earth itself should be dwelt upon. The animal kingdom is closer to Man than the plant kingdom, and the child's attention should be directed to the dependence of all types of vegetation on the conditions obtaining in the cosmos as well as on Earth. The rhythms of the sun and moon should be described in connection with the seasons of the year; how the warmth and light of the sun quicken the plants into growth, and how they are dependent upon climatic conditions for germination and growth. The teacher should point out to the children, again in an imaginative and pictorial way rather than in scientific terminology, how the plant is essentially related to the element of *time*; a plant is never a finished product, so to speak, as an animal is when it is fully grown. Countless plant species go through a continuous process of metamorphosis: root, shoot, stem and leaves, flower and fruit; and after fruiting they die. Even perennials, deciduous and evergreen trees show continuous processes of growth and decay; they cannot truly be said to reach a condition that is static, or permanent.

Steiner contended that if the teacher shows in living pictures how the whole earth is a living being, how it bears the plants as Man bears his hair, although in greater complexity, and how soil and vegetation form a certain vital unity, a kind of expansion takes place in the soul of the children which enables them in later years to appreciate the universe in a living way, and not a dead, mechanical way. Here again the general principle of proceeding from the whole to the parts is applicable: Man's characterization as colonies of animals constitutes the first step in an outer direction, encompassing the globe; the Earth, with its garment of vegetation seen in its relationship to the whole cosmos, represents the second step; Man is thus seen to be firmly established in the universal order together with the rest of Nature. The relationship to the animals is more subjective than that to the plant world, which is quite objective; observing the cycle of the year in terms of changes which occur in the plant world assists in this objectifying process which is appropriate to the child at this time. Helpful, too, in this connection is the imaginative presentation of the differences in the respiratory processes in the plant and in Man.

At about the thirteenth year the children should, if at all possible, be introduced to practical gardening, to bring home to them how much trouble and care is needed for vegetables to thrive and crop well. It may be argued that the expansion of the child's soul to which Steiner referred is effected here also; the feelings of a child towards lettuce, radishes and onions which it has grown itself are far different from those towards vegetables purchased in a shop. Similarly, the attitude of a beekeeper's child towards a jar of honey is far removed from that of the town dweller's child who sees it for the first time on a supermarket shelf; such attitudes are essentially attitudes of *soul*, and are an important consideration.

It should be pointed out to the children something which is quite obvious, namely, the fact that animals are mobile, whereas plants are fixed, and therefore have a much closer connection with the soil on which they grow. Furthermore, the composition of the soil as well as particular climatic conditions are important for plants, and this leads over into the teaching of geography and geology. It is absurd, declared Steiner, to teach botany in isolation, without reference to the Earth as an organism; he deplored any practice involving the study of plants in artificial conditions, such as laboratory or classroom.[28] Later on, of course, pupils will probably study plants scientifically, but it is important that a child's introduction to the plant world be on the level of feelings and not on the intellectual level. Indeed, said Steiner, all the successive soul qualities of the growing child from infancy to puberty can be compared with the plant kingdom, in terms of relative advancement, from the primitive, retiring fungi and algae to the higher plants which produce green sepals and coloured petals in the light and airy conditions of the outside world.[29] The anthropomorphisms of the earlier school years are thus worked out in the manner of treating the plants in imaginative and artistic ways, and above all a living and holistic way. The referential "unit" should not be the plant cell, but the whole cosmos; thus the health-giving principle of going from the whole to the parts and not vice versa is preserved.

Steiner always placed great emphasis on a person's ability to observe accurately, and it is obvious from his lectures that children should be exercised in this. The approach to the physical sciences during the later years of the class teacher period is essentially phenomenological and symptomatological; observation is primary, everything else is secondary, including speculation and theorizing.

At about the twelfth year, teaching of natural history should pass on to geology and mineralogy, to what is even still further removed from the human being, to that which is entirely devoid of life, to that which is inanimate in Nature. Man and the animals depend on the plants for nourishment, and the plants depend on the minerals; the minerals depend on nothing — there with them the life-processes cease. Stones, rocks and the earth generally remain unaffected by the passage of time and are independent of man, animal and plant; chemical and physical processes take place by reference to none other than themselves, by the laws of cause and effect inherent in them. Such processes are mechanical and lifeless, and as such may be grasped purely by the powers of the intellect; now with puberty only a few years away the intellectual faculties of the child are dawning, and the time is ripe for teaching which calls upon the forces of thinking and independent judgement.

Between its ninth and eleventh years, the child builds up its own rhythmic system in a way which corresponds to its inner disposition. This process is helped if the education it receives has paid due consideration to artistic method, especially where this embraces the musical element, that which involves measure and rhythm. The soul-spiritual nature of the child is closely involved in the development of the whole muscular system, and Steiner claimed that there is a hidden connection between the rhythmic system and the muscles during this period, and that everything a child receives into its soul is transformed in such a way as to serve the innermost growth of the muscular system.[30] Until now the bone system conforms to the dictates of the soul-spiritual nature which manifests through the muscles; the effortless ease and grace with which a child of this age moves may be seen to bear witness to this. Between the eleventh and twelfth years, however, the movements become awkward and ungainly as the child adapts itself to the mechanical nature of the skeletal system and thus finds itself having to conform anew to the workings of leverage, balance and so on. This is because the soul-spiritual nature of the child has passed over from the muscles to the skeleton, and therefore has to express itself somewhat differently in terms of dynamics and mechanics in order to effect control over the physical nature. In other words, adaptation to the outer world is now complete.

11   The Dawning of the Intellect

*In order to be ripe for thought, one must have learned to be
full of respect for what others have thought. There is no healthy
thought which has not been preceded by a healthy feeling for
the truth, a feeling for the truth supported by faith in authorities
accepted naturally. Were this principle observed in education,
there would no longer be so many people who, imagining too
soon that they are ripe for judgement, spoil their own power to
receive openly and without bias the all-round impressions of
life.*

Learning from cause and effect

Because the incarnation process is now complete, in that the child's soul-
spiritual nature has now penetrated as far as the skeletal system with its
conformity to the inflexible laws of mechanics, based as they are on the
laws of cause and effect, a kind of reciprocal action takes place. In other
words, the workings of these laws in the skeletal system affords a direct
inner experience and understanding of the laws of cause and effect, in
that the muscular system becomes subject to it and the soul-spiritual
nature influenced thereby. In terms of practical pedagogy the child is now
mature enough to comprehend the laws of cause and effect as manifested in
physical chemistry, mineralogy, geology, geography and history; it is now
able to involve itself not only outwardly, but inwardly. Furthermore, the
powers of the intellect are directly involved, as in all purely scientific and
abstract considerations, and this sets the curricular scene for the period
between twelve and fourteen. During this period the faculty of thinking is
called upon increasingly, as well as the sense of independent judgement;
but with this escalation in intellectual activity comes a corresponding need
for a necessary counterbalance in artistic activity of all kinds. Merely
because the child is now able increasingly to grasp scientific principles
by means of its more powerful intellect, it does not signify that there is

no longer any need for art; indeed it is as necessary as ever, though it may be engaged in with greater self-consciousness and objectivity. This calls for greater efforts on behalf of class teachers, who must throughout permeate all their teaching with the artistic element in addition to evoking in the children a living understanding of art in all aspects. They must strive to impart the impression that the whole world is a work of art, and that Nature is a creative artist. This will help to ensure that the prosaic elements unavoidably present in the civilization and culture of the West may be counterbalanced by that which is essentially human in character — Art. The implications for Society in this argument are profound and far-reaching, and will be discussed later.

The child has no real understanding of historical impulses until it has reached the age of twelve; anything in the way of history before this age should be imparted in the form of stories, preferably those centred on the lives of great men and women. Similarly, any scientific principles expressed in the workings of physics, chemistry and natural history in general should be clothed in pictorial garb and not in the form of abstract laws. Steiner claimed that there is some relation between understanding historical impulses in humanity and understanding the external physical impulses of nature in the human organism.[1] This means on the first count that historical impulses engendered by individuals in the shape of idealistic goals often affect the course of external events: that which has its origin in the human soul and spirit often manifests as historical forces — the inner becomes the outer. On the second count it means that external nature engenders activity in the inner nature of Man: the external stimulus prompts the internal response; for example, in the case of visual stimuli the activity of external nature is repeated in the human being. Steiner argued that both processes require an understanding of the same quality, and for this reason both the inner connections of history and descriptions of how purely physical processes originating in the outer world find their way into the human being through the senses, should not be dealt with by the class teacher until pupils are in their twelfth year.[2] The laws of cause and effect may now be applied to human affairs, both from their inner and outer aspects; pupils now see themselves as members of society on the one hand, and subject to its laws, and members of Nature on the other, and subject to its laws.

Introducing subject-teaching

Rudolf Steiner regarded geography not so much as a separate subject but as a culmination of much of what is achieved in other subjects, and should be accorded the importance it deserves. He suggested that children between the ages of nine and twelve are able to absorb an extraordinary amount of teaching in this area, especially if the subject is tackled in the right way.[3] As might be expected local geography should be dealt with first, and the children encouraged to draw simple maps on which the various natural features of the landscape are represented pictorially and artistically. The elements of economic geography may also be dealt with, by which the teacher explains the importance of local rivers, canals, forest and meadowland, natural resources such as coal and iron, and so on. Simple ideas concerning the economic connections between the natural features of the surrounding land and the conditions of its inhabitants should be discussed; why and when the various towns, villages and hamlets grew up where they did, and the differences between the conditions of life in the country and in the towns and cities. The clear impression should be given of how Man co-operates with Nature as far as he must, but is often able to overcome certain difficulties and problems that arise, and in consequence brings about solutions by building canals, railways, bridges, tunnels, motorways and airports. In all this descriptions of only the external aspects of physical and economic geography need be given, and in so far as they touch on the lives of the inhabitants; political geography and its connections with history should be dealt with after the children's twelfth year.

Natural history in its various forms should be brought in as and when appropriate; what has been learned in connection with mineralogy and geology should be integrated, as well as the distribution of animal life and vegetation in relationship to geographical features. Physics and chemistry are drawn upon concerning climatic conditions and the exploitation of natural resources for industrial and commercial purposes; geometry and mathematics are employed in the drawing of scale maps, graphs and suchlike. A severely demarcated timetable has no place in Waldorf schools; the accent has always been on integration of subject-matter wherever and whenever possible in order to demonstrate the interdependence of human endeavour in widely differing areas. After the age of twelve, descriptions dealing with externalities give way gradually to the cultural conditions and states of the various peoples of the world, together with their historical backgrounds, which need only be sketched in against the framework of world history. The rationale for this approach is the same as that for history, which was discussed earlier in the chapter. After the age of twelve children are able to perceive inner connections both within society and Nature, and between them, and these on a worldwide scale; outer connections will already have been dealt with, certainly in a fundamentally descriptive fashion, and these may now be revised and amplified as necessary by the teacher. The spiritual conditions of the various peoples may be dealt with, particularly their life of rights; how and why certain sections of the world population live in subjection to others, and the extent to which the principle of political equality is recognized. Naturally, such a sensitive and delicate area will demand the utmost tact and care on behalf of the teacher, who must discuss such matters with complete lack of ideological or any other kind of bias.

It may readily be seen from this how geography may be employed to bring unity into the rest of teaching, and Rudolf Steiner was very insistent that this should be done. Geography, he maintained, can really be a vast channel into which everything flows, and from which in return much can be drawn.[4] Effects and their causes across natural or artificial boundaries may now be seen on a universal scale, and the children between twelve and fourteen should be able to grasp them. They should be given a lively impression of the great sweeps of historical impulses as they have affected Man through time, and of the vast extents of sea and land in their various geographical characteristics and how these environmental factors have affected the various civilizations. Steiner, far from denying that intellectuality and all that is connected with it has no place in school, stressed that a child will have stronger powers in this respect if its organism has been allowed to grow strong and firm by educating its feeling and will during the years before puberty. If what is spiritual in human culture is not put before the child in purely intellectual forms, but in artistic imagery, its powers of thinking and cognition are enhanced and it will take less hurt when brought into contact with the stresses and pressures of civilization in later life.[5]

Exercising judgement

Great care must be taken by the teacher not to awaken the intellectual powers of the child too early; as argued earlier, thinking takes place in wide-awake consciousness, and the child does not become fully conscious in this respect until the age of puberty, and it is only then that the real nature of inner freedom may be experienced. Any "freedom" accorded the child before the age of fourteen or so in that it is allowed to exercise powers of independent judgement is far more likely to be more spurious than real, a mere aping of later life. There was in 1920 when Steiner was actively lecturing on educational questions a great inclination to accustom the child at too early an age to independent judgement, and he deplored the pernicious attitudes which prevailed. If it was true then, it most certainly is true of present practice in orthodox education. What Steiner described so graphically then is worth quoting in full:

> Precisely where the child has been taught to look upon
> its educator in the right way, and to accept as truth what he
> presents on authority, by these means precisely we prepare
> the child in the right way to be able to have an independent
> free judgement in later life. If we refuse to stand before
> the child as a natural authority, if we disappear, as it were,
> and try to develop everything out of the child's nature,
> then we work upon the child in such a way that we are
> making demands upon its faculty of judgement at a moment
> when that which we have called the astral body and which
> is set free at the age of puberty is still busy within the
> astral nature of the child. In doing so we imprint as it were on
> the flesh of the child what should only be imprinted on
> its soul. Thereby we prepare something within the child which
> will live as a harmful factor in it throughout life. For it
> makes all the difference whether we attain the faculty of
> judgement after due preparation in the fourteenth or fifteenth
> year when the astral body, which is the bearer of judgement,
> has been set free, or whether we are trained to a so-called
> independent judgement at an earlier age; for in this latter
> case, not our astral faculties, i.e. our soul faculties, are drawn
> upon for such judgement, but our body, i.e. our body with
> all its innate qualities, with its temperament, with its — what I
> should like to call — peculiar blood characteristics, with all
> that produces in it of sympathy and antipathy, in short all that
> gives it no power of being objective. In other words, should
> the child between seven and fourteen already be made to
> use its independent judgement, it will judge out of that part of
> human nature which cannot later be altered unless we see to it
> that it is cared for in accordance with what it demands during
> primary school, namely, authority. If we allow judgement
> too early, the body will judge throughout life, and we shall
> remain as men wavering in judgement, dependent on our

temperament and all kinds of things in the way demanded by
the body, by reason of its own nature. If the child at the
proper time is brought up depending on authority, then that
which is to judge in us will be set free in the right way, and
later in life an objective judgement will be gained.[6]

Much of the judgement exercised by the child before the age of puberty
is subjective rather than objective; common experience vouches for the
tendency of children of twelve and under to bring their critical faculties
to bear in a subjective way. It is often difficult for them to see the points
of view of others, and even if they do no notice is taken of them. It must
not be forgotten that the astral body is the bearer of human love, and if
judgement is implanted into the astral body at the right time, namely at
puberty, then judgement will go hand in hand with kind feeling.[7] Here
again Waldorf pedagogy is seen to carry implications for the common
weal. Steiner rarely drew attention directly to such social implications;
often he preferred to allow such thoughts to linger in the minds of his
audience, for full realization to dawn later. In this, as in other things, he
practised what he preached.

Judgement has a deep relationship with feeling, with the astral nature
which has, as discussed previously, its seat in the chest and rhythmic
system. As in our feelings we are, as it were, dreaming, this means that
we are not fully conscious in their operation; it follows from this that
our judgements are not made in full waking-consciousness but in semi-
consciousness. And this, declared Steiner, is true even of the most abstract
of judgements.[8] The judging process itself takes place in the mechanism
of the hands and arms; only the reflection of it in thought takes place in
the head, which is the true organ for ideation and its processes. Man is
essentially a being who judges; he is, so to speak, destined to employ
his critical powers, his intellectual faculties in his progression through
the stages of civilization. Now the organism comprising the hands and
arms are quite obviously connected to, and with, the chest and therefore
with the rhythmic system it encloses; at the same time, however, it can be
seen that the hands and arms have no part in the rhythmical activity of
heart and lungs — they have been liberated from the continuity of their
rhythmic action. In the physical connection between the rhythmic system
and the liberated organism of the arms and hands, said Steiner, we have a
physical symbol for the connection of feeling with judgement.[9] Reflection
on basic human behaviour supports this notion: we embrace each other
with arms and hands to express love and affection; we ward each other
off with them in order to express the opposite feelings of opposition

and hostility. Thus our feelings of sympathy and antipathy are brought to physical expression in our upper limbs, the extensions of our feeling organs. Feelings of affirmation and denial, which also play a large part in the process of judgement, may readily be seen to correspond to the positive nature of sympathy and the negative nature of antipathy respectively.

When judgements are made, according to the presence of feelings of affirmation or denial in that we say yes or no to something, corresponding degrees of pleasure or pain, joy or suffering are also present as an accompaniment. But the greater the degree of egotism present in what the judgement pronounces as being pleasurable or painful, the less is the person concerned capable of experiencing the whole of life and the world at large as being pleasurable or painful. In other words, the inordinately powerful presence of the ego in such judgements the more subjective they will necessarily be; the bias away from the objective will ensure that this is so. This is unfortunate for the individual, as their judgement is unconsciously more biassed than they perhaps realize, and even more unfortunate for society in general upon which judgements are imposed. Now all this has an important bearing on the awakening of the powers of judgement at the right time in a child's life; if they are awakened too early, namely before the twelfth year, judgements that are made are likely to be subjective, and moreover, subsequent judgements are also likely to be lacking in a proper degree of objectivity. The child whose critical faculties have been aroused too early stands in danger of receiving into itself a built-in bias; in other words, judgements are not originated wholly in the astral body where they rightly belong, but in the etheric body or even the physical body, as indicated earlier in the chapter. Moreover, such a child will probably never overcome such a bias; its power of objective judgement will have been permanently damaged, and the effects of this when translated into action necessarily affect the fabric of the society and subculture in which it lives. For the child's part, it means that it will never be able to experience the true exercise of freedom; it means that such a child's spirit will never be free, as it is virtually shackled to the bodily nature, the "lower nature," and in consequence the innate propensities of the bodily nature gain priority over propensities of spirit and soul. Steiner was devoted to the principle of freedom of the individual, and his philosophy of "ethical individualism" as expounded in his book *The Philosophy of Freedom* amply illustrates this. Hence his great concern for a system of education which would lay the foundations for this in the growing child.

A problem in this connection may be seen in the correctness of a judgement, and how it may be ensured. Clearly, if a judgement is based on sympathy or antipathy exclusively, the danger of bias arises, and this would throw doubt on the validity of the judgement. What can be said is that the correctness of the judgement is experienced through sympathy and antipathy. This is so because the human soul is the arena for the play of sympathy and antipathy, but the judging agent is the ego, whose judgements are experienced by the soul. In order to facilitate optimal correctness of a judgement, the ego, the individuality of a person, must be as free and untrammelled as possible; and this means that there should be involved as few corporeal, psychological and spiritual barriers or hindrances as possible. The correctness or otherwise of any judgement is invariably open to debate, but what will certainly be agreed is that it should be as objective as possible. The degree of genuine freedom wielded by the ego depends directly on the ability to hold the forces of sympathy and antipathy in balance, so that as correct a judgement as possible may be made.

The use of teaching aids

Rudolf Steiner once remarked that he would be really furious if he were to see a teacher standing in front of a class with a book in his or her hand,[10] and the basis for this remark will now be discussed. Naturally, he was referring to Waldorf teachers, and more particularly to teachers of the lower school, the class teachers. One important reason for teachers knowing their subject matter and teaching material so well as to render reference to a book unnecessary is that it strengthens their authority with the children. Closer contact with their pupils is maintained if no book comes between them and their teachers; moreover, if they constantly refer to books or notes, this does not pass unnoticed by the children. Indeed, declared Steiner, as soon as the subconscious, astral nature of each pupil divines that the teacher has not fully mastered the subject but has to look it up in a book first, then the child is justified in questioning whether it is worth all the bother of learning it.[11] The pupil may not appear to notice this consciously, but the impression goes deep, and the teacher's natural authority is thereby undermined; the book becomes the source, the printed word becomes endowed with a spurious and excessive authority which, furthermore, is often appealed to without too much discrimination.

Educational aids of various kinds, particularly computer software now so popular in orthodox schools, tend to operate in a similar way; they detract from the personality of the teacher and from his or her natural authority. It may be argued that such mechanical and electronic aids enable teaching to be as objective as possible, and the personal element represented by the teacher to be eliminated. But this contention ignores the fact that teaching and learning are basic *human* activities; teaching machines, programmed by human beings for the benefit of other human beings, demonstrate that this is necessarily so. Mechanical and electronic teaching aids may register success or failure, but they cannot accord anything but pre-programmed praise or blame; they cannot, in a truly human way, encourage, coax or admonish. They may well possess short-term "recall," but no reflective memories by which to recall past efforts, as do teachers. Such devices are inevitably anti-social in their operation; pupils remain silent and passive when watching a television programme or film. Communication exists in one direction only, and there is little or no feedback. Moreover, however objective film-makers or television producers try to be, such objectivity is eroded by the fact that they have had to be selective in the presentation of their material; mistakes and shortcomings, biases and misrepresentations in the material are absorbed and repeated within the nature of the pupils. In short, those criticisms levelled at teachers who scorn teaching aids may also be levelled at those proxy teachers, the teaching aid devisers, who often successfully give the impression that learning is easy, which it is not.

Situations involving teaching and learning are essentially social situations; the level of operation is the person, and persons are people. The textbook is as impersonal as any other teaching aid; and it is the deliberate aim of most textbook authors to make it so. Scientific method, intellectual preciseness, conceptual exactitude and academic excellence are worthy things in themselves, but their proper place belongs more to the world of the adult than the world of the primary school. The child between the second dentition and puberty is not an intellectual creature so much as a creature of feeling, as argued earlier; therefore the teaching of pupils of this age range should be imbued with feeling. This feeling should not of course be of the sentimental, maudlin kind, but of the aesthetic, artistic kind which has an ennobling and edifying effect which uplifts the soul and exhilarates the spirit. Steiner pointed out that most textbooks, particularly scientific textbooks, quite consciously and deliberately put aside the artistic element, yet there is nothing intellectualistic about the life and development of Nature.[12] He strongly recommended to Waldorf teachers that they assimilate the knowledge contained in such textbooks, but reject the intellectual method in favour of the artistic; everything should be transmuted into the pictorial, so that a corresponding vivification of the imaginative faculties may take place in the children. This mitigates the deleterious effects of growing up in an intellectualistic civilization.

The fundamentally anti-social nature of textbook and teaching aid, the use of which necessarily alienates the pupil from the teacher, is liable to foster anti-social behaviour, or at least a lack of sensitivity for social conventions. If children have not been accustomed to meeting people on the soul level, if they have not been given the opportunity to empathize with flower and insect, wind and cloud, bird and beast, fiend and fairy, they are less likely to be able to empathize with other human beings in later life. Such people would then pass each other by and not really know what stirs in the hearts and minds of others, meeting only on the level of the commonplace and trivial. Instead of fellow-feeling there is likely to be egotism; in place of altruism there is likely to be self-seeking, and instead of generosity, greed. If as children they are not led to have confidence in people, especially their teachers, they are likely to lack confidence in their fellows in later life. A teacher who is looked upon as a natural authority by the pupils is likely to be accorded their confidence also. Steiner went even further than this, saying that the teachers should inspire not only the confidence but also the love of the children, which should be reciprocated in good measure. When personal relationships break down, when there is an erosion of trust and confidence, the fabric of society itself is in danger of collapse. When the personal element is not present, people respond to human situations in a mechanical fashion; their responses are "stock responses," predictable and unthinking as well as unfeeling.

The teacher's kindly humour and geniality is of far more value than any amount of cold logic; children need to feel the humanity of the teacher rather than the impersonality of the textbook. They should not be burdened with the "why's and wherefore's" of things until they can apply the full powers of the intellect, which will then be fresh and vigorous, not stale and tired. Social sensitivity will have been fostered in a thousand subtle ways, and this will remain as a blessing to their fellows in later life; their social consciences will be keen and lively, fresh and perceptive.

The twelve senses

According to spiritual science we possess a total of twelve senses by which we are brought into contact with the outside world, and as Rudolf Steiner saw fit to include more than a passing reference to this tenet in his lectures to the teachers of the original Waldorf School, a review of it should be made. These twelve senses are as follows:

Related to thinking	{ Ego Sense Thought Sense Word Sense Sense of Hearing }	Specifically outer senses
Related to feeling	{ Warmth Sense Sense of Sight Sense of Taste Sense of Smell }	Senses both inner and outer
Related to willing	{ Sense of Balance Sense of Movement Sense of Life Sense of Touch }	Specifically inner senses

If we had not twelve senses, claimed Steiner, we should look at our environment like dullards, we should not be able to experience an inward judgement, a judgement made when sense-perceptions from several senses impinge simultaneously. In this manner a large number of permutations in the combinations of the senses is possible, and this number represents the possibilities of uniting what is separate. Perceptions received through our twelve senses are necessarily disparate, and the manner or degree in which we combine or re-unite these is the measure of the extent to which we participate in the life of things. Orthodox science recognizes only five of the twelve senses and thus formulates theories and postulations around these five which are inadequate and confusing. In the future, claimed Steiner, it will be impossible to educate through such confusion; it is necessary for teachers to know about the twelve senses and how they function so that they may teach the better.

As an example Steiner cites how we perceive a red circle. We not only see the colour red, but also the curve of the circle, the form of the circle, and these two completely different perceptions are looked upon as one. The real activity of the eye — the sole activity, in fact — is perceiving the colour red. We see the form of the circle by making use of the sense of movement in our subconsciousness, perceiving it as such after it has been raised into the realm of conscious knowledge, of cognition. It is not until the circle which has been taken in by the sense of movement is raised into the realm of cognition that what we have recognized as a circle connects itself with the colour red. Steiner argued that the form of the circle — and hence forms as such — are called forth from our whole body by appealing

143

to the sense of movement which extends throughout the body. In other words, it would seem that it is not the actual scanning by the eye of its field of vision that enables forms to be distinguished in their outline, but the sense of movement associated with this activity. The form of the circle is not allowed to remain mere form, as it is to the sense of movement, neither is colour allowed to remain mere colour, as it is perceived by the eye. There is an inner compulsion to combine the two, and this takes place consequent on an act of judgement by the ego.[13] That such acts of judgement take place may be experienced when, for example, we are so engrossed in what we are doing at a particular time that we do not hear words addressed to us. If we have decided inwardly that we are not prepared to hear, we do not hear; we choose to exclude what impinges on us by way of our sense of hearing, while continuing to combine that which comes to us by way of other senses. In this way the ego chooses that of which it shall be conscious.

The human being's ego-consciousness, as awareness of a directing self, is not what is meant by the "ego sense" of the foregoing table. Becoming conscious of one's own ego is not actually a perception; it is itself a perceiving entity whose proper domain is the body and soul and is, in a manner of speaking, agent to the spirit, as discussed earlier. The ego sense perceives the ego of another person directly in a manner analogous to the taking in of any other sense perception. This is Steiner's solution to the "other minds" problem which is still regarded as an unsolved problem of philosophy. He regarded the usual "argument from analogy" along the lines postulated by John Stuart Mill as being quite meaningless; just because other human beings look similar to oneself and their behaviour in given circumstances or conditions similar to one's own, one cannot therefore infer that they have minds. In drawing such an inference and conclusion there is not the slightest real consciousness of what lies behind the wholly *direct* perception of another person's ego or "mind." Steiner insisted that we must ascribe to ourselves an ego-sense, just as we do a sense of sight.[14] The "organ for perceiving the ego" is spread out over the whole human being, and the process of perception is something akin to knowledge. This process is perhaps best described by Steiner himself:

> You perceive a man for a short time; he makes an impression
> on you. This impression disturbs you inwardly; you feel
> that the man, who is really a similar being to yourself, makes
> an impression on you like an attack. The result is that
> you "defend" yourself in your inner being, that you oppose
> yourself to this attack, that you become inwardly aggressive
> towards him. This feeling abates and your aggression ceases;

hence he can make another impression upon you. Then
your aggressive force has time to rise again, and again you
have an aggressive feeling. Once more it abates and the other
makes a fresh impression upon you and so on. That is
the relationship which exists when one man meets another and
perceives his ego: giving yourself up to the other human being
— inwardly warding him off — giving yourself up again —
warding him off; sympathy, antipathy, sympathy, antipathy.
I am not now speaking of the feeling life, but of what
takes place in perception when you meet a man. The soul
vibrates: sympathy, antipathy, sympathy, antipathy vibrate.
This, however, is not all. During the time when sympathy is
active you fall asleep into the other human being; during
the time when antipathy is active you wake up again, and so
on. There is this quick alternation in vibrations between
waking and sleeping when we meet another man. We owe this
alternation to the organ of the ego sense. Thus this organ
for the perception of the ego is organized in such a way that it
apprehends the ego of another in a sleeping, not a waking will
and then quickly carries over this apprehension accomplished
in sleep, to the region of knowledge, i.e. to the nervous
system.[15]

The thought sense is not the sense for the perception of one's own
thoughts, but for the perception of the thoughts of others. Thought is
not always conveyed by speech, which is merely a medium for thoughts;
there are many channels for non-verbal communication which are not
confined to the more obvious gestures such as nodding or winking;
body posture, for example, can well be a means of communication,
of expressing unverbalized thoughts which are correctly perceived and
interpreted, consciously or unconsciously. When the thoughts of another
person have been perceived, one must oneself think in order to understand
their thought in order to bring it into connection with other thoughts of
one's own.

Steiner insisted that listening to words and becoming aware of the
meaning in them is something quite different from hearing mere tone,
mere sound, and therefore is to be distinguished from the more generalized
sense of hearing. He suggested that people with sufficient sensitivity are
able to make a distinction between the sense that has to do with musical
and tonal sounds and the sense for words. The four senses of ego, thought,
speech and hearing are mainly concerned with cognitive activity, as the

will-activity in them is suppressed in a similar manner to that described by Steiner in the passage quoted above. They are mainly directed towards the outer world and concerned more particularly with understanding it, with comprehension and the acquisition of knowledge concerning inanimate and animate objects, human beings included.

The next group of four are related to feeling, and are essentially senses which are concerned with inner experiences connected with external physical phenomena: they are, so to speak, borderline senses which partake of both inner and outer worlds. In a corresponding manner the senses of warmth, sight, taste and smell are all both subjective and objective in character. In general terms, what one person feels in the way of the ambient temperature, or sees, tastes or smells represent inner experiences in themselves, but they can be compared directly with the experiences of others with reference to the same phenomena. For example, a cup of coffee will smell, taste, and look the same to several different people, and they will agree that it is hot, cold or lukewarm without reference to a thermometer. Steiner said that at first the including of the sense of sight with the other feeling senses might seem incongruous, but he maintained that reflection would show that his classification is reasonable. The perception of *colour* is the main function of the eye, as discussed earlier, and colour is related more closely to feeling than may at first be realized; people commonly refer to certain colours as being "warm" or "cool," and the element of feeling is revealed in that people have differing colour preferences; likes and dislikes are often quite irrational. To the objection that the sense of sight is very much an outer sense Steiner pointed out that we are able to close our eyes at will, thus shutting off any visual perceptions originating in the outside world. We close our eyes while asleep, yet by contrast we do not close our ears, which are given up entirely to the outer world and thus hearing is reasonably categorized as an outer sense. As regards the sense of warmth, this is often confused with the sense of touch; but the latter is concerned primarily with the registering of pressure, not of temperature; the genius of language, which after all is only representative of the wisdom of Man, allows reference to "feeling" in respect of both words, but reflection will show that this word has a twin meaning — we "feel" via our sense of touch as well as our sense of warmth.

The senses of balance, movement, life and touch are specifically inner senses and are closely related to the willing faculty. The sense of balance manifests as a consciousness of orientation in space, whereby we become aware of our relationship to our position in terms of right or left, forwards or backwards, up or down, and is susceptible to training to a fine and delicate pitch, as demonstrable by acrobats and gymnasts. The sense of movement conveys to us the state of movement in which we ourselves are, in that we are aware of whether our muscles are flexed or not, whether we are in movement or at rest. The connection with willing is obvious, as it is our sense of movement which facilitates physical activities of all kinds, even to the most delicate operations which demand extremely fine movements involving intense co-operation between hand and eye and muscle co-ordination to an extreme degree. In the sense of life we have the perception of the wellbeing of the body in the widest sense, which corresponds to the homeostasis as defined by biologists and physiologists. It conveys perceptions such as comfort and discomfort, fatigue or lack of it, and so on. The sense of touch registers that which takes place between our immediate environment and our willing activity, and is measured mainly by pressure or resistance, and has not a little to do with body-consciousness with reference to the external world. Thus it may be agreed that these four senses are pronounced inner senses; but what we perceive through them in ourselves is exactly the same as what we perceive in the world outside. The elements of balance and movement are very important in terms of the purely physical — that which behaves in accordance with the laws of physics and mechanics. The sense of life when externally applied enables us to distinguish between the animate and the inanimate, and the sense of touch largely enables us to objectify the physical qualities of external objects.

Thus Rudolf Steiner applied the paradigms of sympathy and antipathy, and the soul-faculties of thinking, feeling and willing to the ways in which Man becomes aware of the outer and inner worlds. He considered an understanding of the twelve senses to be important for the overall understanding of the human being, particularly the growing human being, and as a consequence teachers would be able to educate their pupils better in every way.

12   After Puberty —
the Upper School

The task of the teacher is the greatest self-denial; in the
presence of the child he must so live, that the child's spirit can
develop its own life in sympathy with the life of the teacher.
One must never wish to make the children a mirror of oneself.
That which was in the teacher himself should not live on
in compulsion and tyranny after they have grown up and left
school.

Approaching adulthood

At puberty children reach another turning point in their development, and this sets them on the road to adulthood. With their newly acquired ability to procreate the species, pupils become students, children become young men and women. Now dawns the feeling of a new-found freedom: not the careless, irresponsible kind of "freedom within the law" which characterizes the period between seven years of age and fourteen, but the feeling of self-reliance, independence and the intuition that freedom and self-determination is now a right and not a privilege. Problems, which hitherto were mainly of an external nature are now overwhelmed by those of an inner, personal nature, which are invariably coloured by emotional overtones. Personal relationships tend to become more intense, and unfamiliar urges and compulsions surge up which are surprisingly strong and difficult to manage, manifesting as *gaucherie* and inconsistent behaviour. Underlying all this is that most characteristic of all human emotions — love.

The sexless love of the years before puberty, when it was obliged to remain at the soul-spiritual level, now descends to the physical level. Echoes of the asexual element are carried over to manifest in the form of ideals, a universal love for mankind, a keen social conscience or a generalized desire to help others. Complementary to this, very often,

148

is the idolizing of another person, usually of the opposite sex, which expresses itself as romantic love. This means, in a certain sense, a flowing over into the other on the soul level, and the desire to unite copulatively with the other on the physical level; both are indicative of basically sympathetic tendencies. Antipathetic tendencies, on the other hand, show themselves on the soul level as enhanced faculties of critical judgement, and on the physical level as a heightened antipathy to the environment in the expression of boisterous behaviour at one end of the scale to sheer vandalism at the other. Gone, of course, is the need for authority as well as the wish for it; the child should now be free, but at the same time aware of its responsibilities; the age of reason has been reached. Parents and teachers alike are re-valued and re-assessed, coming under a critical scrutiny that is likely to be harsh and uncompromising, and the main criterion usually applied is that of competence. Parents must be seen to be ideal, teachers must be seen to be expert in their fields; faults hitherto sympathetically accepted are now thrown into sharp relief as a result of intensified antipathy; what went unnoticed before is now revealed in stark detail as the keenness of the newly born intellect is applied.

Nothing is now sacred; old gods are iconoclastically disposed of, old standards are discarded and new ones urgently sought. The vacuum must somehow be filled, and adolescents fill it by accepting the standards of their peers. Childhood, now firmly behind them, is rejected as history, never to be returned to or re-enacted; the world of the adult, seen with fresh eyes as being riddled with convention, hypocrisy and cant, is likewise firmly rejected. Teenagers, having rejected both past and future in a typically antipathetic manner, sympathize with and accept the present, and their present comprises the teenage cult that is perpetuated from generation to generation. This acceptance is reflected in the uniformity of dress, leisure pursuits, ethical and moral standards which is characteristic of the closed world of the adolescent. However, their defencelessness in certain directions is all too often exploited by unscrupulous commercial interests and their gregarious loyalties shamelessly manipulated to financially profitable ends.

The taste of freedom

Adolescents should feel free of authority, but they will only experience this freedom if hitherto they have lived under a regime of authority, however benign. If during their childhood they have not felt that they have been under authority, but have experienced a kind of loose patronage or

149

even *laissez-aller*, they will not so readily notice the change from a spurious kind of freedom to the genuine kind. Rudolf Steiner argued that this was an important experience: young people should first have experienced the dependence on authority, then at puberty they can outgrow this feeling of dependence and begin to judge for themselves.[1] All too often children before puberty are actually encouraged to make judgements for themselves and this, he declared, was positively harmful. Indeed, if teaching and instruction is imparted along intellectual lines these harmful effects are unavoidable, for the very character of intellectual activity involves conceptualizing, judging and drawing conclusions. If, said Steiner, we assume that by the time a child comes to school it is already mature; if we encourage it, as soon as it can talk, to look at things for itself and come to its own conclusions, that will mean we are leaving the child to remain permanently at the stage of having just learned to speak, and want to make sure that it shall not develop beyond this stage.[2] It may here be said, by way of digression, that the so-called "discovery" or heuristic methods of learning which are nowadays so popular have no place in Waldorf education. One would look in vain for a "resource centre" in a Steiner school, apart from the library.

It has been mentioned earlier that the intellect awakens *of itself* at puberty; demands made on it before this time produce results, but only at great detriment to the being of the child. The feeling of freedom which should be experienced at puberty is in direct proportion to the demands which have been made prematurely on the powers of the childish intellect. If during a child's early school years, said Steiner, it has stored up an inner treasury of riches through imitation, through its feeling for authority, and from the pictorial character of its teaching, then at puberty these inner riches can be transmuted into intellectual activity. The child will now be faced with the task of *thinking* what before it has *willed* and *felt*.[3] In soul-spiritual terms, this means that the *spirit* of the child — and thinking is a spiritual activity — which was asleep in its head during the period from birth to the second dentition, and dreaming from then until puberty, is now fully awake. Put another way, also in spiritual-scientific terms: the child, who during the first period of development was awake in its will (limbs and metabolic system), who during the second period was awake in its feeling life (rhythmic system), is now, at the threshold of the third period, awake in its thinking (head system).

If, however, children have not been allowed to imitate properly during the time appropriate to imitation, namely infancy, and have been drained of their intellectual powers prematurely, then, said Steiner, just at the time when they ought to have found a certain security in themselves they will be running after trivialities; in the awkward years of adolescence they will be imitating all kinds of things which please them at the moment.[4] Needless to say, not all things adolescents find in their environment are worthy of imitation, but they instinctively seek for support, and find it among their peers; as members of a sub-culture mutual comfort is sought and given, as mentioned earlier.

Rudolf Steiner often insisted that the intellect only becomes active in its own way when the child has already reached puberty, and not before.[5] He argued that young people can experience true freedom only through an understanding of their own being, and this is impossible if before puberty they have an intellectual education, being forced to absorb abstract concepts or ready-made, sharply outlined observations. This is tantamount to nipping the child's freedom in the bud, so to speak, and amounts to downright interference with the development of the human self, one of the most heinous and reprehensible of pedagogical crimes. It is impossible to impart freedom to another human being — it is something that must be experienced for oneself. Waldorf methodology claims to educate through Nature, to impart to the growing child that which it feels maturationally or developmentally attracted to, namely an environment worthy of imitation during infancy and an authority to look up to during childhood. Then all that has been taken in by means of imitation and pictorial interpretation of the world rises up at puberty, ready to be grasped by the intellect; in other words, adolescents are then ready to lay hold of their own being through their own being. And this, argued Steiner, is as it should be; one should educate all the elements in human beings except their very essence and identity, and then wait for their own being to lay hold on what such education has brought forth within them. One should not lay brutal hands on the development of the human self, but prepare the soul for the development of that self that sets in after puberty.[6] An education which forces the emergence of intellectual powers before they are properly ripe, which calls upon the child before puberty to make judgements and to think abstractly, places hindrances in the path of true self-development of the child. The teacher's task on the contrary, declared Steiner, is to be the removers of hindrances: physical, psychological and as far as possible, spiritual hindrances. This calls for sharpened powers of observation as well as knowledge and insight on the part of the teacher; knowing when and how to act is of course a necessary corollary.

Rudolf Steiner often spoke of the teacher's task as remover of obstacles and hindrances to the development of the child towards freedom; and by this he meant not a spurious kind of "freedom" wherefrom an

151

individual's actions are unpremeditated and influenced by instinct, wishes, and impulses of various sorts which are uncritically allowed to affect them. It is generally the case, it need hardly be said, that to be critical of one's affective and cognitive processes means to be conscious of them; it would entail employment of an extraordinarily high degree of objectifying power, and such is very difficult indeed to achieve. Most people's thinking is more subjective than they realize, as they are not conscious of their own in-built biases, habits and inhibitions which have been acquired by the processes of socialization and education. Steiner's system of "ethical individualism" is fully dealt with in his book *The Philosophy of Freedom*, in which he declared:

> An action is felt to be free insofar as the reasons for it spring
> from the ideal part of my individual being; every other part
> of an action, irrespective of whether it is carried out under the
> compulsion of nature or under the obligation of a moral
> standard, is felt to be *unfree*. Man is free insofar as he is able
> to obey himself in every moment of his life. A moral deed
> is *my* deed only if it can be called a free one in this sense.[7]

He saw freedom as not only being exercised in willing; it is also experienced in feeling and recognized in thinking.

The work of the ego

In the processes of socialization and education parents and teachers bear tremendous responsibilities towards the children in their care; their influences, argued Steiner, extend far beyond childhood and have much greater effects than are generally realized. He insisted that the seven-year rhythm in the development of the human being, easily discernible in childhood and adolescence, is carried on through later life. During the first six or seven years it is the physical body especially which can be developed through external influence; from approximately seven years of age until the age of thirteen or fourteen it is the etheric body which is especially developed, and from puberty until the age of twenty or twenty-one it is the astral body which is particularly accessible to external developmental influences. At about this age the ego is, in a manner of speaking, born; it is after this time that the human being confronts the world as a relatively free, independent being and henceforth is fully capable of working at the development of his or her own soul. Until this age the individual has had little scope for development, even if this were possible: between birth and the seventh year, the ego is entrenched in the physical body, and is affected by everything that it perceives in its environment particularly strongly; from the second dentition until puberty the ego is entrenched in the etheric body, and it is during this time that it is particularly strongly influenced by the external developmental factors which primarily affect the etheric body; between puberty and the age of twenty or so the ego is entrenched in the astral body, and is most strongly influenced by what approaches it in the way of passions, desires and the inner life generally. It is only when the ego becomes free of the astral body that it is able to exert its harmonizing influences on its three vehicles, as briefly mentioned elsewhere.

The period between the ages of twenty and twenty-seven are important for the development of the sentient soul; the years between twenty-eight and thirty-five are important for the development of the intellectual soul (sometimes referred to as the rational soul or mind-soul), and from about the thirty-fifth year the development of the consciousness soul takes place.

The following table may help to make this clear:

Ego entrenched in:		*Special development of:*
physical body	0–7	physical body
etheric body	7–14	etheric body
astral body	14–21	astral body

Birth of ego at approximately 21 years of age

Ego works at harmonizing of:		*Special influence on:*
astral body	21–28	sentient soul
etheric body	28–35	intellectual soul
physical body	35+	consciousness soul

Steiner's contention that the most important period for the development of the physical body as being that from birth to the second dentition has been discussed from other points of view elsewhere. To the objection that the child obviously goes on growing for perhaps ten years or more after acquiring its permanent teeth, it must be said that Steiner stressed that the earlier period is the *most important* precisely because in infancy the physical body is most vulnerable to external influences. At this time the child might be characterized as one extensive sense-organ, devoting itself, surrendering itself to everything that comes towards it from its environment, and it is the time when the ego is most firmly entrenched in its physical body. It may be recalled that it is during this period that that the child imitates what goes on in its surroundings so intensely that its organism is quite literally impressed with what it experiences. Steiner maintained that the physical body bears a mysterious connection with the consciousness soul; he said that if the ego is to acquire strength in later life, namely after the thirty-fifth year, it must encounter no boundaries in the physical body at that time. At this age the ego should ideally attain to inner activity, penetrating and itself becoming penetrated by the forces of the consciousness soul, so that it can finally transcend itself and acquire knowledge of the world.[8] If the individual is to seek free intercourse with the world, and not seek to retire into his or her self, the ego must find the physical vehicle unencumbered by constrictions and maladjustments brought about by undesirable influences during infancy. The more love and happiness, joy and affection experienced by the child at this time, declared Steiner, the fewer will be the obstacles encountered by the ego in its association with the consciousness soul. Conversely, everything in the nature of unkindness, distress and pain which the child suffers during the first seven years of its life creates obstacles for the ego, with the result that such a child, in the corresponding later period, becomes a closed character, one reluctant to face the world and to enter into its manifold activities.

There exists a similar connection between the development of the intellectual soul and the etheric body. The forces aroused by the harmonizing influence of the ego are such that endow a person with initiative and courage, or, on the contrary, tendencies towards cowardice, indecision and vacillation as well as general sluggishness. It is important that, if individuals are to knit the qualities of courage and intrepidity firmly into their character, their ego encounters no obstacles in the etheric body. If people, as children between the second dentition and puberty, have been enabled to experience the presence of indisputable authority and representative truth in their teachers and parents, declared Steiner, inestimable benefits accrue to them in terms of fearlessness in face of life's vicissitudes.

The affinities between the astral body and the sentient soul which Steiner pointed out are perhaps more immediately apparent than in the cases of the corporeal vehicles: physical body and etheric body. If, between puberty and the age of twenty or twenty-one students are deliberately brought into contact with high ideals, great and beautiful ideas which have been formulated by outstanding historical personalities, and selfless deeds of heroic figures who have suffered for what they strove to achieve for mankind, they are invariably fired with enthusiasm for altruistic ideals which become embedded in the sentient soul and consequently embodied in their character. There exists a widespread tendency amongst adolescents to be drawn to positive rather than negative ideals, to optimism rather than pessimism, and the critical faculties being developed at this period often preserve them from definite harm. It is therefore of the greatest importance that young people should encounter only that which represents the very summit of human altruistic endeavour, that they may be themselves inspired by lofty ideals.

Rudolf Steiner insisted that such connections as these were known, albeit instinctively or inspirationally, in times past. He argued that as long as an empirical, scientific approach is made to education, in that the child itself is treated as an experimental subject and the result analysed intellectually, there is little chance that the real being of the child will be reached, and this has been discussed elsewhere. If mature people, because of the presence of wrong influences in their environment as children, or as the result of wrong treatment, find that the ego is unable to overcome hindrances created as a result of these, then they are nevertheless able to take steps to remedy the situation. These steps consist in devoting themselves to deeply meditative consideration of thoughts and feelings that lead to a fuller understanding of the universe, to a frame of mind which leads on to a contemplative pondering of the cosmic mysteries. If they willingly and repeatedly devote themselves to such considerations, then, through the harmonizing work of the ego, their character will gradually be transformed, and any weakness of soul and spirit eventually overcome.

Rudolf Steiner, although undoubtedly familiar with research in this field, entirely disregarded contemporary psychologies of the adolescent, and when he lectured to teachers of the original Waldorf School imminent upon the opening of an upper school, he spoke straight from the results of his spiritual-scientific researches, as well he might, as his audience was comprised mainly of anthroposophists. He spoke, as he always did to close followers, with his audience in mind but in uncompromising spiritual-scientific terms, referring to the supersensible members of the human being as concrete realities, and such clear and consistent reification merits emulation. Readers are thus left to work out their own system of correspondences to modern psychology according to their lights. A man should be paid in his own coin, and this is the well-deserved consideration being afforded to Steiner.

Before puberty, boys and girls are, in a certain sense, unisexual and there is little real difference on the soul-spiritual level. Conventions of dress, life-styles and play habits are largely the result of the general socialization processes and have little basis in the realities of child nature. Adolescents, as mentioned earlier, claim their rights to freedom, even if this is mainly confined to the freedom to conform to the general standards of dress and behaviour of other adolescents; but boys and girls — or more properly, young men and women — at this time differ in their soul-spiritual conformation, and these differences are reflected in their behaviour and attitudes.

It may be recalled that at puberty the astral body becomes free of the organism; it is, in a certain sense, born at this time. As the vehicle for human passions and desires, as the arena for the playing out of sympathies and antipathies on the soul level, indeed the whole life of feeling, it becomes exposed on all sides, so to speak, and its influences are the more directly apprehended from without and felt from within. At the same time its influence on the ego is also stronger, resulting in inner conflicts and personal problems. It may be said that the ego and astral body comprise an individual's subjective members, whereas the physical body and etheric body comprise the objective members. A person's astral body and ego are vehicles of consciousness and sense of self respectively; desires and passions absorb him or her entirely, out of sheer sympathy, unless the ego is extremely strong. When someone *feels* jealousy, joy, anxiety, envy, they *are* jealous, joyous, anxious, envious; even the genius of language itself bears witness to the subjective nature of these members. The etheric body and the physical body are objective in nature. The individual is conscious *of* and *in* these vehicles; in a manner of speaking they belong to the outside world — extensions of Nature into his or her being. They afford the resistance necessary in an essentially antipathetic manner, so as to afford consciousness and selfhood to the subjective members.

Adolescents are now suddenly faced with a very powerful subjectifying force in the newly born astral body, whereby they interpret experiences in a mainly selfish manner, reacting to these as they see fit — in other words, a manner in which they would construe as being "free." Intermixed in the processes of interpretation and reaction is an equally powerful objectifying force which proceeds from their now enhanced intellectual faculties, and which has its basis in the corporeal nature. Their sympathies and antipathies attain to a new dimension of intensity, and with the birth of the ego still some six or seven years away they encounter great difficulties in adjusting themselves to new experiences.

Adolescent behaviour

Steiner said that the astral body of a woman is more highly differentiated, more highly organized than a man's, and that this is already true of the pubescent girl. From puberty until the age of twenty or twenty-one she is almost completely under the influence of her astral body, and only then does she make a supreme effort to attain egohood and assert her real self. During these years she is often very sociable, and rapidly acquires poise and self-confidence, and is therefore able to face the world freely and frankly. She possesses the urge to express her soul qualities in her behaviour, and this is often extended to externalities such as vanity and coquettishness, perhaps together with a penchant for dress, hair styling, and the use of cosmetics, jewellery and personal ornamentation.

Boys and men, on the other hand, have astral bodies which are much less differentiated, and far less open to cosmic influences than those of women. The adolescent boy tends to withdraw into himself; the ego remains in a manner of speaking concealed, and this shows itself in a certain shyness and lack of social grace which in many cases is sufficiently exaggerated to show as rough, boisterous behaviour and crude manners. Steiner said that teachers should be on their guard if boys of this age do not show a certain reserve; lack of it would be a sure sign of probable impending difficulties or abnormalities.[9] If the adolescent boy exhibits a certain surliness or oafishness and behaves in a loutish fashion, this is symptomatic of the concealment of the ego, the wish to hide his real personality, and should be taken as normal. He finds it somewhat difficult to make meaningful connections with the outside world, and this may lead to a certain tendency towards imitation, the inclination to model his behaviour on various people in the attempt to extend his experience. In this way he is able to judge other people's reactions as well as evaluate the appropriateness of different behaviour patterns to his own emerging individuality. The youth must receive wounds and inflict wounds at this age, said Steiner, so that he may be all the more ready to receive the spiritual into himself when his ego comes to maturity at about the age of twenty.[10]

The two dangers to be avoided at this time are allowing the girls to drift off into empty superficialities or letting them gigglingly flaunt themselves, and allowing the boys to develop into young hooligans by letting their natural tendencies to boorishness flourish unchecked.

A problem arising at this age with both boys and girls is often that of eroticism, exaggerated feelings of sensuality. Steiner characterized this as being tormented and oppressed by one's own body, and claimed that there was no better way of restraining eroticism than by a healthy development of the aesthetic sense, a feeling for what is noble and beautiful in nature. However, if such a training in artistic sensibility has not been achieved before puberty, there is little that can be done afterwards to remedy it. Ideally, as Steiner advocated, the child should receive into itself moral and religious impressions during its infancy, and during childhood to have been immersed in the artistic in every conceivable way; a result of this would be that after puberty tendencies to eroticism would then be more able to be contained within proper limits. If a child has learned to perceive the world in all its beauty it is less liable to feel subject to its bodily nature; it feels more free, and less dependent upon its body for pleasurable experiences.

The tendencies towards eroticism are perhaps stronger in boys as they have a more earthy nature, and are more inclined to turn in on themselves in what might often be a morbid way. The boy thus sees the *inner* world as presenting many enigmas, whereas in the case of the girl it is the *outer* world that is problematic. She has not the ability to come to grips with it as the boy has; he has a natural tendency to seek the solution to problems presented by the external world, to find out how things work. This enhances his feeling of control over his environment, of power over the external world which confronts him as an agglomeration of riddles to be solved — which, remarked Steiner, includes even the riddle of woman![11]

On the other hand the adolescent girl, firm in her own inner being but puzzled and perturbed by the many problems presented by the external world, strives to maintain her sense of security by seeking ideals to live by, and having found them, preserves them in her mind as standards for her judgements of value. Being less anchored to the earth and earthly things than the boy, she needs as a counterbalance at this time her attention to be drawn to the *deeds* that have been accomplished on the Earth by outstanding individualities. Conversely the boys, already familiar with worldy problems and how inventors and entrepreneurs have sought to solve them, need *ideals* in order, so to speak, to raise their eyes from pre-occupation with earthly deeds to the more lofty domains of the spirit.

The adolescent, then, during this period of *Sturm und Drang*, needs the firm support of teachers expert in their specialized subjects who are at the same time capable of acting as guides and counsellors. In Waldorf schools, when the children lose their class teachers at the end of Class 8, they are allocated class sponsors from the ranks of the upper school teachers, who administer pastoral care for the rest of the students' time at school; thus a certain modicum of continuity is preserved. Such class sponsors, as must all teachers for that matter, have to be sincere and honest in their dealings with young men and women, and at the same time know how to be tactful and diplomatic. When faced in class by teenagers who rage on finding that the world is different from their expectations, who are disillusioned and critical, scornful and rebellious, teachers may accomplish much of value for the individual and society at large by playing off the future against the past. In other words, if teachers tell their students just how the world has become to be in whatever state it is in, how events have so arranged themselves as to precipitate whatever crises and world problems that are then current, in direct and unvarnished terms, at the same time pointing out the various remedies offered by statesmen and politicians of various colourings, economists of whatever school and spiritual leaders of the different faiths, much will be achieved in that the young people's *wills* are stimulated. Bearing in mind the spiritual-scientific connotations of the will-forces, this means in practical terms sowing the seeds of future action, whether in the sphere of politics, business or social justice. It need hardly be said that teachers should take the most scrupulous care in presenting world situations or social problems in the utmost degree of objective clarity; personal opinions should of course be left unsaid, but at the same time experienced teachers of young people know that, with their heightened critical faculties, they are soon able to detect biassed interpretations and prejudiced viewpoints, not to mention value-judgements, hypocrisy and double standards. Discussions on such matters carry a bonus for teachers too; if they show themselves to be worthy of credibility, young people will gladly accord it, and often respond by elevating their standards of work and behaviour.

Preparation for adult life

The work of Waldorf upper school specialist teachers rests squarely on that of the lower school class teachers, although the nature of their teaching is fundamentally different. As discussed earlier, after puberty the fundamental attitude of pupils to the world finds expression in ideals, which are formulated in ideas. Their new-found intellectual powers seek to exert themselves in that the principle of cause and effect, together with its inherent elemental quality of judgement, now makes appeal to their thinking. It is the ability to judge, to discriminate and to differentiate, which allows the human intellect to weigh the evidence involved in the manifestations of causality. The time is now ripe for teaching along intellectual lines, though this does not mean that the artistic approach, so dominant a feature during the lower school years, should now be abandoned. Rather, art and the History of Art should now become separate upper school subjects, together providing an important counterbalance to the intellectual effort required for the academic subjects.

Furthermore, at this time various social aspects of life may well be nourished in a threefold way. Firstly, the upper school years should be a time when all kinds of preparations for practical life in the outside world should be made. Between the ages of fifteen and twenty the student should be given a thorough grounding in what is involved in agriculture, trade and commerce, and industry and manufacturing processes, as well as the more orthodox subjects usually taught, such as current world affairs, history and geography, physics, chemistry, biology and mathematics. In this way, declared Steiner, students learn to know humankind from their knowledge of the world as a whole.[12]

Secondly, by the very process of inquiry into not only the broad principles of world trade in terms of economics, but also into the finer mechanical details of the workings of the various machines and manufacturing processes which contribute to them, students are brought face to face with the realities of their forefathers' inventiveness, and this tends to instil respect and admiration, albeit unconsciously, for this inventive genius. A consequence of this is the wish and resolve, perhaps equally unconscious, to improve and ennoble that which they have inherited from their forebears.[13]

Thirdly, the importance of knowing how such things as the telephone, the internal combustion engine and electrical and electronic apparatus of various kinds work, and how, for example, soap, toothpaste and other items made use of in everyday life are manufactured, is very great — far greater than is commonly realized. Ignorance of such things, asserted Steiner, contribute not a little to nervousness in people, due to a kind of subconscious confusion engendered by their being surrounded on all sides by mechanical gadgets and processes which they do not fully understand.[14] Machines created by virtue of human genius are, in a manner of speaking, "spiritually transparent"; in other words, every single operation of such machines as well as their construction is the result of spiritual activity, of human powers of thinking and their application to physical materials and their properties. Therefore, that which has been produced by dint of the thinking processes of one human being is capable of being understood by another human being by means of those same processes, and the consequences of this being so are of inestimable value in terms of social life, in that there comes about a greater understanding and a keener appreciation of what is involved in terms of widely differentiated human activities. This is of tremendous importance where modern manufacturing

160

processes are concerned, involving as they do extremely high degrees of division of labour and fragmentation of production, whereby the worker is concerned with the part rather than the whole, with the consequent narrowing of interests and cares, which in turn gives rise to lack of appreciation of other people's problems.

Bridging the generation gap

All this is in line with what Rudolf Steiner aspired for concerning the fundamental brotherhood of Man. Education, for him, was as much the fostering of a certain relationship with the world and its human inhabitants as imparting knowledge and information concerning it. He was insistent that Waldorf teachers reckon with the deep feeling in the young that life must have meaning and purpose. If adolescents have not acquired, by dint of their earlier education, a basis which will be capable of sustaining such a meaning and purpose in the light of their newly-gained enhanced power of judgement, it may well bode ill for themselves and society. They feel, declared Steiner, an urge to bring something new to everyday life, something from their world of ideals.[15] If these ideals are wrongly based as a result of faulty socialization and education they will nevertheless find expression — for the good or ill of society at large. If the young have not been brought into the right relationship to the cultural heritage which is their due, if they misunderstand, disregard, or even reject their cultural birthright, the fault and blame lie with their teachers and parents and not with them. If the young can find no connection with the world they find themselves in, the gulf between them and the older generations is bound to widen; the generation gap becomes synonymous with a credibility gap, and the result is a loss of mutual trust and confidence. There is even a danger that the older generations, unsure of themselves and their natural authority and their values in face of the excessive confidence of the young in theirs, submit to them, so that the danger arises of surrender to adolescent standards and values. Steiner went so far as to say that, if the older generations lose credibility with the younger, authority would so suffer that teachers would eventually find themselves obliged to fall back on the police because they would not be able to keep order in class.[16] In this, as in other matters, Steiner has proved himself to be an excellent prophet.

Creativity with dexterity

Steiner insisted that the original Waldorf School should be co-educational on purely social grounds, and that boys and girls, even in the upper school, should follow largely the same curriculum. Where mechanics and the understanding of devices designed for the convenience of Man's day-to-day living are concerned, the girls should know about spinning and weaving, and the methods used in the production of clothing and household materials, how domestic appliances work, and so on; the boys should be taught woodwork and perhaps metalwork and be called upon to design and construct useful mechanical apparatus or gadgets. The boys should be taught the elements of surveying and planning, and be capable of doing technical drawings and of working from them; the girls should learn the elements of hygiene, simple bandaging, and suchlike. Both sexes would benefit from a course on First Aid, if this could be arranged.[17] Steiner stressed, however, that instruction in the workings of mechanical devices could be justified on purely educational grounds, as being pedagogically correct and suitable for adolescents, and not on any utilitarian grounds. That a boy may make use of such instruction in his later career as a fitter or mechanic is purely by the way; boys who later become bookmakers or surgeons obtain the same benefits in educational terms.[18] Steiner regarded the cleavage between handwork and headwork in any school curriculum, and even in later life, as undesirable if not disastrous. He saw the Waldorf curriculum as allowing those students who were preparing themselves for a career demanding mental facility to be made familiar with manual work, and those students destined to become manual workers to be shown something of the life of the human spirit. Ideally, there should be some kind of work experience scheme whereby students could familiarize themselves with occupational situations and do actual jobs before leaving school. Such a scheme, he declared, would ensure that the students' minds would remain creative and their hands dexterous.[19]

Rudolf Steiner saw the general aim of education as twofold: firstly, that the nature and substance of the curriculum, together with appropriate didactic methods, should satisfy the demands of child nature; and secondly, that teaching and instruction given should enable future adults to find their place in the world in both social and occupational senses, that they should be helped to acquire the requisite skills for their later working life, and that they should get on well with their fellows.[20] He called upon the teachers of the first Waldorf School to submit themselves to the severest self-examination, not only as individuals but as people of their time. He reminded them to make themselves conscious of what had been educated into them, of what they had acquired through their own socialization and training, and of the necessity of growing beyond any constraints and limitations thus imposed on their efforts to master themselves. It would not do, he declared, for them to remain products of their previous education, mere puppets of their time, but to re-appraise their positions as free individuals and their roles as educators and teachers.[21] With characteristic aplomb he strongly recommended that they devote themselves to a through study of spiritual science in order that they may better understand, not only themselves, but the children they seek to teach. In the first place, pedagogy needs a true and accurate knowledge of Man. Such knowledge of the human being as body, soul and spirit does not remain at the intellectual level but passes over into the feelings, thereby stimulating the will. Steiner emphasized frequently that anthroposophy is itself pedagogy in the sense that it becomes pedagogy as soon as the opportunity to educate is present.[22] Just as mere head-knowledge provides little for the inner life, so it is virtually incapable of stimulating the whole person, namely the feelings and will in addition to the intellect. Steiner never tired of pointing out that materialistic thinking alienates people from the real being of the child, hence the urge to experiment with it. It was not that he deplored experiments so much as the narrowing and fragmentation of the field of vision necessitated by empirical methods generally, the concentration on a single aspect to the exclusion of others, attending to the part while disregarding the whole.

13 The Curriculum

A system of teaching which lays down beforehand the
teacher's timetable and every imaginable limitation actually,
and moreover completely, excludes the teacher's art.

Laying the foundations

From 21 August to 5 September 1919 Rudolf Steiner held his main lecture courses for the teachers-designate of the first Waldorf School in Stuttgart. On each of fourteen days he gave lectures entitled *Study of Man* in the morning, *Practical Course for Teachers* in the afternoon, and held seminars in the evening, published in English as *Discussions with Teachers*. As a kind of conclusion to what must be the shortest teacher training course of all time, Steiner gave the three so-called *Curriculum Lectures* on 6 September. Die Freie Waldorfschule opened its doors to its first pupils on the following day.

These lecture courses taken together may be regarded as containing Steiner's basic indications concerning the nature of Man in so far as his educational principles are involved, didactic method, and the actual substance of the curriculum for the first eight classes, variously referred to elsewhere as the lower school or the class teacher period. His main indications concerning upper school pupils are contained in a course given to the teachers of the original Waldorf School in June 1921 entitled *Menschenerkenntnis und Unterrichtsgestaltung*, first published in English as *The Supplementary Course* and later as *Waldorf Education for Adolescence*.

His booklet *The Education of the Child in the Light of Anthroposophy* which appeared in 1909 anticipated in a remarkable way the call to found a school on spiritual-scientific principles which came some ten years later. In the early summer of 1919 he gave *Drei Vorträge über Volkspädagogik* which dealt with the social basis of primary and secondary education in a general way, and in further anticipation of the establishing of a school under his leadership.[1]

Although it was his intention to present systematically the Waldorf

Curriculum in writing, Steiner was never able to do this before his death in March 1925. In the same year, one of the Waldorf School teachers, Dr Caroline von Heydebrand, with the help of colleagues, drew up and formulated his indications and published them. Another early collaborator, Herr E. A. Karl Stockmeyer, has since done very valuable work in the area of the curriculum.[2]

Rudolf Steiner demanded much of his teachers, and his expectations of them appear to be something of a paradox. Although he stressed that the curriculum must be so approached that a teacher should be able to recreate it himself at any moment and not in any circumstances regard it as dogma, he nevertheless expected the basic indications to be strictly observed and not for teachers to do just as they pleased. It would probably be fair to suggest that there are four factors involved in the educational situation:

(a) the spiritual, psychological and bodily needs of the growing child appropriate to its age and rate of development;

(b) the need to connect the teaching/learning content with the circumstances to be met with in contemporary society;

(c) the class of children as a social unit unique in its particular structure in terms of personality, ability, aims and socio-cultural background;

(d) the teacher, with his or her individual gifts and shortcomings, temperamental propensities, professional training and teaching style.

These four factors may then be set against the background of the whole curriculum, and perspectives adjusted according to the demands of the circumstances. Steiner emphasized again and again that the teacher should be able to "read" both the child and the given situation and be able, moreover, to act accordingly within the spirit of the curriculum. Provided the teacher's knowledge of the child's whole being at its various stages of development is accurate and exact, taking into account individual differences from close acquaintance with each particular child, there is little that can go wrong. This assertion is made because of Steiner's oft-repeated axiom that anthroposophy is itself pedagogy; spiritual science, he claimed, of itself gives the necessary enthusiasm and inspiration for teaching, the requisite concern for Man and society and, moreover, a sure knowledge of the overall needs of the growing child at every stage of its development. This claim may seem at best immodest, at worst arrogant, but only those ignorant of Steiner's life, work and teachings would regard it so. Experienced Waldorf teachers are, oddly enough, often amazed when time after time they meet with overwhelming evidence of the essential "rightness" of the curriculum for a given age. They should not, of course, be so astonished, but the very freshness and spontaneity and quality of response from the children if the right thing is given at the right time is an unforgettable experience which invariably confirms one's trust in the curriculum and methodology and, as Steiner asserted, gives increased enthusiasm for teaching.

Interpreting the curriculum

In one sense, therefore, Waldorf teachers are bound in absolute terms to a definite educational philosophy, curriculum and didactic method; in another they are completely free agents, albeit within the "law" of Waldorf methodology. But this places as little constraint on pedagogical behaviour as it would on the conduct of a law-abiding citizen who entertains not the slightest wish nor intention to commit a felony. Steiner stressed at all times that teachers must have enthusiasm and inner mobility; they must be fired with zeal for their task, must possess generous proportions of inventive ability, resourcefulness and imagination, as well as a sense of humour; above all they must not be pedants, stiff and rigid in their thinking. It goes without saying that teachers should be sensitive and observant, individuals of integrity and responsibility, keenly conscious of their power to influence other human beings at a very impressionable stage of their lives. It is quite clear that Rudolf Steiner wished the spirit of the curriculum rather than the letter to be maintained, and that each individual teacher should endeavour to learn to know it as an entity with an existence of its own, as something alive and mobile, not dead and rigid, to be applied by rule of thumb methods. It is this knowledge that prompts the assertion that Waldorf teachers must be anthroposophists first and teachers second; as the first they are enabled to approach the curriculum with true understanding, and as the second they are enabled to implement it also with true understanding. The danger of ossification of the curriculum arises when a Waldorf teacher is a teacher first and an anthroposophist second, because they are then more likely to interpret it by the letter rather than by the spirit, so that the whole pedagogy becomes in danger of being reduced to a kind of mechanical "going by the book" procedure. To deny that a teacher's world-outlook influences the whole approach to his or her vocation would be unrealistic and foolish.

In keeping with Rudolf Steiner's conviction that unprejudiced study of his system of spiritual science leads to a deeper and more real knowledge of the human being, it is reasonable to contend that anthroposophical Waldorf teachers regard themselves as being capable of drawing very close to each child in their care, and hence in a position of advantage to meet its needs. Steiner implied on many occasions that pedagogy is itself therapy; experienced teachers, in their dealings with pupils, should know what to do and how to do it in order to give succour. In order to do this effectively they must be free to act as the situation demands. If their actions are correct in the sense of being in accordance with a child's needs, its reactions will register this correctness, albeit in subtle or covert ways, and teachers must be sufficiently observant and perspicacious to notice them. What thus passes from soul to soul is often more important than that which passes by word of mouth. Steiner exhorted teachers to have in their souls a lively image of the child's nature in every single week of every single year; it is this, he declared, which constitutes the spiritual basis of education.

The late A. C. Harwood, a disciple of Rudolf Steiner and co-founder of one of the first Waldorf schools in England in 1925, described him as an artist among scientists and a scientist among artists, and a universal genius in an age of specialists.[3] The implications of this characterization are strongly reflected in the Waldorf curriculum: the distinction between the sciences and the humanities might be said to exist in name only, and specialization into arts subjects and science subjects is delayed as long as possible — well into the upper school. The artistic element, regarded as essential during the class teacher period, is still regarded as of great importance in the upper school. Whereas during the first eight Classes it forms the basis of the whole teaching method, during Classes 9 to 12, Art crystallizes into a curriculum subject with its various branches, which together with a thorough grounding in the History of Art so effectively reflects the development of Man's consciousness over the centuries. The basic approach to science is phenomenological rather than theoretical, with the stress on observation first and deduction second. As public examination syllabuses and the Waldorf curriculum are so very much at variance, there is usually no attempt to marry the two: curriculum subjects are dealt with in main lesson time and syllabus requirements at any other convenient time. By and large examinations are looked upon as a necessary evil and as a means to facilitate entry into tertiary educational establishments and the professions.

Painting and Drawing

Painting and drawing serve as an introduction to the plastic-formative arts, such as painting, drawing and modelling. The sense for colour should be carefully cultivated, in that the colours should be allowed to speak for themselves, thus preparing a foundation for "soul-perspective" to be developed. For example, certain colours are universally deemed to be cold (blues), while others are considered to be warm (oranges and reds). Similarly, blues give an impression of distance, of receding into the background, while reds and yellows seem to advance towards one. Steiner stressed that, during the first three or four classes in Waldorf schools, the teacher should take the greatest possible care to allow the painting of the children to grow out of the characteristics of the various colours, and not allow them to paint objects of the external world, objective nature. Such a procedure, he claimed, constitutes a fundamental training in aesthetics. Far from allowing the children to paint themes from external nature according to their own whims and fancies, the teacher should take on the responsibility of guiding them at every turn; the time for "free expression" is to come later.

As for drawing, great care should be taken by the teacher not to draw external objects in line, but to lead the children to draw in what may be termed "pure line"; in other words, lines that are expressed in geometrical forms, straight lines and curves, as is done in Form Drawing (see p. 169). Such activity with the children should not, moreover, be confined to drawing in the accepted sense, with pencil and paper; children should be encouraged to "draw" straight and curved forms in the air, and to "draw" giant figures on the classroom floor by walking or running the appropriate outlines, thus fostering an inner feeling for form in a dynamic way. From drawing which has been developed out of painting, the children should be led, by means of the inventiveness of the teacher, through picture-writing to the abstract letter-forms of Roman-type capitals, so that an artistic basis for conventional writing is laid.

As for painting proper, the children should be led by the teacher to develop painting out of the feeling for colours themselves rather than by the mere copying of external objects in a slavish way.

From the fourth class (age 10) onwards the children should be encouraged to work more out of their powers of phantasy and creative inventiveness rather than be guided at every turn by the teacher, and their paintings should reflect their own awakened sense for colour. With the newly developed sense of differentiation from the environment at this age, the children should now be encouraged to copy the forms of outer objects, thus employing more consciously the capacity for drawing straight lines and curves. Modelling in clay, wax or plastiscine should be introduced and developed at the teacher's discretion, but following the general principles prescribed for painting and drawing. In Class 6 simple projections and shadow drawing should be introduced, not only in freehand but with the aid of geometrical instruments, while in Class 7 the children should practise drawing solid bodies which interpenetrate each other, as well as the simpler aspects of perspective. Throughout Class 8 the work of the two previous Classes should be carried on, with greater and greater emphasis on aesthetic and artistic principles. In the upper school the "pure line" principle is followed in that in Classes 9 to 12 Projective Geometry and Geometrical Drawing constitute the main area of drawing as such.

Painting should be continued throughout Classes 6 to 8 with emphasis on the inner experience of colour, and the children should gradually be led to represent landscapes based on observation of the play of light and colour in nature as well as the prevailing mood appropriate to the picture as a whole.

Form Drawing

The drawing of the so-called "forms" is done by the children in Classes 1 to 5 free-hand in coloured crayon as exercises in *pure line*. As discussed earlier, drawing in line of objects in the external world is not encouraged; the purpose of the block crayons generally used is to render the drawing of thin, pencil-like lines impossible. Illustrations accompanying stories or poems in main lesson books or other exercise books are therefore closer to painting than drawing, as the drawings are not made in outline, then to be filled in; rather are the crayons used as a painter uses brushes. Corners or worn edges of the crayons are utilized by the children to draw the thinner lines necessary for clarity and distinction when drawing forms. In the first few classes much is made of simple symmetry and rhythmical repetition, and as the children grow older the principles of metamorphosis and inversion — or both — are employed more and more, so that patterned forms of considerable artistic merit are produced almost as a matter of course. By the time Class 5 is reached freely invented forms and free-hand geometrical forms are often beautifully and sensitively shaded. By Class 6 at the latest geometrical instruments are employed with the gradual transition to the stricter disciplines involved in metrical and modern movement geometry. In the upper school descriptive geometry leads to projective geometry, which will have been developed in some detail by the time Class 12 is reached.

The main characteristic of Form Drawing, namely free creativity in the realm of pure line, allows of no "set" curriculum, but the following indications are widely accepted as being appropriate:

Class 1   The drawing of basic forms incorporating both straight and
(Age 7)   curved lines is introduced, involving for the most part the
            factor of symmetry, as described on page 119.

Class 2
(Age 8)

Whilst maintaining the element of symmetry where suitable, forms may be introduced which reveal metamorphosis. Additionally, exercises that are cursive and rhythmical in character could be encouraged and developed (see below).

Class 3)
(Age 9)

Forms incorporating opposition, inversion and obversion may now be tried out, including coiling and uncoiling spirals, forms which are interlaced, and suchlike, as shown below and opposite.

Classes 4
and 5
(Ages 10
and 11)

The work of the previous classes is carried on with more complex shapes and forms, including those of a more strictly geometrical character. Sensitive shading in compatible colours may be encouraged as and when suitable.

Straight and curved line patterns.

Patterns involving the Letters D & S.

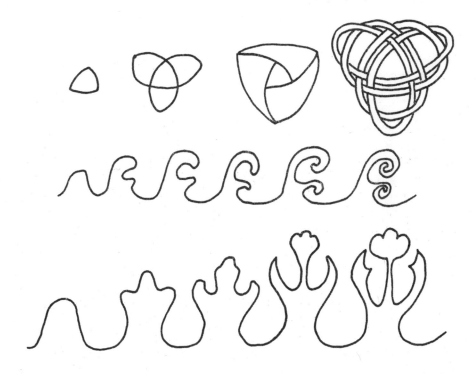

Metamorphic patterns.

English

In Classes 1–3 (ages 7–9), instruction in the fundamentals of the children's native language should cover the three main areas of writing, reading and speech. (See also pp. 113–4, 121ff.) In Class 1, writing should be developed out of painting/drawing as discussed on pp. 167–9 from pictorial representations to the abstract letters, as described in Chapter 10. The children should be led to experience pleasure and delight in creating the letters in this way, and perhaps it is needless to say that the artistic mood should prevail at all times. By the end of their first school year the children should be able to take down simple dictation and write simple sentences of their own choice, employing in the main capital letters. Simultaneously with practice in writing goes practice in reading, for the most part what the children themselves have written, and which for preference has been well rehearsed orally, perhaps in the shape of a poem or verse they have learnt by heart. During the second class the children should be given practice in writing lower case letters. They should be encouraged to write short descriptions of their actual experiences and of things they have learned in class as well as subject-material to the teacher's carefully articulated dictation. Throughout the third class the children should intensify their writing activities in order to achieve fluency and confidence.

Reading should ideally follow writing, and by the end of the first class the children should be familiar with all letter-forms. Throughout Classes 2 and 3, reading skills should be practiced with increasing intensity, great attention being paid by the teacher to clarity of articulation and purity of enunciation when reading aloud. Oral aspects of English should be accorded the primacy they deserve, and any regional accents or dialects should be respected by the teacher, and no attempt made to repress them. So-called "Received Pronunciation" should by no means be insisted upon, but at the same time the children should be taught English that is grammatically acceptable, and those conventions of language which are current among educated people. Needless to say, the teacher must pay the greatest attention to his or her own speech manner and mannerisms, both in day-to-day intercourse with the children and the telling of stories, which in Class 1 should be of the character of fairy tales or *Märchen*. The children should be guided as necessary in the re-telling of such stories, and slight imperfections such as lisping dealt with kindly and gently. Poems and verse should be chosen with great care by the teacher, not only for their artistic and pictorial character but for their inherent musical qualities, expressed in rhyme, rhythm and beat. During Class 2 stories involving animals, especially the traditional fables, should be chosen for re-telling, as well as a selection of regional and national legends in order to characterize the human predicament in artistic ways. Throughout Class 3 stories from the Old Testament should be related for retelling, together with those taken from the chronicles of ancient history. Children should of course be encouraged to tell the rest of the class any items of news from their own family and social circles, such as the acquisition of a pet, a visit from granny, and suchlike. Birthdays as very special occasions provide many opportunities in this direction. During Class 2 the first mention of grammar should be made, but only in the most pictorial of ways. The verb should be dealt with first of all, as being the most "active" and dynamic of all parts of speech, with nouns and adjectives being introduced by the teacher in imaginative and sensitive ways. During Class 3 the construction of sentences should be studied, together with the simpler aspects of punctuation. The main aim of the teacher should be that of gradually making the children conscious of those principles of language of which they have hitherto been unconscious in spite of having employed them.

In Class 4 (age 10), the children should continue writing descriptions and stories, and also be given practice in the writing of letters, even simple business letters. Understanding of the use of the tenses should be aimed at, as well as the peculiarities of preposition usage and other idiomatic features. Story material for Class 4 should be drawn from the myths and sagas of the Celts, Norsemen and Teutons.

The active and passive forms of the verb should be explained during Class 5 (age 11) and, as a parallel to this, direct and reported speech (see p. 125ff). Steiner stressed that it is important for the child to have practice in expressing the thoughts and opinions of other people in contradistinction to its own, and it should be made conscious of such distinctions. In this connection the use of speech marks should be insisted upon, and plenty of practice given in other conventions of punctuation and language usage. Letter-writing should continue as a development of that done in the previous class. The source-material for reading and story-telling should be the myths of Greece and Rome, the great classical stories.

Work on the moods of the tenses should be done in Class 6 (age 12), the teacher taking particular care to foster niceties of style in language usage, with special reference to the subjunctive mood. Letter-writing should continue, again with emphasis on the straightforward business-type letter wherein clarity of expression is paramount; on the other hand jargon often associated with business letters should be avoided. The sense for style should continue to be fostered: the feeling for the essential "rightness" of expression in English should be encouraged at every opportunity. Story material for reading and telling should be sought in the folk-tales of various races and nations.

During Class 7, the feeling for style in language should continue to be developed, and helpful in this respect is the exercise of asking the children to express their thoughts involving wish, wonder and surprise, and getting them to compare such expressions. Titles for composition should still be provided by the teacher, and during this period they should centre round what the children have observed and studied in Nature. Continued, too, should be the practice in writing plain business letters as well as the accurate reporting of actual events. Folk literature and lore should continue to provide material for reading and telling.

Longer works of poetry and prose should be introduced during Class 8 (age 14) in the forms of epic and dramatic verse and the novel. Study of history should interweave with the study of literature during this period, so that the children are enabled to perceive their native culture against the background of the progress of civilization. Emphasis should continue to be placed on the practical aspects of business and everyday life.

Literature

As can be seen from the section dealing with History (see p. 177), Steiner, when giving indications for literary studies in the upper school, stressed that these two aspects of a nation's culture should be so treated as to reveal essential interconnections. The stresses and strains, hopes and fears, freedoms and constraints imposed by important historical events in a nation's life, such as wars, revolutions, cultural impacts resulting from new inventions, scientific advances and so on, are invariably reflected in a nation's literature. Obvious examples taken from English literature are the novels of Charles Dickens which mirror social conditions of his time, the works of Rudyard Kipling which so vividly capture the life-styles of the British military and civilians in imperial India, and the war poems of Rupert Brooke.

Furthermore, literary themes should be chosen which reflect the emotional and intellectual struggles which adolescents experience in their new-found freedom and independence, such as cutting free from family ties and influences and finding their way in the world as individuals, forming significant relationships with members of the opposite sex, and evolving their own particular life-style. When making choices teachers should consider the great classics of other nations and cultures in translation as well as the literary masterpieces readily available in the native language. In this they must abide by the spirit, not the letter, of the curriculum.

Class 9 (Age 15)	Themes should be chosen which give opportunities for discussion concerning problems of aesthetics. Tragedy, comedy and other contrasting universally human experiences should be explored. Essay titles should be distinctly historical in character, for preference those dealing with work covered in the previous year's studies.

Class 9
(Age 15)

Themes should be chosen which give opportunities for discussion concerning problems of aesthetics. Tragedy, comedy and other contrasting universally human experiences should be explored. Essay titles should be distinctly historical in character, for preference those dealing with work covered in the previous year's studies.

Class 10
(Age 16)

Themes dealing with universally human problems should be continued, wherein the riddles confronting the students at their stage of maturational development are mirrored and worked out in illuminating ways. In particular the severing of family ties so common at this age should be featured; including the passing-out from the sphere of non-individualized love into that of intensely individualized love.

Class 11
(Age 17)

Pre-literary works originating in the Middle Ages should form the main source for this class, in which themes illustrating moral ideals are to be found in traditional tales of chivalry. The development of such themes should be traced through in their various developments and transformations right up to the nineteenth century, when more and more strongly individualized themes were explored by writers.

Class 12
(Age 18)

In this class the history of literature is brought right up to date, and modern works studied in order to probe themes favoured by contemporary writers. In this way the students come to grips with the important human and social problems of their time, albeit vicariously, and are better prepared for life in the adult world.

Religious Education

Religion lessons occupy a rather special position in Waldorf schools, and Rudolf Steiner's indications concerning them are so searching and carefully conceived that to do them justice would require a separate volume. The Waldorf School Curriculum as originally conceived made no provision for Religious Education by the teachers, as Steiner thought it best for ministers of the various denominations to be invited into the school to give instruction according to the wishes of the parents. Within a few weeks of the opening of the Waldorf School in Stuttgart, however, anthroposophical parents approached Steiner and asked him to organize religious education lessons for their own children on a non-sectarian basis, based broadly on the anthroposophical world-outlook. He acceded to their request and initiated lessons, but it was not long before parents who professed no religion and were not anthroposophists enrolled their children for this undenominational "free" religious education. As might be imagined, attendance at *any* religion lesson was entirely optional.

In his address delivered at the opening of the school Steiner had publicly stated that he was not founding an ideological school, yet he had now initiated religion lessons based on his system of spiritual science. This involved very delicate handling of the lessons and lesson-material, and the great care with which Rudolf Steiner chose his religion teachers was recognized at the time by the college of teachers, and has since been recognized by every college of teachers in every Waldorf School. Religion teachers are still chosen with great care from within the ranks of the teachers of the school, not usually by appointment but by invitation from the corpus of religion teachers of the school. The task of the religion teachers is therefore seen to be a difficult one; they must so devise their teaching as to strike the very delicate balance between teaching along ideological or sectarian lines and along "spiritual" lines, regardless of the fact that the ideology to which they themselves subscribe is based on a spiritual conception of the world.

What must be emphasized is that it was Rudolf Steiner's wish that religion teachers place undenominational Christianity at the centre of their curriculum, whilst in no way failing to accord respect to the various sects as well as other world religions. In recognition of this difficult position, the college of teachers makes no demands or stipulations of the religion teachers, but leaves them free to devise their own curriculum based on the indications which Steiner gave, and for this reason the briefest of indications are given here. Moreover, it must never be forgotten — and one must be emphatic about this — that the *whole* of the teaching matter and method in Steiner schools is aimed at developing within each child the consciousness that spirit permeates everything in the world.[4]

Rudolf Steiner divided the material for religion lessons according to the stages of development of the child:

Classes 1 to 4 (Ages 7 to 10)	This first stage should be devoted to aspects of nature-religion, whereby the child should be brought to feel that wisdom is expressed through the workings of the divine in nature.
Classes 5 to 8	The second stage represents the more historical side of religion, by which the child is led to perceive that the divine

(Ages 11 to 14)	may be apprehended not through wisdom alone, but through active love also.
Classes 8 to 10 (Ages 14 to 16)	Steiner stressed that as living a picture as possible of the Christ should be the focus of all reflections with the children. The seasons should be dealt with in connection with the important Christian festivals.
Classes 11 and 12 (Ages 17 and 18)	Discussion with the students on such concepts as guilt and atonement, cause and effect should take place. A survey of national religions should be made and comparative religion studied.

Local studies

Classes 1, 2 and 3 (Ages 7, 8 and 9)	Gradually the children should be made more and more conscious of their surroundings, with elements of local history and geography being imaginatively dealt with. Stories about animals and plants, the seasons, the weather and other natural phenomena should be told with the aim of awakening feelings of wonder and respect. In Class 3 the children should be brought into contact with practical activities of everyday life such as building, farming and local industries, and simple business letters written in connection with them.
Class 4 (Age 10)	Local Studies should be further developed along the lines of history and geography as subjects in their own right, though interconnected. The scope of both should be gradually widened so that the children are given some idea of time (through stories of historical personages) and some idea of space (by reference to the various countries and their peoples).

History

Class 5 (Age 11)	The history and culture of the ancient oriental peoples should be briefly sketched in as a prelude to the first really historical concepts as revealed in primary and secondary sources from the Hebrews and Greeks.

Class 6 (Age 12)	Roman times should now be dealt with, with mention being made of the tremendous influence of the Graeco-Roman civilizations and cultures on those of the rest of Europe from BC to the fifteenth century AD.
Class 7 (Age 13)	European history and world history during the fifteenth and sixteenth centuries should now be taught, with special emphasis on this period as the cradle of modern civilization. World exploration and discovery should be dealt with, as well as the rise of the natural sciences.
Class 8 (Age 14)	The period from the sixteenth century to the present day should be covered, care being taken to deal with social history, with special reference to how the great inventions have contributed to civilization: for instance, the loom, steam and internal combustion engines, electrics and electronics, nuclear power, jet propulsion, and so on.
Class 9 (Age 15)	Aspects of history from the Thirty Years' War until modern times previously touched on may now be presented in more detail, the teacher taking care to dwell on the inner and more subtle connections between historical events and processes. The Age of Reason should be dealt with at some length.
Class 10 (Age 16)	The historical development of peoples according to their climatic and topographical circumstances should be substantially dealt with. Also, reversion should now be made to early oriental and Greek history in greater detail, including the period up till the decline of the freedom of the Greek states under Alexander the Great.
Classes 11 and 12 (Ages 17 and 18)	The approach to history in these classes should be by means of studies from history of literature, and how this reflects the mainstream of Man's individual and social development. In Class 11 the "pre-literary" themes of the Middle Ages, such as those revealed in the legends of the Holy Grail, should be followed in their development right through until the end of the nineteenth century, by which time only tradition remains. In Class 12 a complete review of the history of English Literature should be made, and here reference should be made as appropriate to other classics of world literature and the great

literary figures of the nineteenth and twentieth centuries, both national and international.

Geography

Class 5 (Age 11)	From the study of Geography in an elementary, imaginative way during the Local Studies lessons of the first four classes, the children must now be led further afield (see pp. 127–32). Not so much human as physical geography should be taught, but including relevant economic conditions, in such a way that Man's interdependence on one another in universal brotherhood is pointed out sensitively and earnestly.
Class 6 (Age 12)	Work commenced in Class 5 should be continued and extended; world climatic conditions should lead over into a study of the solar system and the elements of astronomy.
Class 7 (Age 13)	Study of the Earth in relationship to the rest of the universe should be continued. Social and cultural as well as economic conditions in various countries of the world should now be dealt with, the teacher taking great care that no comparisons are made that are in any way invidious or disparaging.
Class 8 (Age 14)	The social, cultural and economic conditions of the rest of the countries not dealt with previously should now be studied, and brought to a certain conclusion.
Class 9 (Age 15)	The topography and geological structure of the world's main mountain ranges and their formation should now be studied.
Class 10 (Age 16)	This work should be carried on until the Earth is seen as a structural and ecological whole.
Class 11 (Age 17)	In connection with other curricular work in Surveying and Projective Geometry, Mercator and other projections should be introduced and maps drawn.
Class 12 (Age 18)	A recapitulatory review should now be made of work done in the upper school. Within this survey palaeontology should be dealt with, as well as ethnology.

Mathematics

Class 1 (Age 7)	Teaching and practice of the four arithmetical rules and decimal progression; early work should be confined within 1–20, later work extended to 100. See also Form Drawing on p. 169, and see pp. 114–9.
Class 2 (Age 8)	More widely extended practice of the four rules, mental arithmetic being done according to ability. The children should be taught to memorize number bonds and tables, and be practised in them.
Class 3 (Age 9)	More complex examples, preferably taken from real-life situations, involving the four rules should be given, and number bonds and tables consistently revised.
Class 4 (Age 10)	The teacher should now introduce fractions and decimal fractions and appropriate examples worked.
Class 5 (Age 11)	The work of Class 4 should be continued, with constant revision and practice, so that the children are able to calculate freely and confidently with whole numbers and fractions.
Class 6 (Age 12)	The principle of percentage should now be taught, with practice given in examples of simple interest, discount, etc. The use of formulae is introduced and practised.

Class 6 (Age 12), continued: Geometry should be developed out of the freehand "form drawing" of earlier classes. The children should now be taught to grasp consciously the geometrical concepts of various angles, curves, etc. previously practised artistically, and to construct geometrical forms with the aid of instruments.

Class 7 (Age 13)	The operations of squaring, cubing and so on should now be dealt with, together with negative numbers and simple algebraic equations, preferably with examples taken from practical life. In geometry the children should be taken as far as the Theorem of Pythagoras.
Class 8 (Age 14)	Theoretical and practical aspects of arithmetic and algebra should be continued. In geometry the laws of loci should be

taught, as well as the calculation of lengths and surfaces of plane figures, leading on to the principles of solid geometry.

Class 9
(Age 15)
In arithmetic combinations, permutations and variations should be introduced and problems solved. In algebra linear and quadratic equations should be dealt with, as well as the dissolving of complex brackets and fractions and the binomial theorem. In geometry the study of loci should be continued, and projective geometrical drawing should be introduced.

Class 10
(Age 16)
Arithmetical and geometrical progressions should now be introduced, as well as the use of logarithms in both arithmetic and algebra; also trigonometrical functions and the plane in trigonometry as far as the manipulation of the non-right-angled triangle.

Class 11
(Age 17)
In algebra the students should continue with logarithms and exponential equations. Plane trigonometry should also be continued and spheric trigonometry introduced. The use of mathematics in connection with astronomy and the principles of navigation should be dealt with. Projective geometry should be continued to include difficult examples of the interpenetration of bodies, and shadow construction as regards parallel and central illumination.

Class 12
(Age 18)
A recapitulatory survey of the different branches of mathematics should be carried out. Analytical geometry of the plane, and elements of the analytical geometry of space should be taught, as well as the working out of the first elements of differential and integral arithmetic starting from $\frac{0}{0}$. Study of isonometry should now supplement projective geometry and its practical application to architecture demonstrated.

Language teaching

An outstanding feature of the original Waldorf School in Stuttgart when it opened in 1919 was that two foreign languages, English and French, were taught from Class 1 onwards as part of the normal curriculum. Rudolf Steiner decided this on purely educational grounds, will become clear directly, but wider implications for society may be readily discerned, as is so often the case with Waldorf pedagogy. What is sound from an educational point of view should by definition be sound from a social point of view, and vice versa; any incongruities between the two are symptomatic of sickness, whether manifest or latent.

A fundamental aim of the Waldorf system is to develop the child in such a way that it may later reveal the qualities of full adulthood, and be able also to find its true place in the world. The faculty of speech is rooted in the very depths of Man's being, and the mother tongue, said Steiner, is so deeply rooted in the systems of breathing and blood circulation and in the vascular system that the child is affected not only in soul and spirit, but in body as well, by the way in which the mother tongue comes to expression. This will be readily appreciated when it is remembered that the infant learns to speak during its most imitative period of life, and when body, soul and spirit constitute a unity. Steiner contended that the various languages express various human elements in particular, this being true not only of primitive tongues but of European languages as well. Thus the different elements of will, feelings, intellect, music, imagination and so on come to expression in characteristic form in the different languages, and it is highly desirable from an educational and social viewpoint that the effects produced on the nature of Man by one particular genius of speech be balanced by the effects of another. In this way the ideal of the "universal human" is actively subscribed to, and tendencies towards exaggerated nationalistic or racist development toned down. This does not mean, however, that some kind of universal language should be developed in order to replace or even complement traditional tongues. Steiner claimed that this would be highly undesirable, that a terrible superficiality would lay hold of humanity if a common language such as Esperanto were adopted for widespread use. Such an artificially constructed language lacks the living qualities of established languages, which through their idiomatic expressions reveal much of the national character peculiar to them.

Although the children attending Waldorf schools learn two foreign languages from Class 1 onwards, when the imitative faculty is fading, nevertheless this tendency continues during the eighth and ninth years. It would follow from this that foreign languages teaching during this time should be based on the imitative principle; in other words, it should be confined to oral work, simple conversations, poems, songs and the like. In this way much of the foreign language is learned with little claim being made on the child's intellect; not only are the outer sounds and tones of the foreign tongue imitated, but also its inner musical, soul element. The child thus absorbs the foreign language in a manner similar to that in which it learned its mother tongue, albeit in a much reduced capacity. The emphasis should be on aural comprehension rather than visual comprehension; therefore little or no written work or reading in the foreign language, should be done before the tenth year. All the repetitive work involved in the teaching of foreign languages stimulates the feelings and the will; the intellectual element is almost completely lacking, and this is fully in accord with basic spiritual-scientific knowledge. Direct translation from one language to the other is to be avoided as much as possible, as this heavily involves the handling of concepts and similar intellectual activities.

Grammar and syntax in foreign languages are dealt with at the same time as in the mother tongue, namely, after the eleventh year. Steiner stressed that the grammatical side of language should be taught as independently as possible, by studying sentences expressly intended to illustrate the various rules and devised accordingly. He warned against taking grammatical rules and examples contained in reading matter such as stories and poems — in other words, artistic works; sentences should be quite deliberately devised by the teacher which show clearly the various points of grammar. Furthermore, such sentences should not be written down or copied into notebooks: the rules should by all means be practised, but specific examples should not be preserved. In this way the rules are instilled by way of the feelings rather than the intellect, and therefore may be the better memorized. Sentences illustrating grammatical rules should be designed to be easily forgotten; if the children write them down, too vivid an impression may be left with them of the outward form of the examples; the intention should be for the examples to be forgotten but for the rules to remain. The learning of grammar and syntax in foreign languages, as in the mother tongue, assists in the development of self-consciousness in the child; it helps to impart the requisite inner firmness for coping with the tasks that lie ahead, not only in school, but in later life as well.

Classical languages, such as Latin and Greek, should be introduced into the curriculum only after the elements of grammar and syntax have been dealt with. They are not to be treated in the same way as modern languages, in that the "direct" method is not to be used; methods involving the intellect, such as written translations from and into the classical languages should be used, and the labour and tedium of learning conjugations, declensions and suchlike rendered acceptable.

Modern Languages *(German and French in British schools)*

Classes 1 to 3 (Ages 7 8 to 9)	Songs, poems and games should be used as vehicles for the sounds, rhythms and melodies of the language. Speaking and conversation should be taught by the "direct" method; little writing and no grammar.
Class 4 (Age 10)	Exercises in prose rather than poetry should now be given, and grammatical examples given and rules memorized, beginning with the verb. Reading and writing for general meaning rather than word for word translation should be practised.
Class 5 (Age 11)	The work of Class 4 should be continued, with the teaching of more grammar, including the basic elements of syntax.
Class 6 (Age 12)	Easy readings in the foreign language should be carried on, and idiomatic expressions practised. The general cultural flavour and atmosphere typical of the foreign country should be communicated to the pupils, using such media as folk-tales, proverbs and popular sayings to illustrate national characteristics.
Class 7 (Age 13)	Reading should be continued, again with the stress on general meaning rather than literal translation. Customs and ways of life in the foreign country should be vividly described in anecdote and idiom in order to enhance a feeling for the character of the people who speak it.
Class 8 (Age 14)	The general pattern for Class 7 should be continued; the reading of poetry should now be done more consciously to include metrics.
Class 9 (Age 15)	Studies of the literature and culture of the foreign country should be continued; re-telling of reading matter, and conversation constitute oral practice by the direct method.
Class 10 (Age 16)	Emphasis should now be placed on poetical literature and the various metres used, and practice in individual and choral recitation of suitable verse.
Class 11 (Age 17)	The dramatic classics of the foreign country should now be studied, and play-readings undertaken and plays staged.

Readings in prose and poetry should be chosen to illustrate the beauties of the language.

Class 12
(Age 18)
A survey of the historical and cultural development of the foreign language should now be undertaken in order further to demonstrate and reveal national character. Modern literature should constitute the reading matter for this class.

Classical Languages (Greek and Latin)

Class 5
(Age 11)
Without the use of textbooks the teacher should present the language unsystematically and with no reference to formal grammar. The character and sounds of the language should be dealt with in short sayings and phrases, gradually passing on to short stories and poems. Passages from the New Testament in Greek and Latin already known to the children should be learnt by heart.

Class 6
(Age 12)
Translations from the classical language into English — but not the other way round — should now be attempted, with proper reference to grammar and syntax as appropriate. Myths, legends and stories from ancient history should form the material for reading and retelling.

Class 7
(Age 13)
Work commenced in Class 6 should be continued, with introduction to the works of the classical authors, but without dwelling too long on particularly difficult passages.

Class 8
(Age 14)
Work on Latin grammar should be phased out; readings in the classics should continue, with translation and re-telling alternating. More difficult points should be dealt with as they arise; work should continue with Greek grammar.

Class 9
(Age 15)
In Latin more complex grammatical and syntactical aspects should be taken up; readings in prose should be continued and easy poems learnt by heart. In Greek, grammar teaching should be discontinued, but simple readings carried on.

Class 10
(Age 16)
In Latin the study of syntax, and graded readings, should continue. In Greek, syntax and the use of the different cases should be taught, and suitable passages read from the classics.

Class 11 (Age 17)	In Latin, study of syntax should give way to greater concentration on readings from classical authors. In Greek, syntax should continue, and the more difficult classical authors tackled.
Class 12 (Age 18)	Revision of the more troublesome grammatical and syntactical aspects of both languages should be made, and readings carried on as appropriate, the students' attention being drawn to stylistic peculiarities of the different authors.

Science and nature study

Classes 1 to 3 (Ages 7 to 9)	Nature study should be done imaginatively rather than explanatorily, implicit with moral overtones rather than explicit with scientific reasons. Various characteristics of plants, animals and Man should be dealt with artistically and reverently. (See pp. 127ff)
Class 4 (Age 10)	Nature study should now begin to appeal to the children's understanding, and be more objective. From an artistically based study of the human being at an elementary level, various animals should be studied with reference to their manifold bodily shapes and forms in comparison with that of Man.
Class 5 (Age 11)	From the study of the animals with reference to Man, the children should now study the plant world with reference to the Earth as a living organism, dealing with the climatic or geological dependent of the various plants to be found in various parts of the world.
Class 6 (Age 12)	From the study of plants, the children should go on to study the mineral world as elementary geology, and always in connection with geography. Characteristic features of e.g. granite or limestone mountains in terms of appearance and vegetation should be pointed out, and samples of minerals shown. In physics, a start should be made with acoustics, the teacher leading over from the artistic (as music) to the more scientific aspects of sound. From phenomena of colour and light the children should be introduced to optics, and

186

to heat, electricity and magnetism, again from appropriate phenomena.

Class 7 **(Age 13)**	The study of Man should now be returned to at a more advanced level, and the elements of hygiene and nutrition studied. In physics, studies in acoustics, optics, heat, electricity and magnetism should be carried on. Basic mechanics should be introduced, e.g. the lever, pulley, screw, wheel and axle. In chemistry the teacher should lead over from the phenomena and principles of combustion to other isolated chemical processes. From concepts gained in other natural scientific studies the dependence of industry and transport on chemical and physical processes should be dwelt on at some length, with examples.
Class 8 **(Age 14)**	In nature study the human being should be presented as the epitome of the kingdoms of nature, as a kind of microcosm (see pp. 127–32). Organic functions of the body and their harmonious working should be studied, and the nature of health and disease discussed from the point of view not only of the bodily mechanical processes but of the soul-spiritual nature of Man also. In physics, previous work should be continued to show practical application of scientific principles, e.g. hydraulics, aero-mechanics, climatology, meteorology. In chemistry, its importance in industrial processes should continue to be studied as well as the importance to Man of organic substances such as starch, sugar, protein and fat.
Class 9 **(Age 15)**	In nature study, human science should be continued at a more advanced level. In physics, principles involved in acoustics, heat, mechanics and so on should be explained in their application to industrial processes. Concerning optics, astronomy should be studied at a more advanced level. In chemistry, the elements of organic chemistry should be taught.
Class 10 **(Age 16)**	In natural science human bodily organs should be studied in their relationship to Man's life of soul and spirit. Starting from the individual person, elements of anthropology and ethnography should be studied and links with geography

made, as with mineralogy and crystallography. Formation of limestone and its processes and their significance for the human and animal organisms as well as for the whole Earth should be studied. In chemistry, acids, alkalis and salts should be studied for their various chemical effects, and how processes involving them are manifested in the living organism. In physics, the study of mechanics should be extended to that of actual machines.

Class 11
(Age 17)

In natural science the structure of the cell as a kind of microcosm should be studied. In botanical studies mono-cotyledons should be dealt with, and revisionary work done in connection with the various plants' affinities with the various soils, and indeed with the whole universe. In chemistry, a revisionary survey should be undertaken of work done so far, stressing the importance of starting from chemical processes rather than from chemical elements. In physics, study of the latest developments of practical application in the fields of radio, electronics, and so on should be undertaken.

Class 12
(Age 18)

In botany, the phanerogams should be studied, and a reca-pitulation of zoological and biological studies generally should be undertaken. In chemistry, processes in Man and their corresponding processes in Nature should be studied, and a revisionary survey of all upper school work made. In physics, optics should be studied at an advanced level: photography, mirrors, refraction, polarization, magnification and diminution, the relation of colours, etc.

Eurythmy

Eurythmy is an art of movement originated and developed by Rudolf Steiner himself from purely spiritual antecedents; it has little connection with that which inspires dance, mime or ballet. It was conceived and developed as an art form in its own right, and as well as what might be described as "pedagogical" eurythmy there has been developed a system of "curative" eurythmy which is claimed to be especially therapeutic in its effects, although Steiner maintained that *all* forms of eurythmy are therapeutic. He characterized eurythmy within the Waldorf School curriculum as "ensouled gymnastics." Put briefly, he saw gymnastics and the movements involved in its performance as essentially *physiological*, and those involved in the performance of eurythmy as essentially *psychological*. Basically, there are two kinds of eurythmy: speech-eurythmy, in which the bodily movements are made according to the sounds of the various vowels and consonants, and tone-eurythmy, wherein the bodily movements are made in accordance with musical tones. There are definite principles involved in how the movements are made and the "choreography" devised; nothing is arbitrary. The rationale behind the teaching of eurythmy in Waldorf schools is impossible of brief exposition, being a study in itself; however, it must be said that eurythmy occupies a special position of great importance in the Waldorf curriculum, being compulsory for all children in all classes from 1 to 12, as well as any kindergarten class.

Class 1 (Age 7)	The strong affinities between eurythmy and music are made plain in that the children should run geometric and graphical forms to its accompaniment, so that they feel with their whole being the difference between a straight line and a curved line. In speech-eurythmy, movements for the vowels and consonants should be practised by imitating the teacher's gestures; simple poems strong in rhyme and rhythm should form the basic material. Running and clapping to simple metrical rhythms, the children taking long or short steps as appropriate, should be practised. In tone-eurythmy the movements for the notes C, D, F and G should be imitated and practised in a similar manner, and simple melodies containing the mood of the fifth introduced. Elementary exercises with copper rods should be begun.
Class 2 (Age 8)	The work of the first Class should be continued; in addition, exercises for awakening and developing social feeling should be done, e.g. "We seek one another/We find one another/Quite near."
Class 3 (Age 9)	Work of Class 2 should be continued at more advanced levels. Poems involving alliteration are recommended for speech-eurythmy, while in tone-eurythmy the scale of C major should be continued as well as those intended to assist the children to adjust to their new-found self-consciousness at age nine, e.g. contracting (pain), and expanding (joy), laughing and weeping.

Class 4
(Age 10)

In speech-eurythmy exercises involving elements of grammar should be done, so that the essential nature of parts of speech are grasped not only with the intellect, but with the feelings and the will also. Group exercises designed to promote sociability and awareness of others should be continued. In tone-eurythmy the children should be introduced to the major and minor keys, whose differences should be pointed out, though melodies employed should be mainly in major keys. Rhythmical movements corresponding to the music should be continued.

Class 5
(Age 11)

In speech-eurythmy the work of Class 4 should be continued, though there should be a gradual shift from emphasis on the grammatical content of poems to their meaning content, and appropriate forms practised. Rod exercises should also be continued, and in tone-eurythmy the various major scales should be studied and simple melodies from classical composers practised.

Class 6
(Age 12)

In speech-eurythmy, the work of the previous Class should be continued. There should be more intensive practice with the copper rods in order to strengthen the muscles of the children and develop greater control of the limbs in order to facilitate the soul-spiritual nature's incarnation into the skeletal system. In tone-eurythmy, the interval movements for the whole scale should be practised intensively, and musical introduction for the transforming of triangles and squares in space should be taught.

Class 7
(Age 13)

Exercises in concentration and bodily control, group and rod exercises and geometrical forms should continue to be practised. In speech-eurythmy, the working-out of themes involving wish, wonder and surprise should be done. In tone-eurythmy, work should now be performed to melodies of the old masters in minor keys, and minor scales practised.

Class 8
(Age 14)

In speech-eurythmy, poems should be chosen which express contrasting moods: joy and sadness, humour and tragedy, tension and relaxation, expectation and relief. In tone-eurythmy, working the minor scales should be continued, and melodies practised which modulate from major to minor keys. Rod, group, concentration and bodily control exercises should also be continued.

Class 9 **(Age 15)**	In line with Steiner's maxim that after puberty children should think through what they have previously felt and willed, in the upper school eurythmy is presented to the students from new points of view, in that they are made more conscious of making *visible* that which usually remains *audible*. In connection with the literature lessons, poems chosen to be expressed eurythmically should be those which develop such aspects of speech which are essentially plastic and mobile. In tone-eurythmy, the harmony expressed in the main chords should be emphasized, thus underlining the ideal harmony of thinking, feeling and willing as an aim. Other exercises should continue at appropriate levels of difficulty.
Class 10 **(Age 16)**	In speech-eurythmy, not only the metrical and rhyme structure and content should be studied, but also the poems as expressions of thinking, feeling or willing. In tone-eurythmy, the work of Class 9 should be continued.
Class 11 **(Age 17)**	The difference between the Apollonian and Dionysian approaches to life studied in the art lessons should by now be made apparent in the interpenetration of the grammatical content and the soul content respectively, of poems being performed and studied. In tone-eurythmy, work of the previous Class should be continued, if possible to the accompaniment of music played by other members of the class.
Class 12 **(Age 18)**	As in other subjects, a recapitulatory survey should now be made, and various aspects of work done in speech and music drawn together in some kind of conclusion.

Music

Class 1 **(Age 7)**	The sense for what is and what is not beautiful in music should be cultivated, and simple exercises for training the musical ear practised. All kinds of musical media may be utilized, the children being taught to sing appropriate songs and play simple tunes on instruments according to

ability and suitability within the pentatonic compass. (See pp. 120–3)

Class 2 (Age 8)	Melodies and songs should now be taught within the compass of the octave and the work of Class 1 continued.

Class 3
(Age 9)

Musical notation should be taught, and simple tunes in the key of C major written down and practised. Singing should likewise be extended.

Class 4
(Age 10)

The teacher should now introduce the children to the experience of the major and minor thirds, and theoretical aspects of music explained as appropriate. Reading and writing of musical notation should be continued, and in singing two-part songs and rounds should be practised.

Class 5
(Age 11)

Work of Class 4 should be continued, and the various keys should be studied. Two- and three-part songs and rounds should be continued with.

Class 6
(Age 12)

Work of previous Classes should be continued at appropriately advanced levels, and the minor scales should be practised.

Class 7
and 8
(Age 13
and 14)

In both classes the experience of the octave should be particularly dwelt on, and the singing of part songs continued, both unaccompanied and to the accompaniment of instruments, preferably played by other class members. Theoretical aspects should be continued with, and their practical applications demonstrated and practised. Faculties for musical judgement should be awakened, and appreciation of beauty in music and of the various styles of classical composers by suitable examples.

Classes
9 to 12
(Ages 15
to 18)

Singing in a mixed choir should be practised, and students with suitable ability trained in the school orchestra, if such exists. The aesthetics of music should be dealt with and various musical forms studied. Simple compositions may be attempted and performed. The history of music should be taught, and modern trends discussed.

Art

Class 9 (Age 15)	In the upper school art becomes a subject in its own right. The development of the arts in general from earliest historical times should be dealt with, in the case of painting, say, from Giotto to the time of Rembrandt. Various examples illustrating the concept of the beautiful and beauty should be selected, including some from Greek and Renaissance times.
Class 10 (Age 16)	The art teacher is expected to deal with the principles of aesthetics, not only as they concern the visual and plastic arts, but also the literary arts, more particularly metrics and poetics and figurative language generally. The Dionysian and Apollonian approaches to life should be dealt with and illustrated.
Class 11 (Age 17)	From the differences between the Dionysian and Apollonian concepts of life, students should be brought to a greater understanding of Man in his whole being. As well as the visual arts, the aural arts as expressed in music and song should be dealt with from historical and aesthetic points of view.
Class 12 (Age 18)	The development of the arts through their symbolic, classic and romantic forms, with examples as appropriate, should be reviewed. The history of architecture should be studied, with examples from earliest times to date. The deeply felt need of Man for creative activity should be fully dealt with, together with the role of the artist in society.

Handwork

Class 1 (Age 7)	Both boys and girls should learn to knit with two needles simple, useful things such as a dish-cloth.
Class 2 (Age 8)	The children should learn to crochet, and should carry on knitting more complicated articles such as a recorder bag or plimsoll shoe bag. Simple embroidery should be done to the children's own designs.

Class 3
(Age 9)

The work of the previous Classes should be carried on at suitable levels of difficulty.

Class 4
(Age 10)

Sewing should be taught in this class, practising the various kinds of stitch employed in the making of useful articles such as a handwork bag. Embroidered decorations should be so designed and executed that the specific purpose of the article is thereby expressed.

Class 5
(Age 11)

The knitting of more complicated articles such as gloves should be taught, and stuffed animals and rag dolls made.

Class 6
(Age 12)

The making of dolls and animals should be continued, and the children should make up and embroider more complicated useful garments and articles.

Class 7
(Age 13)

The making up of useful garments such as shirts for boys and blouses for girls should be taught. The manufacture of the various textile materials should be discussed, as well as such properties as wearability, and what constitutes "quality" in a material.

Class 8
(Age 14)

The work of Class 7 should be carried on, larger useful articles being made, perhaps with the use of machines. Darning, mending and other domestic skills should be taught and practised.

Class 9
(Age 15)

Handwork should be extended to the making of other useful articles such as cushions and garments, basket work and other cane work, always bearing in mind that the designs must express the use to which the articles are meant to be put. Posters should be designed, as well as book covers in preparation for bookbinding in later classes.

Class 10
(Age 16)

The work of previous classes should be continued at the appropriate level of difficulty, with emphasis on expressive designs and artistically executed work.

Classes
11–12
(Age 17–18)

Bookbinding should now be introduced alongside previous activities.

Gymnastics

Classes 3-5 (Age 9–11)	Children of these classes should do exercises which express a relationship to the emotions and the imagination, being little removed from the realm of play, e.g. timidity, daring, courage. They should imitate the typical archetypal gestures of human activity in a stylised, rhythmical fashion, e.g. hammering, threshing. Ring games of all kinds may be enjoyed, and free play allowed on the apparatus commonly found in the gymnasium, thus ensuring that each child works to its own pace and within its own physical limitations.
Class 6 (Age 12)	In gymnastics with apparatus the children should be gradually led over from play activity to conscious, controlled and precise movements. Exercises by which the weight of the body is supported by the limbs, hitherto avoided, are now introduced. In gymnastics without apparatus, strongly rhythmical exercises with a pronounced geometrical character, e.g. using the square, circle, triangle, with and without the use of rods should be practised as well as jumping, skipping, javelin throwing and suchlike.
Class 7 (Age 13)	In gymnastics with apparatus, exercises on the ladder bars, rings and parallel bars should be practised with the intention of improving bodily control. In gymnastics without apparatus, rhythmical exercises with and without rods involving geometrical forms should be continued.
Class 8 (Age 14)	Apparatus work of Class 7 should be continued, and jumping over hurdles and the negotiating of obstacles should be practised.
Class 9 (Age 15)	Throughout the upper school gymnastic skills should be developed progressively, using the appropriate apparatus. Exercises involving a vertical fall from the upright position should be done, the actual fall being transformed into jumping, swinging, running or walking movements.
Class 10 (Age 16)	Exercises which develop simultaneously a conscious sense of direction together with an enhanced sense of height should be devised and practised. As well as jumping in varying rhythms, javelin and discus throwing may be practised.

Class 11　　The exercises of Class 10 should now be extended to include
(Age 17)　　the dimension of width as well as those of height and length,
　　　　　　and there should be a conscious shifting in the direction of
　　　　　　movement, such as the tracing of a lemniscatory form by
　　　　　　means of rhythmical walking. Ball throwing may be practised
　　　　　　together with javelin and discus throwing.

Class 12　　The work of the previous classes without apparatus should
(Age 18)　　be carried on, and as a new exercise the students should
　　　　　　practise rhythmically the falling from the upright standing
　　　　　　position and recovering lift of the body through a circular
　　　　　　turn. Running in various rhythms should also be done, as well
　　　　　　as standing still at one particular point in conscious realization
　　　　　　of the body as concentration of the three dimensions.

Bothmer gymnastics

Count Fritz von Bothmer was the teacher of gymnastics at the first Waldorf
School, and Rudolf Steiner asked him to evolve a system of gymnastics
with the aims of imparting an enhanced experience of space, and of
cultivating greater strength of will. Ideally, therefore, gymnastics should
express the connection of the blood processes with the muscles, and should
take account of the flow of blood to the muscles in all movement. For the
first three or four classes physical education is largely confined to the
playing of rhythmical games, ring games and the like, and free activity
such as climbing, jumping and so on, usually done in company with the
class teacher or games teacher. By Class 5 the children should have been
passed on to a specialist gymnastics teacher under whose supervision all
kinds of exercises are done involving apparatus and within the capabilities
of the individual children. Children in Class 6 begin to experience the
forces of gravity and the mechanics of the skeleton in a more conscious
way, as mentioned elsewhere in another connection, and the will becomes
more consciously engaged in exercises involving sheer strength, elements
of decision-making, and awareness of balance and of the position of the
body in space. Social aspects are catered for in that boys and girls
usually attend gym classes together, and the teacher is careful to vary
his or her approach accordingly. Right through the rest of the school the
accent is on attaining goals appropriate to individual needs and abilities
rather than on fostering the spirit of competition or the acquisition of
needless acrobatic skills. Swimming is taught according to availability of
facilities.

Woodwork

Class 6 (Age 12)	Simple objects of practical use should be made, and movable wooden toys shaped and constructed, with stress on the awareness of how beauty and utility can be combined in the same article.
Class 7 (Age 13)	Work of Class 6 should be continued at more advanced levels.
Class 8 (Age 14)	Work of the previous two Classes should be continued, the teacher endeavouring to stimulate the children's imagination and inventiveness, and to foster perseverance and acquisition of skills in order to tackle more difficult work.
Class 9 (Age 15)	More attention should now be paid to the more artistic elements in woodworking and carving in wood and stone. Clay modelling should also be done.
Class 10 (Age 16)	Work of Class 9 should be continued with still greater emphasis on the artistic, and encouragement given for the development of individual talents.

Gardening

Classes 6–8 (Age 12–14)	A three-year course on all aspects of vegetable and fruit culture should be carried out as seasonally appropriate, the necessary care, patience and perseverance for successful cultivation being fostered in the children.
Class 9 (Age 15)	Theoretical aspects should now be dealt with, and crop rotations and various methods of cultivation of fruits and vegetables studied. The various methods of propagation should be discussed as appropriate, and such skills as budding and grafting practised.
Class 10 (Age 16)	The work of Class 9 should be continued; as well as more advanced theoretical considerations, such matters as manuring, composting, pruning, etc. should be studied and practised.

Shorthand

Classes
9–10

Shorthand should now be systematically taught.

Surveying

Class 10
(Age 16)

Surveying of local features should be taught and carried out, and the elements of technical mechanics studied.

First Aid

Class 10
(Age 16)

Principles should be studied and practice undertaken in bandaging and other practical aspects.

Technology

Class 11
(Age 17)

Technological aids to industry of all kinds should be studied, and excursions to factories and works arranged.

Class 12
(Age 18)

Origins of various raw materials and their transformation in the respective industrial processes should be studied, and theoretical aspects dealt with, including economic processes and manpower resources and deployment. Further industrial visits should be arranged as appropriate.

14 Implications for the Future

*There is a direct link between mankind's losing sight of
the real and deeper content of the world and the distress
of our civilization today . . . Education which trains the
citizens of tomorrow is instrumental for the future of mankind.
Our first duty is to use those powers which enable us
to equip the coming generations with substance which the
previous generations had to forgo, and the loss of which led to
the tragic disasters of our civilization. Realizing this, one's
gaze widens beyond the somewhat enclosed domain of school
— sacred though it is for the development of Man — into the
far reaches of mankind's future evolution.*

The roots of orthodox education

During the last century or so much has been written and said about the
desirability of educating "the whole man," which in the main means that
education should not be confined to purely academic subjects. Over the
decades more and more time in State schools has been given over to
practical handwork, arts and crafts, games and gymnastic exercises,
music and drama, and correspondingly less to intellectual pursuits. Most
educationists agree that this trend is a good one, and that a more balanced
curriculum produces more balanced school leavers in terms of all-round
fitness for the outside world. This trend does not seem to have sprung from
any definite conviction on the part of orthodox educationists but rather a
vague and indeterminate feeling that it is somehow "good" for the children
and therefore to be encouraged.

There has, however, been little attempt to justify such a trend on
philosophical grounds, though a certain amount of support has been
forthcoming for ideological reasons. The suspicion is bound to arise that
no sound theoretical framework has been formulated and that pragmatism
has prevailed at all turns. Reflection will show that this was bound to

199

be so, for a century of educational development has coincided with a century of development of materialism. The traditional attributes of spirit and soul have been stripped from the human being, who has been reduced to the status of a mechanistic organism with mental accessories. Materialistic philosophy is bound to deny everything that cannot be traced to physical activity; that such activity is capable of producing phenomena of a non-sensible nature does not signify, for elimination of the matter in question incurs inevitable disappearance of the phenomena. Hence any advancement in philosophical terms must be made from the standpoint of the material-physical, and it follows from this that any development must be pragmatic in nature and content. That this argument is correct is confirmed by the manner of educational progress that has gradually become more and more firmly established, namely, procedure by trial and error.

Educationists are in the main well-intentioned, sincere and humane, as are the growing numbers of educational psychologists, researchers and experimenters. There is no question of the honesty of their motives; their methods are scrupulously scientific in their manner of approach, and their findings are rigorously scrutinized, checked and evaluated. It cannot be said, however, that no false steps have been made, that no contradictions have been revealed, but these are minor considerations in view of the fact that no overall philosophy of education has been evolved which would sustain a pedagogical art worthy of the name. That certain methods have appeared to succeed may well be due to the infinite capacity for adapting to changing circumstances which is a distinguishing feature of human society. Progress has been piecemeal and sporadic, and in spite of unstinted efforts of experimentalists and pragmatists it is likely to continue in this manner, at least until a sound philosophy of education has been established.

The limits of empiricism

Rudolf Steiner maintained that the need for experimental research involving human beings indicated that the real being of Man has been lost sight of. Each age produces the theories and ideas of education which correspond to the understanding of human nature in that age. But this knowledge of human nature is in its turn only the reflection of the knowledge of the world which has been attained to date.[1] As discussed just now, the present age is a materialistic age, and its research methodology is essentially pragmatic and empirical by nature. Steiner went on to say that even though the scientific view of the

200

world be based on observation and experiment, the instrument used by Man in the interpretations of his observations is the *intellect*. It therefore follows that contemporary mankind has an intellectual conception of the world.[2] The hallmark of the scientific method, of purely intellectual ways of observation and interpretation is, said Steiner, the law of cause and effect. The logical application of this law to any science of teaching entails treating the child absolutely as a link in the chain of cause and effect, as any other mechanistic bit of nature. The practical outcome of this is that the child's essential humanity is excluded and in consequence is treated as a being who exhibits, not human nature, but the laws of cause and effect.[3]

Intellectual rationalism, claimed Steiner, is in fact powerless in the face of reality, and for this reason one cannot educate by its means. Since it leads away from Man, and from the understanding of him in his true nature, it can never be the basis of a science of teaching; and since teaching involves a relationship between human beings it must be based on human nature. Such a real knowledge of human nature is claimed by spiritual science.[4] It is to be expected that an intellectual age would seek to educate not only by the standards of the intellect but also by intellectual means and methods. Modern orthodox educational methods seek to induce the formation of concepts by the child at the earliest possible age so that it the more readily understands what is placed before it in conceptual form. As concepts are expressed in words it follows that a wide vocabulary is desirable for rapid assimilation of knowledge, and it follows from this that the earlier the child is taught to read the better. Hence the emphasis placed on the teaching of reading automatically places emphasis on the cognitive powers of the child and their rapid development; its equally important faculties of feeling and willing are effectively ignored.

Logical though the above is from an *intellectual* point of view, Steiner educationists tend to accept Steiner's contention that intellectual "solutions" to any problem must be suspect. If Steiner is right in his assertion that no child is ready for educating along intellectual lines before the age of twelve at the very earliest, then the enforcement of early intellectual development represents none other than pedagogical vandalism. According to Steiner such enforcement is the sowing of the wind; the whirlwind is reaped later in life in terms of the enfeeblement of the will and of the emotional life, insomnia, nervous disorders and indifferent bodily health as well as a general inability to face the ordinary vicissitudes of life.

Such claims are admittedly difficult to justify or prove to the satisfaction of hide-bound empiricists, but a careful study of the theoretical grounds

201

for many of Steiner's assertions could be rewarding and instructive. Unfortunately, such grounds are not easy of exposition, and this is one certain reason why few Waldorf educationists have attempted to argue from them against protagonists of empirical methodology and intellectual rationalism. The question is bound to arise: theoretical considerations apart, which Waldorf school practices might profitably be adopted in State and other schools? Rudolf Steiner himself maintained that in many respects Waldorf schools were "method" schools, in that if certain teaching methods are adopted, certain results will follow. Teachers in orthodox schools might well adopt certain Waldorf practices without being fully conversant with the principles behind them, however desirable this may be. Analogous to this would be the fact that most people switching on a television set have little real knowledge of the principles involved in its operation. The main objection to adopting a practice without being fully cognizant of its principle is that the methodology would be in danger of degenerating into a rigid system to be applied by rule-of-thumb. Moreover, it is hardly to be expected that members of the teaching profession, however intelligent and enlightened they may be, would be willing to adopt new practices unless they understood them and their rationale reasonably well.

There are two Waldorf school practices which could be adopted by State schools easily and to great advantage: they are the class teacher system and the main lesson system, discussed in earlier chapters. Furthermore, these practices have the advantage of being easily justified from an ordinary intellectual, common-sense point of view. The class teacher system carries all the advantages of continuity of teaching and learning; any objection on the grounds of teacher/pupil incompatibility is trivial, and in any case easily avoidable in schools with parallel classes. The main lesson system completely avoids the tremendous waste of time and energy involved in coping with the fragmented timetable as ordinarily implemented, less so in modern primary schools but certainly so in secondary schools. The economies in teaching effort are immediately apparent, and when practised in conjunction with the class teacher system the advantages are indeed great.

Some of the less obviously advantageous practices, such as the teaching of writing before the teaching of reading, and the slower approach to these skills necessitated by the use of the practice of developing the letter-forms from painting and drawing could, if adopted widely, be very successful indeed, especially in more confident reading and more accurate spelling and sentence construction. The very great overall advantage would of course come with any appreciable degree of emphasis on the artistic approach rather than the intellectual approach, though such advantage would not be so immediately apparent.

All children enjoy drawing "forms", and there is little doubt that they benefit enormously not only in development of the artistic sense and the rhythmical sense, but in surer co-ordination between hand and eye. The imagination is tremendously stimulated by exercises in form drawing, and the children, when given freedom to develop their own forms, often show artistic creativity of a high order. Moreover, exercises in the metamorphosis of forms promote mobility of thinking and facility with ideas. Form drawing could be introduced into State schools for these reasons, apart from the great pleasure afforded the children.

The teaching of eurythmy is unique to Steiner schools, and it is taught only by specialist teachers who have undergone a comprehensive three- or four-year training. The implications at both personal and social levels are profound, and eurythmy is therapeutic in that the movements do much to harmonize the corporeal and soul-spiritual natures, thereby strengthening resistance to injurious influences regardless of their origin. The very practice of eurythmy as "soul gymnastics" serves to emphasize the view Rudolf Steiner took of the essential wholeness of Man: bodily practices have their spiritual effects, and vice versa. Its importance may be judged from the fact that eurythmy is the only compulsory subject in the Waldorf school curriculum. The principles and practice of this entirely new art of movement are much too involved for adequate treatment in the present study, and the chances of eurythmy appearing on the timetables of orthodox schools are extremely remote.

Free or conditioned society?

The moral implications inherent in the Waldorf methods of teaching general subjects, particularly arithmetic and nature study, are too involved for detailed discussion here. Furthermore, adequate justification for teaching pictorially and artistically during the primary school period in particular would require searching argument involving profoundly esoteric reasons, and this again is outside the scope of this study. The tremendous importance of providing an environment worthy of imitation for the infant and the right kind of authority during childhood, with the necessity of working towards a real and not spurious freedom for the adolescent, are all felt and recognized by Waldorf educationists, and to convince orthodox educationists of this importance is undoubtedly a challenging but by no means hopeless task. Indeed, the implications for the life of society of the Steiner philosophy, pedagogy and didactics are far-reaching indeed, but very worthwhile studying and attempting to work out.

To give one instance, Rudolf Steiner recommended strongly that teachers of the first Waldorf school visit the homes of the children in their care in order to see for themselves what kind of environment had been provided for their imitation as infants, so great was the importance he attached to this factor. This task, formidable as it was more than seventy years ago, before the advent of domestic radio and television, is practically insurmountable today. It is well-known that many children watch television/video for more hours per week than they attend school; and as discussed in an earlier chapter, Steiner never tired of emphasizing that *whatever* goes on in an infant's environment is quite literally impressed upon it, imprinted into its very physical organs, thereafter to affect it for its whole lifetime. Taking this to be so, the effects of what is *incorporated* into young children by means of television programmes in terms of negative influences such as violence to person and destruction of property must be staggering indeed. A society which condones — indeed demands — such programmes in the name of entertainment may be said to be fully deserving of the consequences.

It bears repetition that social scientists may be judged by their ability to predict the social consequences of a given social situation. Rudolf Steiner predicted that the police would be needed to keep order in schools if the confidence gap between older and younger generations kept on widening, and in this he has been vindicated. If Steiner was right, the inevitability of the working-out in their environment in later years of the influences that children have imbibed, is a horrific prospect. If, zombie-like, adolescents and adults have no option but to play out, albeit unconsciously, what has been impressed into them as children; if Steiner was right in this assertion, western civilization may well shudder in face of the future. And the future is already here, in that the cohorts so influenced are today's adolescents and young adults, to be followed inevitably by others with similar predispositions and propensities. Steiner insisted at all times that genuine freedom in adulthood may not, will not, indeed *cannot* be experienced if wholesome influences have not been provided in the childhood environment for intensive imitation. If he was right, then we are already on the threshold of a nightmare world in which words such as "conditioning" and "behaviourism," already in common use, will take on far more sinister connotations.

If Steiner was right, unless the principle of authority is scrupulously cultivated by parents and teachers during the period when children need it, namely between the second dentition and puberty, then when such children become adults they will not be equipped to appreciate the ideal of equal rights in the social organism. People will *talk* about rights, he declared, but will *act* out of a striving for power. As symptomatic of this, the strong-arm tactics of certain trade union factions on the industrial front, the nakedly bigoted attitudes of both left and right extremists on the political front, not to mention the pitiless campaigns of various terrorist factions, suggest the unbelievably paradoxical maxim: Be my brother or I'll batter you to death.

Economics is anything but an exact science or even a skilfully practised art, as the economic conditions prevailing over the past century have amply demonstrated. Rudolf Steiner always accorded to economics the distinction of being regarded by the proletariat as the only reality, from which such tenuous notions as freedom of the individual and social justice rise like vapours. He maintained that unless the ideals of universal brotherly love are actively and consciously cultivated in schools during the years after puberty, the economic life of the world would remain chaotic, and so unwieldy as to defy effective management. Symptoms of national and international economic malaises are too blatantly obvious to bear repetition — they are never absent from the headlines; but if Steiner was right, economic "realities" will remain shifting shapes, intangible and unmanageable, until the principle of universal brotherhood inspires sound management of the world's resources.

Rudolf Steiner was a man of great vision, whose ideas are not yet fully appreciated by educators and sociologists, much less by politicians, and it is fair to assert that since 1919, when he broached the ideas just discussed, advances in understanding and improving the social, political and economic conditions in the world have been minimal. If Steiner's predictions of catastrophe were fulfilled — and who, after World War II and world events since would deny this? — then further troubles inevitably threaten us now. If they have been avoided in the past by expediency and manoeuvre, will human ingenuity and resourcefulness somehow continue to avoid them in the future?

As originator of the philosophy of "ethical individualism," Steiner sought to impart the necessary impulse to a healthy development of individual freedom and social liberty in Western civilization. He saw history as the evolution of consciousness from pre-historic Man, with his extensive vision into the spiritual realm combined with limited knowledge of material things, to modern Man who has limited awareness of the supersensible but a rapidly deepening understanding of the material world.

Steiner claimed that for true personal freedom and social liberty to come about, there must be a progressive emancipation from every externally imposed constraint on behaviour, with each individual discovering the realities of truth and freedom from within. A modern art of education, urged Steiner, should prepare future generations for a deep personal insight into the great spiritual values — liberty, equality and fraternity — by which civilization progresses. This he saw as a necessary task, an historical demand, and it is one which Waldorf schools all over the world seek to fulfil.

References

Sources of chapter quotations from Rudolf Steiner
Thematic quote: Berne, 13 April, 1924. *The Roots of Education.*
Chapter 1. Dornach, 9 August, 1919. *Education as a Social Problem*, p. 4.
Chapter 2. *Occult Science*, p. xiii.
Chapter 3. Stuttgart, 21 August, 1919. *The Study of Man*, p. 7.
Chapter 4. Oxford, 16 August, 1922. *The Spiritual Ground of Education*, p. 47.
Chapter 5. Arnhem, 18 July, 1924. *Human Values in Education*, p. 47.
Chapter 6. Munich, 9 January, 1909. *The Four Temperaments*, p. 6.
Chapter 7. Stuttgart, 6 February, 1923. Waldorf School Teachers' Meeting.
Chapter 8. Basel, 22 April, 1922. *The Renewal of Education*, p. 49.
Chapter 9. Dornach, 29 December, 1921. *Soul Economy and Waldorf Education*,
    p. 119.
Chapter 10. *Education and Art*, in *Das Goetheanum*, Vol. II, no. 34.
Chapter 11. *The Education of the Child in the Light of Anthroposophy*, p. 50.
Chapter 12. Oxford, 19 August, 1922. *The Spiritual Ground of Education*,
    p. 60.
Chapter 13. Stuttgart, 2 September, 1919. *Practical Course for Teachers*,
    p. 147.
Chapter 14. Basel, 21 April, 1920. *The Renewal of Education*, pp. 36–7.

Text references
Chapter 1
1 Steiner R. *Education and Modern Spiritual Life*, pp. 38–69.
2 Edmunds L.F. *Rudolf Steiner Education.* Harwood A.C. *The Way of a Child*,
    Harwood A.C. *The Recovery of Man in Childhood*, Moffat P.S. *Forward
    toward What?* Carlgren F. *Education towards Freedom.*
3 Steiner R. *Education as a Social Problem*, p. 17.
4 See pp. 20f, 166.
5 Harwood A.C. *The Way of a Child*, p. 111.

Chapter 2
1 Steiner R. *The Course of My Life*, p. 11.
2 *Ibid.*
3 *Ibid.*
4 Steiner R., *op. cit.* p. 16.
5 Steiner R., *op. cit.* p. 167.
6 Steiner R., *op. cit.* p. 41.

7 Steiner R., *op. cit.* p. 76.

Chapter 3
1 Steiner R. *The Threefold Commonwealth*, p. 25.
2 *Ibid.* p. 26.
3 Kirton R.J. in Harwood A.C. (ed) *The Faithful Thinker*, p. 234.
4 Steiner R., *op. cit.* p. 70.
5 See Wachsmuth G. *The Life and Work of Rudolf Steiner*, p. 363.
6 See Hahn H. in von Poturzyn M.J.K. *Wir Erlebten Rudolf Steiner*, pp. 84–5.
7 *Ibid.* p. 97.
8 Childs G.J. *Rudolf Steiner Education as Historical Necessity*, Ph.D. thesis, University of Wales 1981.

Chapter 4
1 Steiner R. *Theosophy*, pp. 6–8.
2 *Ibid.* p. 8.
3 *Ibid.* p. 13.
4 *Ibid.* pp. 50, 51, 55. See also Steiner R. *The Education of the Child in the Light of Anthroposophy*, p. 9.
5 Steiner R. *Theosophy*, p. 23
6 For Steiner's methods of acquiring the necessary powers of perception (Imagination, Inspiration, Intuition) see his *Knowledge of the Higher Worlds and its Attainment*. See also *A Road to Self-Knowledge and The Threshold of the Spiritual World*.
7 Steiner R. *The Education of the Child in the Light of Anthroposophy*, pp. 12–13. Steiner insists that plants have no sensations as such. Certain plants (e.g. the Venus Fly-trap) respond to external stimuli, but *inner* feeling is absent. Unless this criterion is maintained, one would be justified in saying that blue litmus-paper has a sensation of certain substances, because it turns red by contact with them.
8 Steiner R. *The Education of the Child in the Light of Anthroposophy*, p. 15.
9 *Ibid.* p. 16.
10 Steiner R. *Theosophy*, p. 41.
11 *Ibid.* p. 60.
12 *Ibid.* p. 93.
13 *Ibid.* p. 77.

Chapter 5
1 Steiner R. *The Education of the Child in the Light of Anthroposophy*, p. 7.
2 Lecture to members of the Giordano-Bruno Union, 8 October 1902.
3 Steiner R. *Education and Modern Spiritual Life (A Modern Art of Education)*, p. 134.
4 Steiner R. *The Renewal of Education through the Science of the Spirit*, p. 21.
5 *Ibid.* Lecture 7 of 14, 29 April 1920.
6 Steiner R. *The Roots of Education*, p. 86.
7 Steiner R. *The Education of the Child in the Light of Anthroposophy*, p. 20.

8 Steiner R. *The Kingdom of Childhood*, p. 19.

9 *Ibid.* p. 20.

10 Steiner R. *The Study of Man*, p. 139.

11 Steiner R. *Practical Course for Teachers*, p. 9.

12 See Lecture 8/5, in Steiner R. *Waldorf Education for Adolescence.*

13 Steiner R. *The Spiritual Ground of Education*, p. 21.

14 Steiner R. *Education and Modern Spiritual Life*, p. 56.

15 Steiner R. *The Roots of Education*, p. 64.

16 Steiner R. *The Renewal of Education through the Science of the Spirit*, p. 20.

17 Steiner R. *Erziehungs-, Unterrichts- und praktische Lebensfragen vom Gesichtspunkte anthroposophischer Geisteswissenschaft.* Lecture given in The Hague, 27 February, 1921.

18 Steiner R. *The Spiritual Ground of Education*, p. 106.

19 Steiner R. and Barfield O. *The Case for Anthroposophy*, p. 69.

20 *Ibid.* p. 77.

21 Steiner R. *A Theory of Knowledge Implicit in Goethe's World-Conception*, pp. 116–18.

22 *Ibid.* p. 118.

23 Steiner R. *Die pädagogische Bedeutung der Erkenntnis des kranken und gesunden Menschen.* Lecture given in Dornach, 26 September, 1921.

24 *Ibid.*

25 Steiner gives full details in his *Knowledge of the Higher Worlds and its Attainment.*

26 Steiner R. *Human Values in Education*, p. 132.

27 Steiner R. *Education and Modern Spiritual Life (A Modern Art of Education)* p. 82.

28 *Ibid.* See also note 25 above.

29 *Ibid.* p. 30.

30 *Ibid.* p. 31.

31 Steiner R. *The Renewal of Education through the Science of the Spirit*, p. 172.

32 "Idea" used in the Goethean sense, as referred to on p.35.

33 Steiner R. *The Study of Man*, p. 12.

34 *Ibid.* p. 35.

35 *Ibid.* p. 51. See also development of this in his *Wahrheit und Wissenschaft.*

36 Steiner R. *The Renewal of Education through the Science of the Spirit*, p. 43.

37 Steiner R. *The Study of Man*, p. 157.

38 *Ibid.*

39 *Ibid.* p. 159.

40 Steiner R. *The Education of the Child in the Light of Anthroposophy*, p. 46.

41 Steiner R. *Education and Modern Spiritual Life*, p. 90.

42 *Ibid.* p. 92.

43 Steiner R. *Practical Course for Teachers*, p. 99.

44 Steiner R. *The Study of Man*, p. 13.

45 *Ibid.* p. 14.

46 Steiner R. *Konferenzen mit dem Lehrerkollegium der Freien Waldorfschule*. Lectures given in Stuttgart, 3 February, 1923.

47 Steiner R. *Drei Vorträge über Volkspädagogik*, Lecture 2.

48 Steiner R. *The Study of Man*, p. 10. Further discussion may be found in his *Occult Science — an Outline*.

49 *Ibid.* p. 11.

50 *Ibid.* p. 14.

51 *Ibid.* p. 16.

52 *Ibid.* p. 22.

53 *Ibid.* p. 23.

54 *Ibid.* p. 26.

55 *Ibid.* p. 32.

56 *Ibid.* p. 27.

57 *Ibid.* p. 38.

58 *Ibid.* p. 40.

59 *Ibid.* p. 77.

60 *Ibid.* p. 57.

61 Steiner R. *Theosophy*, p. 41. See also Steiner R. *Occult Science an Outline*, pp. 24–38.

62 Mead G.H. *Mind, Self and Society*, p. 140. See also Argyle M. *The Psychology of Interpersonal Behaviour*, pp. 119 and 128.

63 Steiner R. *The Study of Man*, p. 101.

Chapter 6

 1 Steiner R. *The Four Temperaments*, p. 1.

 2 Steiner R. *The Education of the Child in the Light of Anthroposophy*, p. 25.

 3 Steiner R. *Waldorf Education for Adolescence*, p. 24.

 4 *Ibid.* p. 25.

 5 Steiner R. *The Four Temperaments*, p. 5.

 6 *Ibid.* pp. 6–7.

 7 *Ibid.* p. 9.

 8 Steiner R. *Discussions with Teachers*, p. 12.

 9 Steiner R. "Karma." Lecture 7 in *Vor dem Tore der Theosophie*.

10 See Chapter 4.

11 Steiner R. "Karma." See note 9 above.

12 Steiner R. *Discussions with Teachers*, p. 18.

13 *Ibid.* p. 46.

14 Steiner R. *Psycho-analysis in the Light of Anthroposophy*, p. 10.

15 Steiner R. *Discussions with Teachers*, p. 34.

16 Steiner R. *The Four Temperaments*, pp. 16–19.

17 Eysenck H.J. *The Structure of Human Personality*, p. 346.

18 Steiner R. *Discussions with Teachers*, p. 31.

19 Steiner R. *The Essentials of Education*, pp. 14–20.

20 Steiner R. *Curative Education*, p. 39.

21 *Ibid.* pp. 39–40.

REFERENCES

Chapter 7

1 Steiner R. *Ancient Myths, their Meaning and Connection with Evolution*, p. 93.
2 Steiner R. *The Study of Man*, p. 102.
3 Steiner R. *Spiritual Ground of Education*, p. 23.
4 *Ibid*. p. 28.
5 Steiner R. Lecture 2 in *The Renewal of Education through the Science of the Spirit*, p. 26.
6 Steiner R. *The Three Fundamental Forces in Education*, p. 16.
7 *Ibid*. p. 8.
8 *Ibid*. p. 15.
9 Steiner R. *Human Values in Education*, p. 126.
10 Steiner R. *Lectures to Teachers* p. 31.
11 Steiner R. *The Roots of Education*, p. 21.
12 *Ibid*. p. 42.
13 *Ibid*. pp. 38–9.
14 Steiner R. *The Study of Man*, p. 161.
15 Steiner R. *The Kingdom of Childhood*, p. 31.
16 Edmunds L.F. *Rudolf Steiner Education — the Waldorf Impulse*, pp. 21–2.
17 Steiner R. Lecture 1 in *The Renewal of Education through the Science of the Spirit*.
18 Chomsky N. "Language and Mind," p. 132.
19 Slobin D.I. *Psycholinguistics*, p. 61.
20 Harwood A.C. *The Recovery of Man in Childhood*, p. 15.
21 Steiner R. *Education and Modern Spiritual Life*, p. 112.
22 Steiner R. *Human Values in Education*, p. 72.
23 Steiner R. Lecture 1 in *The Child's Changing Consciousness and Waldorf Education*, passim.
24 *Ibid*.
25 Steiner R. *Die pädagogische Bedeutung der Erkenntnis des kranken und gesunden Menschen*. Lecture given in Dornach, 26 September, 1921.
26 Steiner R. *Education and Modern Spiritual Life*, p. 118.

Chapter 8

1 Steiner R. *The Study of Man*, p. 129.
2 *Ibid*. p. 65.
3 Steiner R. *Human Values in Education*, p. 59.
4 Steiner R. *Konferenzen*, 17 January, 1923.
5 Steiner R. *The Study of Man*, p. 105.
6 Steiner R. Lecture 4 in *Waldorf Education for Adolescence*, p. 49.
7 Steiner R. *The Study of Man*, p. 165.
8 See Hudson L. *Contrary Imaginations* (1967), and *Frames of Mind* (1970), Penguin Books.
9 Steiner R. *The Study of Man*, p. 166.
10 Steiner R. *The Younger Generation*, p. 118.

11 *Ibid*. p. 138.
12 *Ibid*. p. 141.
13 *Ibid*. p. 133.
14 Steiner R. *The Kingdom of Childhood*, pp. 47–8.
15 Steiner R. Lecture 2 in *Die pädagogische Praxis vom Gesischtspunkte geistes-wissenschaftlicher Menschenerkenntnis*, given in Dornach, 16 April, 1923.
16 Steiner R. *Human Values in Education*, p. 127.
17 See note 15 above.
18 Steiner R. *Spiritual Ground of Education*, p. 121.
19 Steiner R. *Education and Modern Spiritual Life*, p. 127.
20 Steiner R. *The Study of Man*, p. 186.
21 Steiner R. Lecture 1 in *Waldorf Education for Adolescence*, p. 3.
22 *Ibid*.
23 *Ibid*. p. 7.
24 *Ibid*. p. 11.

Chapter 9

 1 Steiner R. *Education as a Social Problem*, p. 55.
 2 Glas W. *A Historical Study of the Philosophy and Methodology of Speech Education in the Primary Grades of Waldorf Schools*, p. 49.
 3 Steiner R. *The Roots of Education*, p. 23.
 4 Steiner R. *The Kingdom of Childhood*, pp. 75–6.
 5 Steiner R. *The Study of Man*, p. 202.
 6 Steiner R. *Education as a Social Problem*, p. 46.
 7 Steiner R. Lecture 14 in *The Renewal of Education through the Science of the Spirit*, p. 185.
 8 Steiner R. *The Study of Man*, p. 139.
 9 Steiner R. *The Younger Generation*, p. 84.
10 Steiner R. *The Essentials of Education*, p. 76.
11 Steiner R. *Education and Art*. Reprinted from *Anthroposophy*, May 1923.
12 *Ibid*.
13 Steiner R. *Practical Course for Teachers*, p. 57.
14 Steiner R. *The Education of the Child in the Light of Anthroposophy*, pp. 41–2.
15 Steiner R. *The Study of Man*, p. 139.
16 *Ibid*. p. 65.
17 *Ibid*. p. 116.
18 Steiner R. *Education and Modern Spiritual Life*, pp. 183–5.
19 Steiner R. *Konferenzen*, 14 June 1920.
20 Steiner R. *The Kingdom of Childhood*, pp. 82–3.
21 Steiner R. *Konferenzen*, 19 June 1924.
22 Steiner R. *Konferenzen*, 14 June 1920.
23 Steiner R. Lecture 9 in *The Renewal of Education through the Science of the Spirit*, p. 115.

24 Slobin D.I. *Psycholinguistics*, pp. 39–66.

25 Steiner R. *Practical Course for Teachers*, p. 59.

26 *Ibid*.

27 Britton J. *Language and Learning*, pp. 97–125.

28 Steiner R. *Knowledge of the Higher Worlds and its Attainment*, pp. 38–41. See also Patterson C.H. *Counseling and Guidance in Schools*, Harper & Row, New York 1962, *passim;* and Ohlsen M.M. *Group Counseling*, Holt, Rhinehart & Wilson, New York 1970, *passim*.

29 Steiner, R. *The Younger Generation*, pp. 125–6.

Chapter 10

1 Steiner R. *Practical Course for Teachers*, pp. 51–2.

2 Steiner R. *Human Values in Education*, p. 91.

3 Steiner R. Lecture 10 in *The Renewal of Education through the Science of the Spirit*, p. 127.

4 Steiner R. *Practical Course for Teachers*, pp. 10–11.

5 Steiner R. *The Kingdom of Childhood*, p. 86.

6 Steiner R. *Education and Modern Spiritual Life*, p. 160.

7 Steiner R. *Human Values in Education*, p. 160.

8 Steiner R. *Spiritual Ground of Education*, pp. 74–5.

9 Steiner R. *Education and Modern Spiritual Life*, p. 156.

10 Steiner R. *Practical Course for Teachers*, p. 37.

11 Steiner R. Lecture 10 in *The Renewal of Education through the Science of the Spirit*, p. 130.

12 *Ibid*. Lecture 11.

13 Steiner R. *Lectures to Teachers*, p. 53.

14 Steiner R. *Human Values in Education*, p. 150.

15 Steiner R. Lecture 2 in *Zwei Vorträge für Waldorflehrer und Musiker*, given in Stuttgart, 8 March, 1923.

16 Steiner R. *Practical Course for Teachers*, p. 46.

17 Steiner R. *Speech and Drama*, *passim*.

18 Steiner R. *Practical Course for Teachers*, p. 28.

19 *Ibid*. p. 29.

20 Steiner R. *Education and Modern Spiritual Life*, p. 179.

21 Steiner R. *Practical Course for Teachers*, p. 161.

22 Steiner R. *Lectures to Teachers*, p. 76.

23 Steiner R. *Practical Course for Teachers*, p. 132.

24 *Ibid*. p. 134.

25 Steiner R. *Kingdom of Childhood*, p. 129.

26 Steiner R. *Practical Course for Teachers*, pp. 93–4.

27 Steiner R. *Education and Modern Spiritual Life*, pp. 147–150.

28 Steiner R. *The Kingdom of Childhood*, pp. 50–2.

29 Steiner R. *Discussions with Teachers*, pp. 132–3.

30 Steiner R. *Lectures to Teachers*, p. 69.

Chapter 11

1 Steiner R. *Practical Course for Teachers*, p. 107.
2 *Ibid.*
3 *Ibid.* p. 139.
4 *Ibid.* p. 147.
5 Steiner R. *Education and Modern Spiritual Life*, p. 119.
6 Steiner R. Lecture 11 in *The Renewal of Education through the Science of the Spirit*, pp. 138–9.
7 Steiner R. Lecture 3 in *Die pädagogische Praxis*, given in Dornach, 17 April 1923.
8 Steiner R. Lecture 2 in *Waldorf Education for Adolescence*.
9 *Ibid.*
10 Steiner R. *Human Values in Education*, p. 67.
11 Steiner R. *The Kingdom of Childhood*, p. 68.
12 Steiner R. *The Essentials of Education*, p. 40.
13 Steiner R. *The Study of Man*, pp. 125–6.
14 Steiner R. *Man as a Being of Sense and Perception*, p. 7.
15 Steiner R. *The Study of Man*, pp. 120–1.

Chapter 12

1 Steiner R. Lecture 8 in *Waldorf Education for Adolescence* p. 96.
2 *Ibid.*
3 Steiner R. *The Roots of Education*, p. 85.
4 *Ibid.*
5 Steiner R. *The Essentials of Education*, p. 88.
6 *Ibid.* p. 81.
7 Steiner R. *The Philosophy of Freedom*, p. 138.
8 Steiner R. *Metamorphoses of the Soul*, pp. 116–122. For a detailed exposition of Man's soul and spirit members see Steiner's *Theosophy*, pp. 25–54.
9 Steiner R. *Waldorf Education for Adolescence* p. 60.
10 Steiner R. *Lectures to Teachers*, p. 83.
11 *Ibid.* p. 84.
12 Steiner R. Lecture 1 in *Drei Vorträge über Volkspädagogik*, given in Stuttgart, 11 May, 1919.
13 Steiner R. *Lectures to Teachers*, p. 86.
14 Steiner R. Lecture 14 in *The Renewal of Education through the Science of the Spirit*, p. 182.
15 Steiner R. Lecture 8 in *Waldorf Education for Adolescence*, p. 96.
16 *Ibid.* Lecture 7, p. 85.
17 *Ibid.* Lecture 5, p. 66.
18 *Ibid.* p. 67.
19 Steiner R. *Lectures to Teachers*, pp. 87–8.
20 Steiner R. Lecture 6 in *Waldorf Education for Adolescence*, p. 70.
21 *Ibid.* p. 74

22 *Ibid.* Lecture 7, p. 93.

Chapter 13
1 Apart from the fundamental Stuttgart lectures, Rudolf Steiner gave important
  lecture courses in many other European towns and cities. His lecture courses
  for teachers in August 1922 at Oxford, in August 1923 at Ilkley, and in August
  1924 at Torquay attracted the attention of many contemporary educationists.
  Apart from his lectures as such, he gave much in the way of suggestions
  and advice for dealing with day-to-day problems during meetings with the
  teachers of the original Waldorf School during its early years, and the
  indications he gave, known collectively as the *Konferenzen,* have not been
  published in English.
2 The *Lehrplan* of the first Waldorf School compiled by Dr von Heydebrand
  was translated by the late Miss Eileen Hutchins, who supplemented it with
  valuable indications and suggestions concerning the teaching of English
  Language and English Literature in British schools. A translation of
  Stockmeyer's painstaking compilation of Steiner's indications from many
  sources concerning the curriculum was made available in 1969 by the Steiner
  Schools Fellowship.
3 Harwood A.C. *The Recovery of Man in Childhood*, p. 9.
4 Steiner R. *Drei Lehrplan-Vorträge*, given in Stuttgart, 6 September, 1919.

Chapter 14
1 Steiner R. *Lectures to Teachers*, p. 10.
2 *Ibid.* p. 11.
3 *Ibid.* p. 14.
4 *Ibid.* pp. 15–16.

Bibliography

Books and lectures by Rudolf Steiner

Ancient Myths, their Meaning and Connection with Evolution, Steiner Book Centre, Toronto 1971.

The Case for Anthroposophy, (with Owen Barfield), Rudolf Steiner Press, London 1970.

The Child's Changing Consciousness and Waldorf Education, Anthroposophic Press, New York 1988.

The Course of My Life, Anthroposophic Press, New York 1951.

Curative Education, Rudolf Steiner Press, London 1972.

Discussions with Teachers, Rudolf Steiner Press, London 1967.

Drei Lehrplan-Vorträge. Lectures given in Stuttgart, September, 1919.

Drei Vorträge über Volkspädagogik. Lectures given in Stuttgart, May–June, 1919.

Education and Art. Reprinted from *Anthroposophy*, May, 1923.

Education and Modern Spiritual Life, Anthroposophical Publishing Co., London 1954. (Re-issued as *A Modern Art of Education*, Rudolf Steiner Press, London 1981.)

Education as a Social Problem, Anthroposophic Press, New York 1969.

The Education of the Child in the Light of Anthroposophy, Rudolf Steiner Publishing Co., London 1938.

Erziehungs-, Unterrichts- und praktische Lebensfragen vom Gesichtspunkte anthroposophischer Geisteswissenschaft. Lecture given in The Hague, 27 February, 1921.

The Essentials of Education, Anthroposophical Publishing Co., London 1926.

The Four Temperaments, Rudolf Steiner Publishing Co., London 1944.

Human Values in Education, Rudolf Steiner Press, London 1971.

The Poetry and Meaning of Fairy Tales, Mercury Press, Spring Valley, N.Y. 1989.

The Kingdom of Childhood, Rudolf Steiner Press, London 1964.

Knowledge of the Higher Worlds and its Attainment, Rudolf Steiner Press, London 1976.

Konferenzen mit dem Lehrerkollegium der Freien Waldorfschule. Lectures given in Stuttgart, February, 1923.

Lectures to Teachers, Rudolf Steiner Press, London 1931. (Re-issued 1986 as *Soul Economy and Waldorf Education*, Anthroposophic Press, New York.)

Man as a Being of Sense and Perception, Steiner Book Centre, Vancouver, British Columbia 1981.

Metamorphoses of the Soul, Rudolf Steiner Press, London 1983.

Occult Science — an Outline, Rudolf Steiner Press, London 1979.

Die pädagogische Bedeutung der Erkenntnis des kranken und gesunden Menschen. Lecture given in Dornach, 26 September, 1921.

Die pädagogische Praxis vom Gesischtspunkte geisteswissenschaftlicher Menschenerkenntnis. Lecture given in Dornach, 16 April, 1923.

The Philosophy of Freedom, Rudolf Steiner Press, London 1979.

Practical Course for Teachers, Rudolf Steiner Publishing Co., London 1937. (Re-issued 1976 as *Practical Advice for Teachers*, Rudolf Steiner Press, London.

Psycho-analysis in the Light of Anthroposophy, Anthroposophic Press, New York 1946.

The Renewal of Education through the Science of the Spirit, Kolisko Archive Publ., 1981.

A Road to Self-Knowledge and The Threshold of the Spiritual World, Rudolf Steiner Publishing Co., London 1938.

The Roots of Education, Rudolf Steiner Press, London 1968.

Speech and Drama, Anthroposophical Publishing Co., London 1960.

The Spiritual Ground of Education, Anthroposophical Publishing Co., London 1947.

The Study of Man, Rudolf Steiner Press, London 1975.

A Theory of Knowledge Implicit in Goethe's World-Conception, Anthroposophic Press, New York 1940.

Theosophy, Rudolf Steiner Press, London 1973.

The Threefold Commonwealth, Anthroposophical Publishing Co., London 1923. Reissued as *Towards Social Renewal*, Rudolf Steiner Press, London 1977.

The Three Fundamental Forces in Education, Anthroposophic Press, New York 1944.

Vor dem Tore der Theosophie. Lecture given in Stuttgart, 28 September, 1906. Published as *At the Gates of Theosophy*, Rudolf Steiner Press, London 1943.

Waldorf Education for Adolescence (Translation of *Menschenerkenntnis and Unterrichtsgestaltung.* Lectures given in Stuttgart, 12–19 June, 1921), Michael Hall, Sussex, UK, 1980.

The Younger Generation, Anthroposophic Press, New York 1969.

Zwei Vorträge für Waldorflehrer und Musiker. Lectures given in Stuttgart, March, 1923.

Works by other Authors

Argyle, M. *The Psychology of Interpersonal Behaviour.* Penguin Books, Harmondsworth 1967.

Barfield, O. and Steiner, R. *The Case for Anthroposophy*, Rudolf Steiner Press, London 1970.

Britton, J. *Education towards Freedom*. Pelican Books, UK, 1972.

Carlgren F. *Education towards Freedom*, Lanthorn Press, Forest Row 1977.

Chomsky, N. "Language and Mind," in Cashdan, A. and Grugeon, E. (eds) *Language and Education*. Routledge & Kegan Paul, London 1972.

Edmunds, L.F. *Rudolf Steiner Education — the Waldorf Impulse*. Rudolf Steiner Press, London 1962.

Eysenck, H.J. *The Structure of Human Personality*. (3rd edition), Methuen, London 1970.

Glas, W. *A Historical Study of the Philosophy and Methodology of Speech Education in the Primary Grades of Waldorf Schools*. M.A. Thesis, Wayne State University, Detroit.

Harwood, A.C. *The Faithful Thinker*. Hodder & Stoughton, London 1961.

—, *The Recovery of Man in Childhood*. Hodder & Stoughton, London 1958.

—, *The Way of a Child*. Anthroposophical Publishing Co., London 1942.

Heydebrand, C. von *The Curriculum of the first Waldorf School*. Steiner Schools Fellowship.

Mead, G.H. *Mind, Self and Society*. University of Chicago Press, Chicago 1970.

Moffat, P.S. *Forward toward What?* The Rudolf Steiner Educational Association, Edinburgh 1968.

Ohlsen M.M. *Group Counseling*, Holt, Rhinehart & Wilson, New York 1970.

Patterson C.H. *Counseling and Guidance in Schools*, Harper & Row, New York 1962.

Poturzyn M.J.K. von *Wir Erlebten Rudolf Steiner*, Verlag Freies Geistesleben, Stuttgart 1956.

Slobin, D.I. *Psycholinguistics*. Scott, Foresman & Co., Glenview, Illinois 1971.

Wachsmuth, G. *The Life and Work of Rudolf Steiner*. Whittier Books, New York 1955.

Stockmeyer, E.A.K. *Rudolf Steiner's Curriculum for Waldorf Schools*. Steiner Schools Fellowship, 1969.

Index